The Ageless Woman

How to Navigate the Transition Naturally
for a Long Life of Vibrant Health and Radiant Beauty

NANCY K. LONSDORF, MD

Also by Nancy K. Lonsdorf, MD
   • *A Woman's Best Medicine*
   (Co-authored with V. Butler, MD, M. Brown, PhD)

© 2016 Nancy K. Lonsdorf. All rights reserved.

Published by
Maharishi University of Management Press
Fairfield, Iowa. United States of America

No part of this book may be reproduced or utilized in any form or by any means, electronic or mechanical, including photocopying, recording, or by any information storage or retrieval system, without permission in writing from the Publisher. Inquiries should be addressed to Maharishi University of Management Press, 1000 N. 4th Street, Fairfield, IA 52557

Cover Design: Elinor Wolfe

ISBN 978-0-923569-67-9

[SM]Maharishi Ayurveda, Maharishi Amrit Kalash, Amrit, and Maharishi Rejuvenation, are service marks used under license by Maharishi Ayurveda Foundation. ®Transcendental Meditation, TM, TM-Sidhi, Yogic Flying, Maharishi, Maharishi Vedic Vibration Technology (MVVT), Vedic Science, Maharishi Gandharva Veda are protected trademarks and are used in the U.S.A. under license or with permission from Maharishi Foundation.

This book is dedicated to Maharishi's goal of establishing a disease-free society, permanent world peace, and heaven on earth in this generation.

Disclaimer

This book provides an educational guide for developing a healthy lifestyle at midlife and for correcting imbalances according to Maharishi Ayurveda. No part of this book is intended to diagnose or treat any disease or to replace standard medical care. Athough preventive in intent, these guidelines do not replace modern preventive medical approaches recommended by your doctor. All information in *The Ageless Woman* is given with the understanding that the reader accepts full responsibility for her own health and well-being. While the self-care approaches outlined in this book have been safely used by hundreds of women, as with any health approach, the results cannot be guaranteed. The author and publisher are not responsible for any adverse effects that may result from the herbal and self-care approaches outlined in this book. Consult with your health-care professional before beginning any herbal products, remedies, or procedures described in this book and before making any changes in your current medical treatment.

The views represented in this book are those of the author and do not necessarily represent those of Maharishi Foundation or any of its subsidiaries.

Contents

Foreword to the Paperback Edition *ix*
This Book is for You *xi*
Introduction *xiii*

PART I: Creating Health: The Key to A Smooth Transition

1. The Search for a Natural and Healthy Menopause *3*
2. Achieving Balance Through Nature's Intelligence *23*

PART II: How to Restore Balance and Relieve Your Symptoms

3. The Wisdom of the Doshas: Understanding Your Mild Midlife Symptoms *39*
4. Creating Balance for Relief of Your Mild Symptoms *59*
5. Your Metabolism: Key to Resolving Your More Serious Symptoms *81*
6. Purification for Relief of Your More Serious Symptoms *105*

PART III: How to Overcome Specific Health Issues

7. Your Heart: Healthy and Happy, Naturally *127*
8. Your Bones: Strong Without Drugs or HT *147*
9. Your Mind: Out of the Fog into the Light *169*
10. Your Emotions: Transforming Blues to Bliss *187*
11. Your Skin: A Program for Ageless Beauty *211*

Epilogue: The World Is Your Family *229*
Glossary of Ayurvedic Terms *235*
References *239*
Resources *249*
Index *253*

Foreword to the Paperback Edition

When I was just married, at age twenty-five, my husband used to tell me, "You'll be incredible when you're thirty-five." I couldn't understand what he meant, assuming as most American women do at virtually any age, that getting older means getting less attractive, less pretty, and less desirable. His message at age twenty-five of "you're not getting older, you're getting more beautiful" planted a seed idea in my mind that has refused to wither, even past the ripe "old" age of forty-five. After twenty years, I am convinced that older *can* mean more attractive, beautiful, and desirable — at any age. Healthy aging is a factor that is largely in our control. How you age is more a matter of how you treat yourself than of how life treats you.

This book was originally written to help dispel the myth that menopause is an estrogen-deficiency disease that must be treated with hormone replacement. To give women a truly natural, nonhormonal approach to menopause and their future health was its primary aim. Fortunately, the findings of the Women's Health Initiative (WHI), released in July 2002, changed overnight the way women and the medical community view menopause and women's health thereafter. Hormone replacement therapy (HRT) has become officially hormone therapy (HT), acknowledging the fact that replacing hormones does *not* improve health, but creates damaging side effects.

As I toured the country in 2002, speaking to women about the ancient natural approach to health described in this book, I kept hearing, "This book covers so much *more* than just menopause." They were amazed at how deeply and completely its natural approaches addressed a wide variety of their health issues — and how personalized the program was. I was encouraged by their response to revise, update, and retitle this book for its paperback edition, so that women from age forty onward could have this practical ancient wisdom to smooth their menopause transition, and once through "the change," to stay healthy, beautiful, and youthful.

A Truly Natural Medicine

The findings of the Women's Health Initiative documenting HT's failure to deliver many of its previous claims, along with the high risk of serious side effects, have opened the door to a plethora of alternative approaches. A positive shift has occurred, moving away from the concept of menopause as a disease requiring drugs and "replacement" hormones to an understanding of menopause as a natural transition, potentially smooth and disease-free. Herbs, foods, and lifestyle changes are coming to the forefront as viable and preferred alternatives to dangerous hormones and drugs.

Yet, with the enthusiastic shift toward "natural" therapies, some caution must be exercised to ensure that what we utilize is truly safe. The term "natural," although widely used in advertising to create an aura of safety, does *not* guarantee freedom from side effects. A number of these therapies, such as bioidentical, or so-called "natural" hormones, are promoted with unsubstantiated claims such as "proven safe and effective." In some cases, these assertions are even contrary to the available evidence.

A truly natural therapy not only has no side effects, but also has side *benefits*. It engages the entirety of Nature's intelligence and helps the body heal itself. It does not create dependency while it promotes the healing of the body. Truly natural approaches help establish a state of resilient health that remains even after the catalysts for healing are withdrawn.

Our health system is based on the idea that a "magic bullet" contains the answer to our health problems, most commonly in the form of a pill.. A risk-free magic bullet for health is a contradiction in terms and may forever be outside our grasp. For women who wish to be truly healthy, now is the time to face a simple truth: Health before, during, and after menopause cannot be found in a pill, no matter how natural. There is simply no substitute for creating a lifestyle that supports the healing and balance of your body and mind. After all, a healthy body and mind *at any age* depend on healthy living.

This Book is for You!

This book is for all women everywhere who wish to improve their health at midlife and enjoy a long, healthy life thereafter. Women who want a truly natural approach to good health at menopause and in the decades that follow, without drugs or hormones of any kind, will find a personalized, complete, and holistic approach in this book. If you are not sure whether "natural" is right for you, this book will help you understand your choices. It will explain clearly the latest research on the risks and benefits of various options and will provide an abundance of practical tips for a variety of concerns including memory, emotions, weight, heart health, bone density, and beauty.

For those of you who are on hormone therapy (HT) and feel uneasy about it, this book will give you a way to address your menopause symptoms at their root and help you eliminate the need for HT. Finally, but no less importantly, this book is for all women who take HT and love the way they feel on it, because you will learn safer ways to feel good and be healthy without the risks of HT. And if you choose to continue HT, you will know you are correcting the underlying factors that promote disease, thereby creating glowing health and youthfulness from within. This book will help every woman discover and actualize the infinite sustaining wisdom of Nature within — the key to safely creating radiant good health at midlife and beyond.

INTRODUCTION

The basic premise of this book is that Nature knows best. According to Maharishi Ayurveda (muh-<u>har</u>-shee <u>ah</u>-yur-<u>vay</u>-duh), the comprehensive system of natural medicine on which this book is based, menopause is both *natural* and *for the best*. It is part of Mother Nature's plan for the female physiology. And, contrary to the prevailing view, Mother Nature does *not* intend for a host of health problems and accelerated aging to plague women at midlife and beyond. Rather, menopause has a nurturing purpose — to support a woman's health in her later life by preventing reproduction, which is too taxing for the more mature physiology. Understanding menopause as a positive and purposeful event, rather than a harbinger of problems or deficiencies, empowers us to take steps toward a smooth transition without the need for hormones, natural or otherwise.

According to Maharishi Ayurveda (MAV), "women's wisdom" is Nature's wisdom, functioning deep within our minds and bodies. This innate wisdom of Nature guides our bodily functions in perfect balance, just as it upholds every aspect of the universe in complete harmony. Nature's intelligence is the coordinating force that holds the planets, stars, and cosmic bodies in perfect order in space. It is the unifying force of evolution guiding the infinite diversity of life in every ecosystem, whether it be a woods, an ocean, a rainforest, or the universe itself. Left to itself, without mankind's intervention, perfect balance reigns in our bodies and everywhere in Nature.

This is the model of women's health provided in MAV. We are *naturally* healthy. We can stay healthy or regain health, naturally. We simply have to begin to live in harmony with that inner intelligence of Nature that is already organizing our minds, bodies, behavior, and environment in perfect balance, perfect health.

The Origins of Maharishi Ayurveda

Nature's inherent wisdom is the foundation of the Maharishi Ayurveda approach to health. *Ayurveda* literally means "knowledge of the totality of life." The term *Veda* means "pure knowledge." It refers specifically to Nature's intelligence — the cosmic blueprint or orderliness that underlies and governs the function and evolution of everything in the universe, including our human physiology. The human physiology as an expression of the Veda has recently been documented scientifically in a monumental, seminal work by physician and neuroscientist Tony Nader, M.D., Ph.D., International President of Maharishi Universities of Management, formerly of Harvard Medical School and M.I.T.

Ayurveda originated in the Vedic civilization of ancient India and is known to be the world's oldest system of natural medicine. In ancient times, Vedic sages, or *rishis* (rih-sheez), recognized the pure knowledge of the Veda, the total structure of natural law, deep within their own consciousness. Vedic knowledge is structured within every fiber of creation, in what modern physicists call the "unified field," an all-pervading field from which all matter and energy arise. Just as the unified field gives rise to immutable laws of Nature that govern chemistry and physics, it also gives rise to universal laws of Nature that govern health. These laws for health are recorded in six *samhitas*, or complete works, which codify the essence of Ayurvedic knowledge.

Ayurveda has been in continuous practice for over five thousand years. It is still practiced today in India, supported by state-sponsored and accredited Ayurvedic medical colleges and hospitals. However, it is far removed from the original version. Much of the original knowledge of Ayurvedic healing was lost — most regrettably, the understanding of how consciousness and physiology (mind and body) are connected. Aspects of healing elaborated more fully in the Vedic literature, such as yoga asanas, Transcendental Meditation, Vedic sound and vibration therapies, and techniques to improve the health and peacefulness of humankind on a societal level also fell out of use or continued only in a fragmented form.

In 1983 in the United States, His Holiness Maharishi Mahesh Yogi, founder of the Transcendental Meditation technique, assembled some of the most prominent Ayurvedic physicians and scholars to restore the complete practice of Ayurveda, including age-old, traditional healing techniques lost to modern practice. We know from the ancient classical texts of Ayurveda that thousands of years ago, when disease was rampant on the earth, an assembly of Vedic *rishis* led by Maharishi Bharadwaj gathered together to re-enliven the full value of Ayurveda on earth. Similarly, a Maharishi of our modern day gathered with the world's finest Ayurvedic scholars to restore this ancient health science to its original form. This complete restoration of Ayurveda, which acknowledges as its source the Veda known by the *rishis*, is today referred to as *Maharishi Ayurveda*.

Today's MAV is a complete medical system with a theoretical basis that encompasses our modern biomedical model. But MAV expands beyond the range of our modern medicine to detail the interconnection of the body with consciousness, mind, and emotions, and in a larger context, with the Veda, the totality of Nature's intelligence. MAV emphasizes the development of consciousness as the foundation of health, as well as every aspect of lifestyle and behavior — eating and sleeping habits, exercise, herbal supplements, living space and greater environment.

The therapies and theories presented in *The Ageless Woman* are derived directly from the classical texts of Ayurveda, as taught by some of today's foremost Ayurvedic scholars and physicians. This council of over eighty Maharishi Ayurveda physicians, or *vaidyas* (*vai*-dyuhs), ensures that the application of this knowledge is authentic. I have had the great privilege of working with a number of these *vaidyas* over the past ten years, jointly seeing hundreds of patients and applying the treatments of Maharishi Ayurveda for women of all ages. This collaboration has resulted in the many practical tips for women's health described in this book, including careful and insightful adaptation of the traditional Ayurvedic tips and formulas to meet the unique physiological needs of Western women.

How To Use This Book

In reading *The Ageless Woman*, you will effortlessly learn the basics of MAV through stories and examples that illustrate Ayurvedic principles. You will be shown how to apply these principles in treating your specific symptoms and health conditions at midlife and beyond. More than just a Band-Aid for symptom relief, this approach lays a foundation for optimal health for the rest of your life.

For any woman over thirty-five, the most significant single physiological event is the menopausal transition. Therefore, the book begins with a focus on midlife health issues, especially menopause. In Part I, you will see how menopausal and midlife symptoms arise from underlying imbalances that have developed over time, but are now unmasked due to newly shifting hormones. In Part II, you will see how knowledge of two basic underlying principles guiding your physiology — your *doshas* and your tissues — can be used to eliminate symptoms. Then you will learn how to design your own self-care plan based on your individual symptoms. If you are concerned about specific disorders, such as weight-loss, heart disease, osteoporosis, memory loss ("brain fog"), mood swings, or aging skin, the chapters in Part III offer explanations and natural self-care tips for each of these areas of women's health. In the glossary, you will find definitions of Sanskrit terms that appear in the text to help in your understanding.

My hope is that this book will guide you to rediscover your natural state of inner balance and the radiant health that is every woman's birthright. Maharishi Ayurveda provides a simple, time-tested approach that can lead you toward a state of balance and true health without harmful side effects, trade-offs, risks, or compromises. And best of all, the core of this knowledge lies not outside yourself, but *within* yourself, in the totality of Nature's intelligence that lies within us all. *You* are your own best medicine.

Part I

Creating Health: The Key to a Smooth Transition

* 1 *

THE SEARCH FOR A NATURAL AND HEALTHY MENOPAUSE

*True healing of any condition means to restore the mind, body, and spirit
to their naturally balanced states.*
— *the* Charaka Samhita

A profound realization is dawning in the collective psyche of women today: Our bodies are *natural*, and our medicine, to be truly effective and safe, must be natural as well. For decades, women have put their faith in the technology of modern medical science and relied on it for the answers to health problems. Since the startling findings of the Women's Health Initiative on the hazards and limitations of hormone therapy (HT), we are questioning the wisdom of this approach.

The old-fashioned medical model, in which we complacently accept our doctor's view of what needs "fixing" and prescriptions for how to do it, no longer meets our needs. We realize now that the drugs doctors offer don't get at the root of our problems and, in addition, usually cause side effects.

As the traditional caretakers of our own and our families' health, we know from our healing intuition that there must be a better way. We are looking for a natural medicine that uses Nature's infinite power to *heal* rather than man-made technologies that harm.

In The Midst Of A Transformation

In this search for a completely natural medicine, women today are dramatically transforming the practice of medicine. As health consumers, women are voting with their pocketbooks, sending doctors scurrying to educate themselves in the knowledge of natural approaches, including herbs and diet. Even doctors now realize that for effective prevention and treatment of chronic health disorders, the tide has irreversibly turned in the direction of natural approaches.

Women of the baby boomer generation are leading the way. Many of us in our forties and fifties are in the midst of our own transformation, entering menopause in record numbers. Soon, for the first time in history, there will be more women beyond menopause than have yet to go through it. For us, the demand is clear: "Our bodies are *natural*, our menopause is *natural*, and our *treatment* for menopause must be natural!" We find ourselves in a double transformation, one happening *within* — in our bodies, minds, and hormones — and another happening *without* — in our culture's healing revolution.

A New Direction

More and more women are looking beyond the modern medical model to older, more time-tested solutions to their health problems. We intuitively sense that menopause is not a mistake or failure of our physiology, but a deeply significant developmental shift that should be honored and embraced. The wisdom offered by older traditions, along with a deepening trust in our intuitive experience of what's right for our bodies, points in a new, promising direction — toward a more natural approach to menopause.

Maharishi Ayurveda, the world's most ancient system of medicine, offers a truly natural approach to menopause for women today. Maharishi Ayurveda is our planet Earth's original health science, created by Nature herself — Nature's *own* medicine. It is also scientifically validated and complete in theory and practical application. And unlike other traditional approaches, MAV provides a firm intellectual understanding of why we have the symptoms we do and how certain lifestyle changes can reverse them. Over six hundred research studies have been published in medical journals on the benefits of healing modalities from MAV, including over $20 million given for studies funded by the U.S. government's own National Institutes of Health. However, the most important validation of MAV must come from your experience of its simple, completely natural principles and healing approaches in your own life. Whatever is truly natural will illuminate the wisdom of Nature already within *you* and bring your health back into alignment with what Nature originally intended for you — a smooth menopause transition and a long, blissful life in radiant good health.

Our Menopause Is Natural

For women, change is programmed into our bodies in the cycles of hormonal shifting that occur throughout our female life span. We accept the experience of changing hormones as natural. Even so, major hormonal shifts may cause some discomforts, such as acne and mood swings at puberty, morning sickness during pregnancy, or the "baby blues" after delivery. Menopause is no exception. Fluctuating and declining hormones commonly bring on symptoms we are all too familiar with: changes in body temperature, mood shifts, and sleep interruption, to name a few.

In the past, doctors offered women the only helping hand they had, a therapy then called hormone replacement therapy, along with a warning that we must accept their "treatment" to replace our declining estrogen or suffer the consequences — hot flashes, osteoporosis, heart disease and general physical decline. The implication was that menopause itself is a disease of "estrogen deficiency," treatable only with strong "magic bullets," whose promised benefits are worth the risk of potentially serious side effects. Many women were so frightened by this disease model that they took the hormone therapy in spite of their concern that cancer or other harmful side effects may develop later on.

Fortunately this unfounded and erroneous approach to menopause came to a screeching halt in July of 2002 when the Women's Health Initiative (WHI), the first randomized, controlled trial of hormone therapy in women, was stopped three years early, due to excess of side effects in the group taking hormones. Those women taking both estrogen and progestin had an increased incidence of heart attacks, strokes, blood clots, and breast cancer, as compared to the placebo group — so much so that it was necessary to prematurely end the trial.

The WHI findings resulted in a 180-degree shift in the medical community's thinking about menopause. Doctors suddenly realized what women have known for millennia — that menopause is *not* a disease. In fact, nothing could be further from the truth. In a broad, biological sense, menopause occurs for good reasons and is a completely natural and healthy process of the female physiology. The purpose of menopause is to bring about the cessation of the menses and prevent the possibility of pregnancy and childbirth at a time when your body cannot bear the stress of these events. Your menopausal transition is actually a health *advantage*, curtailing the monthly loss of iron, blood, and protein at a time in life when your body assimilates nutrients less efficiently and needs to work harder to get adequate nutrition. This most natural event — yet one more cyclical hormonal shift like puberty and pregnancy — is clearly what Nature intended. It is not a cause of disease or degeneration.

Let's take a look at how Nature has programmed your body to make this shift naturally and with good health.

The ABCs of Your Hormones

The major hormonal event occurring at menopause is the fluctuation and decline of your female hormones, estrogen and progesterone. (See the sidebar "Hormone Terms Defined.")

A hormone is a substance secreted by your glands that travels in your body to other organs and tissues, where it produces effects necessary for healthful functioning. Hormones are very potent messengers. Extremely minute quantities can create major shifts in your entire body. Many hormones, including estrogen, directly affect your basic genetic material, your DNA, stimulating cell growth and proliferation. This is why hormones are so powerful and why they can have serious side effects when taken as a medicine.

Estrogen is a generic term that applies to a certain class of reproductive hormones that are all chemically similar. Yet, to borrow a phrase from a researcher in the field, "All estrogens are not alike." In fact, no estrogen is exactly like any other. Your body itself makes three different types of estrogen: estrone (E1), estradiol (E2), and estriol (E3). Estradiol, the most potent form, is the predominant form during our reproductive years. Estrone, a less potent form, is most abundant after menopause. Estriol, the weakest of the three, is produced mainly by the placenta and is highest in your body during pregnancy. Only one form of *progesterone* is produced by your body, and it is called just that, "progesterone."

At perimenopause (see the sidebar "Menopause Terms Defined"), your hormones begin to fluctuate and decline until after your last menstrual period, when they gradually stabilize. Even after your periods have ceased, your ovaries continue to produce lower levels of estrogen, primarily in the form of *estradiol* and *estrone*, the two main types of estrogen in your body. In addition, your ovaries and your adrenal glands (the organs that also secrete stress hormones) produce a hormone that is converted to *estrone* by an enzyme in your fat, skin, and muscle tissue, providing additional estrogen support. *Testosterone* (yes, women have some, too) also continues to be produced by your ovaries, but drops off relatively less at menopause than do your "female" hormones. Continued production of all these hormones supports your body after menopause and helps to ease the transition.

The Myth of "Estrogen Deficiency"

The prevalent medical belief that falling estrogen levels are solely responsible for all the symptoms we currently attribute to menopause is a mistake. While there is a very definite drop in estrogen and progesterone during perimenopause and menopause, women in their forties and fifties are showing other signs of aging that may have been going on for decades. You may notice that muscle tone, skin firmness, youthful complexion, and your figure are no longer what they were, due to the effects

Hormone Terms Defined

Bioidentical Hormones — Manufactured hormones that exactly match your body's own hormones in chemical structure.

"Natural Hormones" — A commonly used term for bioidentical hormones. Many women mistakenly believe that bioidentical hormones occur naturally in plants. However, although they are derived originally from hormone-like substances in plants, the substances must be chemically altered in the laboratory before they match your body's own hormones.

Phytoestrogens — A class of compounds found in plants. They are similar in structure to human estrogen, and affect hormonal balance in a woman's body when consumed.

Estrogen — A general term referring to any of three similar hormones naturally occurring within a woman's body that are involved in reproduction: estrone (E1), estradiol (E2), and estriol (E3).

Progesterone — The hormone produced by a woman's body that plays a complementary role to estrogen in the reproductive cycle.

Progestin — Any synthetic molecule that has actions similar to the body's own progesterone.

Progestogen — A term for any molecule that has progesterone-like action; includes both bioidentical progesterone and synthetic progesterone.

of time, unhealthy lifestyle, and stress on your body. For many women, age forty marks the onset of a noticeable slowing of metabolism and digestion, particularly if they are sedentary.

Most men at midlife go through a similar transition due to aging — developing middle-aged spread, wrinkles, and flagging libido, even forgetting a name here or there — yet they are not suddenly losing estrogen. A study of more than fifteen hundred men and women in rural England showed little difference between the genders for midlife health symptoms. In fact, only two symptoms occurred more often in middle-aged women than in their male peers: hot flashes and vaginal dryness! It just goes to show that many of the symptoms attributed to changing hormones at perimenopause or later are due to other, more fundamental disturbances that occur equally in men and women.

Cultural differences further highlight the question of whether menopausal symptoms and disease are the inevitable result of estrogen decline. The Japanese language, for example, has no word for "hot flashes," because they are so rarely reported by Japanese women. Their absence is commonly attributed to the Japanese diet, which is high in soy and contains substances called *phytoestrogens*, or plant estrogens that mimic the effect of estrogen in the body.

In tribal and rural India, women living simple, low-stress lives rarely have menopausal symptoms. Physical exertion and a diet of fresh foods (especially wild yam), grains such as quinoa and amaranth, and spices with estrogenic effects all have a modulating or balancing effect on fluctuating hormone levels. I have noticed that when Indian *vaidyas* (Ayurvedic physicians) come to the West, they are usually very surprised by the many reproductive problems Western women have, including

> ## *Menopause Terms Defined*
>
> **Natural Menopause** —
> (1) *Medical definition*: Menopause that occurs according to the body's own timing and not due to any medical intervention, such as hysterectomy or chemotherapy.
>
> (2) *Common definition*: Menopause that occurs according to the body's own timing *and* does not involve any prescribed medicines, such as HT or drugs, for treating symptoms or complications.
>
> **Perimenopause** — The six years or so immediately before natural menopause when changes begin, up to the point when there have been twelve consecutive months without a period.
>
> **Menopause** — The acknowledged end of menstruation. Technically, only one day in a woman's life, when she has gone twelve months in a row without a period or her ovaries are removed or damaged.
>
> **Postmenopause** — All the years of a woman's life after menopause.
>
> **Premenopause** — All the years from puberty until perimenopause begins.
>
> **Premature Menopause** — Menopause that occurs naturally before age forty.

menopausal symptoms, as well as premenstrual syndrome (PMS), dysmenorrhea (painful menstrual periods), weight gain after pregnancy, and postpartum depression. All of these occur far less often in India.

Even in our own culture, not all women experience menopausal symptoms or complications. One study found that one out of five women does not experience hot flashes at all. It is also important to remember that (despite what drug companies may tell us) not every woman gets osteoporosis or has a heart attack, yet every woman goes through menopause. If menopause alone caused these problems, then every woman would have them. This leaves us to ponder the possibility that health problems at midlife and beyond are due to something more than declining estrogen.

The Bigger Picture of Menopausal Problems

If conditions such as osteoporosis and cardiovascular disease are not caused by estrogen deficiency, as our modern medical theory would have us believe, what does cause them? According to Maharishi Ayurveda, (and today's more enlightened medical experts) these diseases are primarily due to the cumulative effects of unhealthy lifestyle habits during our entire premenopausal lives and are only partially aggravated by shifting hormones when perimenopause and menopause arrive at our doorstep.

The best academic medical minds in our country are coming to realize that drugs and hormones cannot replace what years of poor lifestyle have destroyed. In light of recent evidence, it seems foolish to rely on drugs and hormones to magically grant us healthy golden years, including freedom from heart disease and osteoporosis.

These magic bullet treatments do not bestow real health, and they carry with them side effects that in the long run are not worth the risk.

With all of this growing evidence, a more complex picture of menopausal complications is emerging. Rather than scapegoating estrogen decline as the ultimate problem, we must instead take into account how aging, cumulative lifestyle factors, and the body's underlying state of health at the time of menopause affect the body's ability to *adjust* to the loss of hormones.

Could it be that if the body maintains a healthful balance — all physiological and psychological factors coordinated and functioning as Nature intended — then it will more readily adjust to a change in estrogen levels? If so, symptoms will be minor and long-term complications such as osteoporosis and cardiovascular disease will not occur. This is the upbeat prediction of Maharishi Ayurveda across the millennia. I have seen it verified over and over again in my own clinical practice today.

THE SPECTRUM OF APPROACHES: DEFINING WHAT IS NATURAL

When it comes to choosing a natural, healthy approach to menopause, women today are faced with a mind-boggling array of treatments, therapies, and prescriptions — enough to confuse even the most well-informed. Like most women, you have probably asked: Should I take "natural hormones"? Are soy products safe? Do I need to take something, *anything* to compensate for my lack of hormones? But nowhere are the answers clearly spelled out, nor are there comparisons of how safe and natural each therapy is.

To help address this situation, I designed Table 1.1, which summarizes the benefits and hazards of a broad spectrum of treatment approaches, from the most high tech to the most natural. At one end of this spectrum are the drug and hormonal interventions for menopausal health problems; at the other end are approaches that have no side effects and are completely natural. In between these two extremes are the mixed approaches of "natural hormones" and alternative approaches using food and herb-based supplements.

Along the spectrum I have placed six different approaches, each considered from the perspective of how natural it is, how safe it is, and how thoroughly it addresses women's midlife health needs. Let's look more closely at each of these approaches, starting with the least natural category, which I am calling *synthetic* because it is made up of traditional HT and the new designer version of HT, selective estrogen receptor modulators (SERMs).

Table 1.1 Spectrum of Naturalness

Most Natural ....

NATURAL	MIXED	MIXED
Maharishi Ayurveda	**Phytoestrogens**	**Bioidentical Hormones**
Overall health-balancing approach.	Dietary approach.	"Replacement" approach, usually individualized.
Multiple approaches that support the body's innate ability to adjust to lower hormone levels.	Consumption of plants, herbs and foods to balance the hormonal transition.	Replacing the hormones which are lost at menopause.
Psychophysiological imbalances that lie at the root of menopause symptoms are removed through:	Ingestion in the diet as whole foods is completely natural and safe.	Bioidentical hormones are hormones that are chemically identical to your body's own hormones.
1) Balancing biorhythms with a daily routine in tune with Nature's cycles. 2) Reducing mental stress through the Transcendental Meditation technique. 3) Optimizing diet and digestion as well as including phytoestrogen-rich foods, herbs and spices. 4) Herbs and highly absorbable minerals to balance hormones and bodily tissues. 5) Maharishi Rejuvenation Therapy (MRT), *panchakarma,* for eliminating wastes and toxins and quickly restoring overall balance.	Concentrated herbal or extract formulas have the potential to create side effects and should be used with proper guidance and ideally not for more than one year until more is known about their long-term effects. Examples: Dietary-soy, wheat, cashews, apples, almonds, turmeric, fennel and many others. Herbs-*Angelica sinensis* (Dong Quai,), *Cimicifuga racemosa* (black cohosh,) licorice, red clover, and others. Extracted phytoestrogens-genestein, diadzein, others.	They are "natural" in the sense that they exactly match your body's natural hormones, and because the raw material for them is from plants. They are *unnatural* in that they are given to the body at a time (i.e. after menopause) that the body would not naturally have such high levels of hormones. Also, they are given according to arbitrary amounts and schedules, rather than guided by your own body. Examples: estradiol, estriol, estrone, Climara, Alora, Estraderm, FemPatch, Vivelle; natural progesterone, Prometrium, Crinone.

....Least Natural

SYNTHETIC	SYNTHETIC
"Traditional" HT	SERMs
"Replacement" approach, usually standardized.	"Designer" approach to hormone replacement.
Replacing the hormones that are lost at menopause.	Replacing the estrogen that is lost at menopause with a chemically-designed estrogen-like drug that would ideally supply only the positive effects of estrogen without any negative effects.
"Traditional" HT here refers to conjugated equine estrogens, (a complex combination of over 17 different estrogenic substances found in pregnant mare's urine, hence the name "Premarin"), along with a synthetic progesterone-like compound called "Provera." Premarin is "natural" in the sense that it is naturally found in the horse. However, it is not natural to the human body. Provera is not natural in any way in that it is synthesized chemically in the laboratory and it does not exactly match the body's own progesterone. "Traditional" HT is unnatural to the body for the same additional reasons that bio-identical HT is unnatural.	SERMs are completely man-made molecules that are designed to be proestrogenic in desirable sites such as the bones, and anti-estrogen in sites such as the breast and uterus where estrogen can cause cancer or other side-effects, So far, SERMs are available that can increase bone density, lower cholesterol, and block breast and uterine cancer. However, hot flashes, blood clots, and potentially negative effects on the brain, mind and emotions are still possible side effects. Examples: Tamoxifen, Raloxifene (Evista).

"Traditional" Hormone Therapy

Today, in the post-WHI era, the decision to take HT is really only an issue for those women who have persistent, severe hot flashes or sleep disturbance, in spite of treatment with other, safer therapies. Hormone therapy remains the fastest and most effective treatment for reducing hot flashes, night sweats and sleep disturbance associated with the menopausal transition. However, according to current guidelines, intractable menopausal symptoms are the only reason that women should be prescribed HT, due to the serious potential side effects.

The findings of the Women's Health Initiative (WHI), released in July 2002, definitively established that the risks of combination HT outweigh the benefits. The WHI followed more than 16,000 women over a 5.2 year period who were ages 50-79 (average age 63), still had an intact uterus, and were taking a combination of estrogen and progestin (Premarin, derived from mare's urine, and Provera, a synthetic progestogen). HT increased the risk of disease by the following amounts: breast cancer by 26 percent, heart attacks by 29 percent, strokes by 41 percent, and blood clots by 100 percent. In addition, significant increases in dementia and ovarian cancer were noted. Contrary to popular belief, quality of life, including general health, vitality, mental health, depressive symptoms and sexual satisfaction proved no better in the hormone group than in the controls. On the positive side, colon cancer was 37 percent less in the hormone group, and all fractures were reduced by 24 percent. However, the latter benefits were not enough to offset the increased risks.

Since the risks of HT are cumulative, taking HT for two to four years around the time of menopause is currently considered reasonably safe. However, the catch is that women taking HT for hot flashes quite often experience a return of their symptoms when they try to stop the hormones several years later. They end up facing the same dilemma all over again, this time with the added pressure of more immediate increased health risks from the hormones.

For this reason, taking HT for menopausal symptoms should be understood as a temporary solution only. Beyond that, the current medical approach falters, offering only more hormones or a variety of drugs. An approach that makes women *truly healthier* during their 2-3 year "grace period" on HT is desperately needed so that women can eventually wean themselves off hormones without experiencing a return of their symptoms.

Cathy's Story

Cathy was 48 years old and in the middle of a difficult marital situation when she first came to my clinic at The Raj. She was taking "time out" for a week, she explained, to help clarify her feelings toward her marriage, to recover from a string of life stressors in the past several years, and to learn what she could do naturally to ease her menopausal transition. She had been on hormones for over two years, since her periods had become irregular, and hot flashes had begun to keep her awake at night. She had tried several other natural approaches, including black cohosh and soy extracts, without relief.

I explained to Cathy that mental stress and accumulated imbalances in her body were interfering with its ability to adjust to her shifting hormones. Hormone therapy was temporarily helping her symptoms, but in a way also masking deeper imbalances. In contrast, her MAV treatment would address the root causes of her symptoms, making her body truly healthier and better able to adjust to this most natural transition. I felt confident that her week-long treatment at The Raj, followed by some simple lifestyle adjustments at home would provide her with a momentum of inner balance and health that could propel her beyond the need for hormones.

Six months later, Cathy wrote me to report her amazement that, despite the stress of an ongoing divorce, she had indeed been able to wean herself off the hormones, was sleeping well and having only mild "warm flashes" a few times during the day. "I am pleasantly surprised at how well I am handling the stress of a divorce, and doubly pleased that I have been able to come off the hormones, as you suggested. This treatment has been nothing short of a miracle for me."

HT: A Reality Check

In spite of HT's original promise as a hormonal fountain of youth, women in my practice would often report to me that they tried HT but stopped because it gave them side effects, such as weight gain, depression, tender breasts, facial skin spots and rashes, hypoglycemic tendencies, or just plain "feeling awful." In fact, studies report that only 20 percent of postmenopausal women in this country took HT in the pre-WHI era, and of these, 70 percent stopped within six months. In my experience, only a minority of women who begin HT report a return to their "old" selves. The majority continue to experience problems such as fatigue, overheating, depression, weight gain, high blood pressure, and rising cholesterol, long after more immediate symptoms such as hot flashes or vaginal dryness have resolved.

Why Were Women So Mislead About HT?

Obviously, the WHI findings were shocking because they followed on the heels of decades of rosy press reports on HT's supposed benefits. So why the sudden turnaround? The answer lies in the *type* of research from which conclusions are drawn. The initial positive studies on HT were mainly "observational" studies, which look backward in time, comparing those who chose to take HT versus those who did not. However, the women who chose to take estrogen back in the sixties and seventies were not randomly assigned to HT, as by a "coin toss" (the "gold standard," randomized, double-blind trial). They may have been more health conscious and followed better diets and exercise regimens than their non-HT-taking peers. Indeed, HT users have been found to be more highly educated and thinner than nonusers.

The failure to find any benefit of HT in randomized trials indicates that such lifestyle factors were the most likely cause of the reduction in heart attacks among these women.

New Low-Dose Estrogens: Will They Solve the Problems?

Within months of news-breaking research findings on the disappointing results of HT for heart disease and stronger evidence regarding HT's cancer risks, journals began arriving in my mailbox with articles and ads proclaiming the promise of "new, low-dose" HT regimens. Indeed, initial studies show that doses that are about half of standard are effective at reducing hot flashes and vaginal atrophy with fewer short-term side effects, such as breakthrough bleeding.

Recently, "ultralow-dose" estrogen (one-quarter of the "usual" dose) was found to significantly increase bone density in postmenopausal women without giving any reported side effects in three years. Whether that will translate long-term into fewer fractures and an absence of side effects is yet to be determined.

Overall, less is likely to be better. However, in women with ovaries intact, *any* amount of estrogen taken as therapy is still more than the body is making naturally — a setup for long-term side effects. Keep in mind that it will take at least ten years to get an accurate picture of the long-term safety of low-dose estrogen regimens.

SERMs: The New Designer HRT

In another attempt to reduce the side effects of estrogen therapy, a new category of synthetic estrogens called *selective estrogen receptor modulators* (SERMs) has been created by medical science. Similar in molecular structure to estrogen, SERMs were designed to bring about positive effects without the negative effects of estrogen. They do this by acting like estrogen in some organs but blocking estrogen's effects on others. So far, raloxifene and tamoxifen are the main SERMs available.

These drugs, while beneficial in certain circumstances, are far from perfect. Tamoxifen is useful in treating breast cancer initially. However, it actually *increases* breast cancer risk if taken for more than five years. It also increases uterine cancer risk and clotting problems, can cause hot flashes, and may cause depression and memory problems. Raloxifene (better known by the trade name Evista) improves bone density, slightly reduces cholesterol, and reduces breast cancer risk in the first years of use, but causes hot flashes in many women. Most importantly, long-term studies on its safety and effectiveness are yet to come.

As breast surgeon and women's health advocate Dr. Susan Love wrote in *Dr. Susan Love's Hormone Book*, "Will we ever get the perfect hormone? Or is that what we really should be looking for? Stay tuned, but remember that anytime someone tells you they have developed something that sounds too good to be true, it probably is."

"Natural Hormones" (Bioidentical Hormones)

As more and more bad news about the risks of HT is reported, many women are turning to so-called "natural hormones," in hopes of a safer, more natural form of hormone replacement. While these hormones may be safer than designer or traditional HT, we still need to ask: Are they safe enough? (Remember, a truly natural approach should be without side effects because it is not interventional, but rather works along with your body.) Let's see just how natural "natural hormones" are.

Earlier in this chapter, I explained how your own natural hormones — estrogen and progesterone — work. Now let's look at how they actually interact with your cells in order to understand where they fit in the spectrum of naturalness and safety.

Estrogen hormones act within your cells by combining with tiny molecules called *receptors*. A receptor is similar to a keyhole and designed so that only certain "keys" fit into it. However, unlike a key, which must fit a lock precisely, a wide variety of estrogen-like "keys" can fit into an estrogen receptor, including your body's own three forms of estrogen, commercial estrogens like Premarin, SERMs, and the estrogen-like molecules called phytoestrogens that occur naturally in a variety of foods, herbs, and spices. Remember, not all estrogens are alike. Due to their varying structures, each of these different estrogens causes its own unique effects as it connects with the receptors on the various cells in tissues and organs of your body.

Are "Natural Hormones" Really Natural?

So-called "natural hormones" are manufactured hormones that exactly match your body's own hormones, including estradiol, estriol, estrone, and progesterone. They fit your body's receptors in the same way your own hormones do, thereby earning the label "natural." However, they are not natural in the sense of being derived directly from soy or wild yam, as many women assume. Rather, the estrogen-like substance is extracted from the plant and then altered chemically in the laboratory to make an exact replica of your body's own. Since these substances do not naturally occur in the form you eventually take, but do match your body's own hormones, a more precise term for them is *bioidentical*.

There is a second and more important way in which these bioidentical hormones are not natural to your body. *Nature did not put them in your body in the first place.* Like HT, bioidentical hormones are introduced into your body from an outside source, with a preset amount and timing that do not fit your body's needs and natural cycles. Such a situation cannot possibly create the precise and intricate state of *natural* balance within your body that is the foundation of health. It is a setup for potentially dangerous side effects.

Nonetheless, bioidentical hormones are promoted as "proven safe" by several popular authors, physicians and natural pharmacies. But this pronouncement is premature, misleading, and likely to be proven wrong. The long-term side effects of bioidentical hormones have not yet been studied in human trials, and there is no proof that they are any less carcinogenic than Premarin and Provera. Rather, many medical experts believe they are equivalent to Premarin and Provera in carcinogenic effects and several other side effects. According to the latest medical guidelines, all estrogens must be assumed to be as risky as those studied in the Women's Health Initiative, until proven otherwise. Whether large, randomized controlled trials on bioidentical hormones will ever be done is currently being questioned due to the high expense of such trials, and the ethical concern that women would be put unnecessarily at risk. Considering the large proportion of women who are currently being lead to believe that bioidentical hormones *are* safe, it may be prudent to do some long-term studies to definitely test these claims.

After all, our body's *own* estrogen, when present in higher levels or with longer exposures, can increase our risk of cancer. Women with dense bones, a marker of high estrogen, have an increased risk of breast cancer. So do women who started their menses at an earlier age or stopped them at a later age, giving them more years of exposure to their own bodies' estrogen. Indeed, laboratory estrogens as a whole, including the popular bioidentical form of estradiol, were recommended for classification as "known carcinogens" by the National Institute of Environmental Health Sciences' National Toxicology Program in 2001.

In their favor, the bioidenticals may have fewer side effects in the short term. Synthetic progestins, for example, have been found to increase cholesterol significantly, but bioidentical progesterone that exactly matches your own does not raise cholesterol nearly as much, and women report fewer side effects with it.

Preliminary studies suggest that one bioidentical estrogen, estriol (E3), may be less cancer-promoting, yet deliver significant benefits to bone health while reducing vaginal atrophy, urinary tract infections, and hot flashes in menopausal women. While it is doubtful that any hormone taken as therapy will ever be totally "proven safe," it does seem that estriol deserves to be studied on its own in well-designed clinical trials to properly assess its benefits and side effects. Meanwhile, I would advise you to approach estriol treatment with as much serious consideration and caution as any other hormone therapy.

Is "Natural" Progesterone Safe?

Proponents of bioidentical progesterone downplay its risks, and I have yet to meet a woman taking it who did not assume that it was completely risk-free or even

> ## *Yam Scam?*
>
> I commonly see women who are taking *wild yam*, a popular herbal product for menopause symptoms available in both cream and tablet form. Wild yam is marketed as a natural plant source of substances that both act like progesterone in your body and can be converted by your body into progesterone. However, these promotional claims are not substantiated by clinical research. What little research there has been so far indicates that wild yam gives no progesterone effects and is not converted to progesterone by the body. In fact, two studies by researchers Zava and Beckham found that women taking wild yam had much *lower* levels of progesterone than the control group. This suggests that diosgenin, the natural compound and active ingredient in wild yam and some other herbs, may actually suppress progesterone synthesis and lower progesterone levels — not exactly the effect women are looking for.

anticarcinogenic. However, while bioidentical progesterone has been shown to protect against the uterine cancer-causing effects of estrogen when taken orally (as does Provera), it has *not* been shown to protect against the cancer-promoting effects of estrogen on the breast. Given recent findings that taking synthetic progestogens with estrogen for ten years doubles the risk of breast cancer over taking estrogen alone, we must assume, until we see proof to the contrary, that bioidentical progesterone carries a similar risk, whether taken as a capsule or as a cream rubbed into the skin.

All told, bioidentical progesterone has not yet been proven safe, and a recent randomized trial indicates that it also does *not* increase bone density significantly, contrary to popular belief. While it has been shown to reduce hot flashes, there are safer options, such as dietary and herbal treatments, that should be tried first. If you do choose to take bioidentical progesterone, take it for as short a time as possible to minimize your risks.

Alternative Approaches: Vitamins, Herbs, and Food Concentrates

A growing number of women who are dissatisfied with the fragmented approach of modern medicine — a cardiologist for high blood pressure, a gynecologist for Pap smears, and a psychiatrist for our chronic anxiety — are visiting alternative practitioners. They hope to find a more holistic approach to menopause symptoms and related health conditions. Treatments may include taking supplements such as vitamins, herbs, and food concentrates.

How Safe Are Alternative Approaches?

Is the alternative approach really more holistic? Is it even safe? Some women find they are dealing with just as many different practitioners: a chiropractor for their back pain, a naturopath for their hot flashes, and an acupuncturist for their sinus headaches. Add to this the bewildering array of supplements and vitamins available at the health-food store, and the vastly differing opinions of health-food store clerks, and it seems that alternative approaches can be just as fragmented and confusing as the mainstream medical model.

In regard to safety, vitamins, herbs, and food concentrates are designed like a magic bullet — the same way traditional HT, SERMs, and bioidenticals are designed. Both try to use an isolated substance to bring about a cure. A woman may feel she is helping herself by taking garlic capsules for her high cholesterol, or echinacea for her immune system, but treating a symptom with a supplement does not treat health as a whole. Alternative endeavors cannot counter the effects of a lifetime of poor eating habits and an unbalanced lifestyle. This is not to say that many alternative or complementary therapies are without benefit. Certainly many are helpful and relatively safe when compared to drugs and surgery. A number of studies indicate that black cohosh is helpful for hot flashes, and safe for a six-month period of use, possibly longer. For overall health, however, over-hyped, largely unsubstantiated claims of reduced heart disease or cancer risk can lull people into thinking that lifestyle is unimportant — maybe their lack of exercise is all right, since they are taking their vitamin E and coenzyme Q10. The fact is that despite decades of research, no substitute for healthy living has ever been discovered. The experience of Gina illustrates one way supplements can do more harm than good.

Gina's Story: When Less Is More

Gina, a forty-nine-year-old nurse, came to me for an evaluation because she had been having episodes of heart palpitations for over a year. She had gotten a complete cardiac workup from her previous doctor, who had told her that her symptoms were due to her perimenopausal condition. Gina did not want to take HT, her doctor's recommendation, and came to me for a more natural, herbal approach.

In the course of her evaluation, Gina pulled out her bag of seventeen supplements, ranging from black cohosh to CoQ10 to high-dose multivitamins to blue-green algae — all of which she had been taking for over a year. She gave me a logical reason for taking each one, based on studies she had read, proclaiming how great each substance was for health. When it came time to write her prescription, I found myself unable to add anything to the confusing conglomeration of substances she was already taking. On a hunch, I suggested that she gradually wean off the supplements over a few weeks and then return for a follow-up visit. In addition, I recommended a diet of fresh, whole foods, based on her individual needs, as well as other lifestyle changes.

Sure enough, four weeks later, Gina returned with a smile and a healthy glow on her face. "I have good news for you," she reported. "The palpitations have completely disappeared." Not only that, but she had lost 4 pounds without trying and attained a state of energy and vitality that she had been striving for, but that all her supplements had been unable to deliver.

But Aren't Vitamins Naturally Safe?

Vitamins are naturally occurring substances found both in foods and in the body. However, taking them in high concentrations in isolated form rather than as they are naturally found in whole foods is not natural to the body. In fact, it's just one more magic bullet that can throw you off balance. Over time, imbalances in your body's biochemistry may lead to side effects. In January 2000, a panel from the Institute of Medicine established, for the first time ever, upper limits of vitamin C and E intake to prevent such adverse health effects.

The bulk of the evidence now indicates that vitamins naturally occurring and consumed in foods are much more powerful, and safer, than vitamins taken in supplement form. The Iowa Women's Health Study found as much as a 50 to 75 percent reduction in heart attack risk in postmenopausal women consuming high amounts of vitamin E naturally in their diet. In contrast, taking vitamin E as a supplement has shown variable benefits, with a 35 to 40 percent heart attack reduction at best, and at worst, an increase in strokes and bleeding problems. The Iowa Women's Health Study further discovered that those with high vitamin E intake from their diet who also took supplemental vitamins had *less* benefit than those with a healthy diet who didn't take vitamins at all.

It is a policy in my practice to ask new patients to bring all their supplements to their first visit. I am frequently astonished by how large a bag they bring, often overflowing with bottles and jars! With studies showing that just one supplement in high doses can throw the body out of balance, imagine what taking dozens of them at a time might do.

Generally, the safest approach to "supplementing" your diet is simply to optimize your intake of a variety of whole foods. If a woman feels she really needs to take certain vitamins that she may not be getting in her diet, I generally advise her not to take them every day, but just once or twice a week. This minimizes any unbalancing effect that they may have and reduces any strain on your body that may come from excreting the excess nutrients. If your body is really low in a nutrient, its "affinity" for it — meaning its ability to absorb it from the intestines — increases dramatically, making megadoses or daily supplements rarely truly necessary.

How Naturally Safe Are Herbs?

Herbs in their whole form, or as whole components, behave much like foods in your body and are therefore generally balancing. However, by definition, herbs have stronger physiological effects than most foods and so must be used in a balanced and knowledgeable fashion.

Natural medicine, as practiced today in the West, tends to mirror the modern medical model of treating a symptom with an isolated magic bullet — albeit an herb.

For example, modern herbalism commonly recommends St. John's wort for everyone who feels depressed and the herbal resin guggulu to anyone with high cholesterol.

In traditional natural medicine systems, including Maharishi Ayurveda, single herbs specific to one symptom or ailment are rarely used alone. In MAV, precise understanding of the art and science of herbal preparation is combined with a sophisticated understanding of how to match the right formula to the right patient. For example, guggulu is often used in the treatment of high cholesterol, but only when the problem is caused by particular imbalances and never as an isolated ingredient. Supportive herbs are always combined with guggulu to enhance its action and to balance its inherent heat-increasing effects, which otherwise may cause heartburn, skin rashes, or other inflammatory conditions.

The principles that influence herbal safety and efficacy are important because herbs are fast emerging as popular treatments for menopausal symptoms such as hot flashes, vaginal dryness, mood swings, and sleep disturbances. Traditional Ayurvedic herbs and spices will be used later in this book in a highly individualized program to help eliminate your menopausal symptoms and correct the underlying physiological imbalances that have given rise to them.

Phytoestrogens: Hormonal Intelligence from Your Food

We have seen how taking any kind of "magic bullet" to replace or enhance what is already naturally in your body is unnatural and therefore carries the risk of side effects. But Nature, in her infinite compassion and wisdom, did provide one powerful, yet gentle option for hormonal support at menopause: our food. *Phytoestrogens*, those plant estrogens that exist in foods, spices, and herbs, enter your body through your diet every day. This ebbing, flowing, and partnering with your body's own hormones is an intricately choreographed, intelligent dance of hormonal health.

Phytoestrogens in your diet technically come from outside your body, but in their naturally-occurring food form, they do not create side effects. This is because your genes have evolved *with* phytoestrogens over millions of years, and they are fully integrated into Nature's plan. Classified in at least eight different botanical categories, phytoestrogens are found in common fruits, vegetables, nuts, cereals, spices, seeds, legumes, and herbs. In foods, phytoestrogens are present in relatively low doses and occur in wide variety, so no one hormonal signal can overwhelm your body's delicate hormone-balancing act, and thus create side effects.

Furthermore, phytoestrogens in plants are natural SERMs — they act like estrogen in some organs and block its effects in others. But not all these hormone-balancing herbs and spices act like estrogen in your body. Research has found black cohosh to be the most effective isolated herb against hot flashes, but surprisingly, it doesn't act at all like estrogen in your body. It doesn't even attach itself to the estrogen receptors in your cells. Yet, many phytoestrogenic herbs do interact directly with your hormonal system: Licorice and red clover work by directly stimulating your estrogen receptors much as estrogen does, while soy has mixed stimulating and blocking effects. The total effect of phytoestrogenic herbs and foods, when taken properly, is to *balance* your hormones and support your body, rather than overstimulating the body, causing damaging side effects.

Isolated Phytoestrogens Are Not Safe.

Research has shown that eating a phytoestrogen-rich diet that includes soy products can reduce hot flashes and may lead to modest gains in bone density and a lowering of cholesterol. Countering the "magic bullet" mentality, recent research has found that soy phytoestrogen can be more powerful when given as whole food than when concentrated into a pill.

An NIH-sponsored workshop held in 1999 to review the known health effects of phytoestrogens found that whole soy foods seem to provide greater health benefits than isolated extracts. For example, one study found that isolating the phytoestrogen substances, called *isoflavones*, from soy and giving them as a pill was not as effective at lowering cholesterol as giving intact soy protein.

Isolating and ingesting the "active ingredients" in phytoestrogen-rich foods may also create side effects. While soy food consumption in general is associated with a reduced risk of breast cancer, concentrated isoflavones have a variable effect on cancer cells growing in the laboratory. In one study, they actually stimulated cancer growth when given in low doses. While phytoestrogen-rich foods in their whole form may be helpful, isolated and concentrated isoflavones act more like drugs. Medical experts caution against their use until more research is done. It just may end up that isolated isoflavones carry the same risks as the drugs and hormones women are trying to avoid.

Maharishi Ayurveda (MAV)

By now, you have seen that a variety of therapies other than MAV are promoted as natural or healthy. None of them except for phytoestrogenic and vitamin-rich whole foods deserve those descriptions. MAV's position on the "most natural" end of the spectrum of therapies for menopause suggests that it is a purely and totally natural approach.

MAV doesn't rely on intervention by a foreign substance to correct or replace the hormones your body has been using all of your life. Instead, it supports your health during menopause by strengthening your body's own self-healing and balancing mechanisms. Enlivening the inner intelligence of the body for total healing, not simply targeting symptoms, is the primary goal of every treatment modality in MAV.

MAV herbal prescriptions are not applied according to the magic bullet theory. Rather, combinations of herbs are prepared together in precise formulas to create a synergistic enhancement of herbal effects and to increase bioavailability. These herbal formulations always include select ingredients that balance out the potential side effects of the primary herbs in the formula.

Herbal preparations from MAV, when applied correctly, are free of dangerous side effects. Achieving this high degree of safety, however, requires a meticulous attention to detail and a thorough understanding of how to combine and prepare the formulas to minimize negative effects. An herb prepared properly can be very safe even when modern research on that same herb used in isolation and in high doses finds potentially dangerous side effects.

YOUR MAHARISHI AYURVEDA PROGRAM FOR HEALTH AFTER FORTY

The MAV approach outlined in this book will provide you with an individualized, focused approach to optimizing your lifestyle for radiant good health at menopause and beyond. You will also be given a tailor-made herbal and dietary program to correct the underlying imbalances in your body that are the *real* cause of most health problems before, during and after menopause.

Regardless of what other choices you make for your health during this important transition, your personalized, totally natural MAV menopause program will support your body's inner healing ability and help you create a stable foundation for vibrant health in the decades to come, without harmful side effects.

* 2 *

ACHIEVING BALANCE THROUGH NATURE'S INTELLIGENCE

Any treatment that attends only to the symptoms is not a good therapy. The best treatment is one that balances the whole and does not create other disorders.
— *the* Charaka Samhita

Perfect balance is the natural state of your body, mind, and spirit, according to Maharishi Ayurveda. Nature created you whole and complete. Even if you no longer feel whole, healthy, or in balance, your body's inner healing intelligence nonetheless has the capability to re-create perfect health within you. Getting truly healthy depends on restoring that natural balance, which at menopause includes supporting the intricate interplay of your hormones for a smooth and trouble-free transition.

Modern medicine knows this natural balance as *homeostasis*, the built-in tendency of your body to return to a state of equilibrium and health when temporarily thrown off balance by stress or illness. According to MAV, this natural mechanism of self-healing represents your body's intelligence working to restore balance, its naturally healthy state. Restoring your inner balance is the key to keeping you free of symptoms and disease. How you can achieve this during midlife and later is the subject of this chapter.

TREATING THE WHOLE, NOT THE PARTS

Being women influenced by our Western culture, we automatically tend to look *outside* ourselves for the solution to our health problems, most often in the form of a pill to target and correct our symptoms. But, as we saw in Chapter 1, adding one more piece, such as an extra hormone, drug, vitamin, or herb is not the best way to effectively manage the symptoms of menopause or your overall health. These isolated magic bullets may help in one area of your body, but they tend to disturb another and, in addition, can cause harmful side effects. Even more detrimental, the magic bullet approach allows the underlying causes of your symptoms to remain hidden, postponing treatment and risking that symptoms may pop up again later as more serious disorders and disease.

The classic children's nursery rhyme "Humpty Dumpty" reminds us of the wisdom we know instinctively to be true. When he was dashed to pieces by his fall from the wall, "all the king's horses and all the king's men couldn't put Humpty together again." Likewise, after investing billions of dollars and decades of scientific research, even the most brilliant medical professionals and scientists have not found the key to restoring true health. Their failure lies not in a lack of sincerity, effort, or intellect but in a medical approach that tries to put pieces back together again, as if health were simply a matter of manipulating the parts to regain the health of the whole.

At midlife, this approach attempts to replace your waning hormones with a manufactured substitute, as if Nature has made a mistake and needed to be corrected. The price of our modern medical solution is often uncomfortable and dangerous side effects, not to mention deadly diseases. Many alternative approaches are also founded in this replacement theory and promote piecemeal hormonal therapies that carry similar risks, despite their claims to be "natural" and "safe."

But there *is* a better way — a safer and longer-lasting approach that harnesses your body's homeostatic, self-balancing mechanisms to re-establish the inner health that Nature meant for you to enjoy — at menopause and beyond. The story of my patient Joanna shows how restoring balance can resolve menopausal complications and eliminate other ailments as well.

Joanna's Story: Restoring Balance without Magic Bullets

When Joanna, a forty-four-year-old computer programmer, came to see me for her menopausal symptoms, she was struggling with chronic back pain from an injury that had occurred eight years earlier. The resulting pain, fatigue, and depression had forced her to quit her job and turned her into a "full-time patient," in dramatic contrast to the athletic and energetic life she had led before her injury.

To add to her problems, Joanna's menstrual periods were becoming irregular and she was waking several nights a week with drenching sweats and disturbing hot flashes that kept her up for hours. She had refused to take the hormone therapy offered by her gynecologist because she feared breast cancer, a disease that was prevalent in her family. Now, between chronic back pain, debilitating fatigue, and increasing perimenopausal symptoms, her life was barely tolerable.

Joanna came to see me, looking for a natural solution for her complex condition. She had been diagnosed and treated with conventional medicine for the last eight years. She had tried many therapies, including back surgery, physical therapy, and antidepressant medication, but with limited success. Six months before she came to see me, she had discovered a prominent, well-respected physician who integrated alternative medicine with standard medical therapies, a practice commonly called *integrative medicine*.

Hoping this new approach would work for her, Joanna underwent a wide-ranging battery of tests. These included hair and blood mineral analyses, stool analysis, 24-hour stress hormone level tests, estrogen and progesterone level tests, and the standard blood count, blood chemistry, and thyroid function tests. Her doctor said the results indicated she was lacking in nutrients and her adrenal function was abnormal, most probably the source of her extreme fatigue and depression. As might be expected at perimenopause, her progesterone level was low and readings of other hormone levels correlated with her experience of approaching menopause.

Joanna's doctor described his integrative approach as "holistic" and assured her it addressed all aspects of her mind, body, and emotions. He proceeded to prescribe four pharmaceutical drugs, including two antidepressants, sleep medication, and Ritalin, a drug sometimes used on adults to alter mood. He also recommended more than twenty supplements, among them thyroid hormone, glandular extracts (providing cortisol-like substances from animal adrenal glands), DHEA, pregnenolone (a building block for most of the body's hormones), melatonin for sleep, progesterone for hot flashes, and high-dose vitamin and mineral supplements. Each drug, hormone, and vitamin was justified in this physician's logic to restore some natural substance that was missing or abnormally low, according to the many tests Joanna had undergone.

After six months of this rigorous therapy, Joanna still had symptoms, and to make matters worse, her body showed signs of rebelling. A routine test revealed liver enzymes more than *six times* the normal level, indicating that the supplements and drugs were seriously taxing her liver, the organ responsible for breaking down and eliminating these substances from her blood on a daily basis. The treatment that was supposed to restore her health was actually throwing her body out of balance and doing more harm than good.

Joanna's experience is extreme, but it illustrates how even an extremely well-informed physician, working with fragmented parts of the body — a hormone here, a vitamin there — cannot recreate the balance that Nature so effortlessly displays when you are in good health. Her doctor had failed in his attempt to imitate the inimitable.

I explained to Joanna that I would not be intervening with drugs and supplements to target and "fix" the separate systems and organs involved in her symptoms. Instead, my goal was to support her own internal balancing mechanisms, the natural tendency of her body to return to health.

I was concerned that her supplements were overloading and damaging her liver, so my first goal was to help her feel better with fewer or no supplements. In their place, I prescribed a lifestyle routine that would help to realign her bodily rhythms through an early bedtime and regular mealtimes; improve her digestion and elimination through a fresh, wholesome, home-cooked diet containing organic, phytoestrogen-rich vegetables, whole grains, and spices; and reduce her stress level through the Transcendental Meditation technique, a scientifically valid meditation technique I'll discuss in a later chapter. I was confident that these treatments could provide the foundation for her own inner healing response to begin to reintegrate the disjointed functioning of her body and mind. Joanna agreed to follow the program I prescribed.

At her follow-up visit two months later, I was delighted to hear that Joanna's hot flashes were abating and she was sleeping "better than in years." Not only were Joanna's perimenopausal symptoms decreasing, but her back pain was noticeably improved as well. She had begun to experience a lift in her mood and breakthroughs in her psychotherapy, which had been stalled for many months due to "mental blocks" she couldn't seem to overcome. Both her massage therapist and her osteopath reported that her body seemed more flexible, another reflection of the stress relief and inner healing she was experiencing from the program.

For Joanna, the healing she had sought for so long and from so many different approaches came spontaneously once she stopped trying to fix her isolated organs and systems and made some significant lifestyle and dietary changes. Clearly, her symptoms had been due to her body's lack of balance, not to a disease state in need of repair. With Nature now doing the work, she was well on her way to health, using an approach that was quicker, easier, and safer than drugs — and *truly* natural.

Quick Relief Is the Norm

You may be wondering if it is really that easy to get relief from your symptoms. For most of the patients I treat, the answer is a definite yes. Getting significant relief within the first month is the norm. It is reassuring to see, as with Joanna, that even very simple changes in lifestyle can trigger the body's innate sense of balance and quickly lead to improvement in symptoms.

The speed of the relief you can expect from such treatments depends on two factors: how out of balance you are and how committed you are to following the prescriptions to restore balance. At the end of this chapter, I offer a self-rating assessment scale that will help you place yourself in a range of balance from mild to moderate to severe. Once you have rated your own level of balance, you can apply the guidelines and recommendations I provide in the next chapters according to your individual needs.

You may also be wondering what underlies this natural power to heal and restore functioning so effortlessly compared to other approaches. For the answer to this, MAV expands on the Western notion of homeostasis, the body's own balancing mechanism, and goes directly to the source — the infinite natural intelligence that not only runs your body, but also underlies and coordinates the whole of the universe.

Nature's Intelligence: The Source of Your Inner Balance

The approach I used with Joanna was based on the principles of the most ancient healing modality known to humans, that of Maharishi Ayurveda. MAV is rooted in the understanding that your body has an inborn intelligence — Nature's intelligence — which knows exactly how to maintain a balanced state of health for body, mind, and spirit.

Nature's intelligence is built into your physiology as a kind of program — an original, living blueprint of how your body is designed to function automatically in perfect health, without disease or problems. When you support your inner intelligence by honoring your body's signals and needs, you are restoring the pure, radiant vitality and unshakable well-being that are your birthright and the hallmarks of lasting health.

MAV understands that the most silent level of your mind — your *Atma* in Vedic terminology — is the home of Nature's intelligence within you. At this deep, quiet level within yourself, your mind and body are one. Waking up your Atma through direct experience of it is key to enlivening the healing intelligence of Nature programmed within you. The therapies of Maharishi Ayurveda all work from this deep, inner level of Nature's intelligence, where mind and body are one — strengthening your body's healing ability in a most profound way.

Joanna's recovery was made possible when she began to enliven her body's inner intelligence through Transcendental Meditation and support her body's healing process with healthier lifestyle habits. These simple lifestyle changes allowed the healing process to occur spontaneously from *within*, establishing a new state of balance, in which her perimenopausal and chronic pain symptoms improved automatically.

Balance and Your Symptoms at Menopause

According to Maharishi Ayurveda, the basis of health is *balance*, which can be defined as the intelligent and coordinated functioning of all the parts in a unity that is greater than the sum of those parts. When your inner intelligence is able to express itself fully throughout your body, keeping all systems running smoothly, you experience good health. But when your natural intelligence is thwarted — by toxin or waste buildup, inadequate sleep, or poor diet — your body does not function optimally and you begin to experience symptoms that may be warnings of later disease.

As we saw with Joanna, stress, injuries, unhealthy lifestyle habits, and even overuse of supplements can lead to an imbalance that blocks the body's innate healing wisdom. Nature's healing program is still present, but it becomes overwhelmed, and no amount of magic bullets will help.

According to MAV, how you fare in the midlife transition is largely determined by how balanced your body is at this time. If your body is in balance when you reach age forty or fifty, your inner healing intelligence will orchestrate the hormonal shift smoothly and you will have an easy transition. But if you are out of balance, when menopause arrives (meaning your body's healing system is in a state of disrepair from years of stress and unhealthy lifestyle habits) you are likely to have more troublesome symptoms.

The story of two Indian sisters dramatizes how your lifestyle choices can affect your inner balance and determine how smooth or bumpy your menopausal transition will be.

Two Sisters: An Indian Menopause Story

A distinguished Ayurvedic physician with whom I have consulted in treating over three hundred of my patients shared with me his observation that menopausal problems, while rampant in the West, are nearly nonexistent in India. He noted, however, that menopausal symptoms are showing up more today in those Indian women who have adopted a Western diet and lifestyle.

He related his experience of treating a pair of sisters who grew up in a rural village in Eastern India. One sister moved to Bombay when she came of age, adopting a fast-paced lifestyle with a high-powered business job. The other remained in the small village, caring for her family, cooking wholesome food, and leading the physically active life of an Indian village woman. At menopause, the sister in Bombay consulted with him for severe hot flashes, night sweats, and mood swings. Yet her village sister had none of these menopausal symptoms, nor did their mother or other women in the family.

There are three important factors that probably contribute to the relative lack of menopause problems and complications such as osteoporosis in rural Indian women. First, they eat a diet rich in phytoestrogen-containing vegetables, whole grains, and legumes, and cook all their meals with phytoestrogen-rich spices. Second, they keep a regular routine of going to bed early, getting up early, and eating their meals on a regular schedule. Their schedule is more relaxed, with less pressure and more time spent enjoying the simple pleasures in life, including family activities and worship. Finally, exercise is an integral part of their lifestyle, with weight-bearing activity virtually impossible to avoid.

Indian village women live closely attuned to nature and are in balance automatically because of the simplicity and traditional values in their lives. Impossible as it may seem, this same balance can exist for modern women today. In our fast-paced Western culture, women can get back into balance even after menopause by paying closer attention to those quiet whispers of Nature's intelligence within — that wise-woman intuition we all have that tells us what is right to do. We can all begin to obey the nonverbal signals our bodies' inner wisdom uses to communicate its needs. We can eat when we are hungry, slow down when we feel stressed, and go to bed when we are tired, instead making one last phone call, performing those extra chores, or answering our e-mail late into the night.

Listening to our heart and seeking to satisfy our spiritual and emotional needs are also important parts of this journey back to balance. Such a simple but profound shift in how we are leading our daily lives can be the catalyst for the complete renewal of our health, as well as the resolution of many menopausal discomforts.

NATURE'S PLAN FOR YOUR NATURAL, HEALTHY MENOPAUSE

Nature has a plan for a natural, *healthy* menopause for every woman, despite our loss of estrogen at this time. This plan is essentially twofold. It combines an internal hormonal backup system that kicks in at menopause and an external hormone-building supply of food sources rich in phytoestrogens. By taking advantage of the two-pronged support system nature provides, you can be doubly assured that your menopause will be balanced, healthy, and emotionally rewarding instead of a bothersome drain or a time of illness and discomfort.

Let's look first at how your body's hormonal backup system functions and then at how foods can support it to provide the balance you need at the time of your transition.

Your Internal Hormonal Backup System

You may recall from Chapter 1 that your body does not completely lack estrogen after menopause. Your ovaries continue to make small amounts of estradiol even after your menstrual cycles stop, and your adrenal glands make androstenedione, which is then converted by your skin, muscle, and fat cells to estrone, the most abundant estrogen in your body after menopause. This backup system allows your body to continue to receive estrogen after menopause and helps it adapt slowly and smoothly to the reduced level with minimal symptoms.

For your backup system to operate effectively and support your smooth transition, however, four factors are involved. First, your ovaries, adrenal glands, and peripheral tissues must *produce* enough of the hormones estradiol, estrone, and androstenedione. Second, these hormones must be secreted in a *timely* manner to serve the needs of your various organs. Third, they must be *delivered* to their target sites, such as the vagina, brain, and urinary tract. Finally, your hormones must *interact* with specific estrogen receptors in your cells to provide their beneficial effects.

Only if all four of these factors are working will your own hormones be able to perform those functions that are vital to smooth menopause, such as stimulating adequate lubrication by the vagina, metabolizing cholesterol in the liver, and helping the hypothalamus in your brain regulate your temperature and minimize hot flashes. Anything that interferes with this hormonal balancing act will hinder your hormonal adjustment at menopause, making you more prone to persistent menopausal symptoms and long-term complications. Anything that supports it will help you achieve hormonal balance naturally, leading to good health for the long haul.

These four functions are critical to the smooth, balanced operation of your hormones during the menopausal transition. Let's look at what weakens them and how they can be strengthened.

When Your Hormonal Backup System Goes Awry

Maharishi Ayurveda confirms what common sense should tell us, that menopause is supposed to be easy. Nature took everything into account with her perfect plan. However, just as any beautiful, perfectly-balanced ecosystem (like a forest) can be damaged by man-made interference, like acid rain or traffic exhaust, your own naturally healthy state can be damaged by years of the wrong food, lack of sleep, and generally unnatural living. Then, the perfect balance that is programmed into your body becomes distorted, leaving you without the ability to adjust to a sudden change or challenge. Just as a high wind downs the weakest tree branches, the challenge of menopause unmasks any physiological weaknesses that have lain hidden beneath the surface for so many years.

Simply put, a rough menopausal transition means your hormonal backup system has malfunctioned in some way. If your mind-body system is out of balance, too much or too little hormone will be secreted or your amount of hormone secretion will fluctuate greatly. If your internal biorhythms (cycles of hormones, sleep, digestion, elimination, and other cyclical functions) are out of sync, the timing of your hormonal secretions can be thrown off. If your body is clogged with wastes and impurities from years of poor diet and lifestyle habits, the delivery of your hormones to your body's tissues (vagina, brain, skin, etc.) will be disrupted, even if your hormone supply is adequate. All of these problems can add up to a bumpy ride at menopause and poor health later on.

Recent cutting-edge research by Phyllis Wise at the University of Kentucky supports this ancient Ayurvedic theory of the menopausal transition. Dr. Wise's research indicates that at midlife, subtle irregularities in the circadian, or "pacemaker," part of the brain, which governs daily physiological rhythms including hormonal cycles, play a key role in the development of irregular menstrual cycles and eventually menopause itself.

It makes sense that the more widely fluctuating our sleep habits are, the greater the irregularity in the brain's 24-hour pacemaker function will be, and these irregularities in our hormonal functions lead to more hot flashes and other menopausal symptoms.

Hormonal Help from Plants

Remember that Nature has built in a second prong of your hormonal backup system — a rich supply of phytoestrogens in a wide diversity of food sources, including vegetables, cereals, grains, and legumes. Plant estrogens are Mother Nature's own version of HT, programmed into the very fabric of human sustenance and provided automatically when you have a wholesome and balanced diet. Nature's hormone-balancing cuisine, along with your body's own estrogen production, exercise, and a balanced lifestyle, are all designed to make menopause a gentle transition to support your health in later years — just as Nature intended.

Addressing Your Hormonal Adjustment

Each of these fundamental causes of menopause symptoms will be addressed in turn in the chapters that follow. In Chapter 3, you will learn how the underlying causes of menopausal and midlife symptoms, imbalances in your mind-body system, generally fall into one of three categories, each with its own unique healing strategy. Chapter 4 gives you practical self-care tips to balance your own unique symptom profile and normalize your hormonal system naturally.

In Chapter 5, you will learn how accumulated toxins and wastes can cause midlife symptoms by clogging your body's microcirculatory channels. Chapter 6 tells you how you can rid your cells of wastes that may be clogging the entry ways and blocking what little estrogen action you do have at this time. Eliminating this cellular junk is essential to improving your own natural hormonal function and relieving the symptoms of menopause in a truly natural way, without taking HT. This lets your body make the most of the decreased estrogen it produces during menopause, and it benefits your overall health at the same time.

> ### "A Little Dab'll Do Ya"
> The value of enhancing your own hormonal function after menopause is supported by recent research, which indicates that even a very small amount of estradiol produced by the body itself (less than one-tenth the amount found in women who are taking HT) helps protect your bones from osteoporosis. When your body makes the hormone itself, according to its own timing and delivery systems, a little can go a long way and protect you naturally without the risks of taking hormones from the outside.

Surgical and Chemotherapy Effects on Hormone Adjustment

Unfortunately, women who have their ovaries surgically removed during a hysterectomy no longer have the advantage of the small amounts of estrogen produced by the ovaries after menopause. Even women who have had hysterectomies or tubal ligations without removal of the ovaries usually lose some ovarian function due to the reduction of blood supply to the ovaries.

If your ovaries have been surgically removed, you are indeed more likely to have severe symptoms of menopause than women whose bodies have a longer, more gradual adjustment period and whose ovaries continue to make small amounts of estrogen. Similarly, if you have gone through menopause suddenly as a result of chemotherapy or Tamoxifen (an anti-estrogen drug used to treat breast cancer), you may have a more difficult transition and more troublesome menopausal symptoms.

But since most of the estrogen in your body after menopause originates in the adrenal glands, not your ovaries, your hormonal backup system is not completely disabled. You also have the option of including a rich variety of phytoestrogens in your diet to support your own hormonal production. In my experience, the balancing approaches of MAV are especially helpful in the case of ovarian compromise because they help you make the most of your remaining hormonal power.

THE POWER OF MAKING CHANGES NOW

Now that you know your midlife health problems are the result of imbalances acquired from a lifetime of stressful lifestyle factors, you may be feeling a bit overwhelmed or discouraged. But there is some good news: Midlife is not too late to turn your health around and begin to enjoy a really vibrant and vital state of being.

The Critical Decade

When I began my practice in MAV in 1986, the majority of my patients were in their thirties and came to see me for what we doctors call functional symptoms. Functional symptoms, such as fatigue, insomnia, low back pain, and indigestion, usually indicate disturbances in the normal function of the body; disease is not usually present. We often attribute these symptoms to diet, stress level, overwork, or other lifestyle factors. Fifteen years later, however, when most of my patients were in their late forties, I began to notice a distinct shift in the symptoms that brought them to my office. Their chief concerns were now more serious disorders — elevated cholesterol and high blood pressure, adult-onset diabetes, and hypothyroid conditions — real signs that disease is progressing.

My patients who fit this profile are in what MAV calls the "critical decade," that period between ages forty-five to fifty-five. This decade is critical because it is then that the foundation of future health is laid. It is also your last chance to correct imbalances that, if left untreated, may make you vulnerable to diseases such as cancer, heart disease, and osteoporosis. I like to think of this important time as a window of opportunity for establishing good health and longevity, a time to correct your imbalances and sail into your later years with excellent health, strength, and purpose.

It's Not Too Late

The importance of cultivating good lifestyle habits during the critical decade is underscored by a study called the Women's Healthy Lifestyle Project, which is under way at the University of Pittsburgh Graduate School of Public Health. At first glance, these researchers tell a discouraging tale: By middle age (forty-five to fifty-five), it is already clear who is at high risk for heart disease. Damage has already been done. They claim that by midlife it is too late to get healthy, because years of unhealthy lifestyle have already set the course for chronic disease in later life.

In spite of its gloomy prognosis, this report actually supports an important point I am making in this book: Health problems don't simply pop out of nowhere when your estrogen levels start to fluctuate and fall off. Rather, it is those damaging lifestyle habits, accumulated over a lifetime (smoking, sedentary living, eating unwholesome foods, and any number of others), that set in motion chronic degenerative diseases well before menopause.

But the report's conclusion is overly pessimistic. The good news is that with the complete natural healing system offered by MAV, these conditions and their effects are reversible much later in life. Modern medicine doesn't have a clue how to reverse them and thus gives up, consigning millions of women to a dim outlook. Fortunately, the tradition of MAV, as well as further research that I will review in later chapters, reassures us that meaningful changes and reversal of health problems are indeed possible long after menopause.

WHAT YOUR SYMPTOMS ARE TELLING YOU

According to MAV, your symptoms are telling you just how out of balance you are. Remember, how you fare in the menopausal transition is largely determined by how balanced your body is at this time. If your body is functioning optimally at the onset of menopause, then the symptoms you experience will be minor and your body will adjust quickly. However, if your body is already out of balance when you reach menopause, you are more likely to experience troublesome symptoms.

In MAV, your symptoms at midlife and their severity reveal your underlying imbalances and their causes. Knowing how you rate on the spectrum of imbalance will enable you to design your own self-care program according to the directions given in later chapters of this book.

Your next step is to take the self-rating quiz "How Balanced Are You?" to find out where your symptoms fall on the continuum of balance.

Assess Your Midlife Symptoms

Please turn to the self-rating quiz "How Balanced Are You?" on pages 37-38. You will see that the section on the far left lists the menopausal symptoms you may experience. To the right are four columns, labeled according to degree: balanced, mild, moderate, and severe. In each of these columns is a description of the symptom as it occurs to that degree.

How to Rate Yourself on the Scale

For each symptom on the left, read the descriptions of degree going across to the right. Circle the one that most closely describes your experience. If you are not sure, then choose the one that is more severe to ensure getting the most helpful recommendations in later chapters. When you are finished, add up the number of circled symptoms in each degree category and put each total at the bottom of its column.

Once you have assessed your level of balance, you are ready to apply the principles of Maharishi Ayurveda to find solutions. The results of your assessment will guide you to the chapters in *Part II: How to Restore Balance and Relieve Your Symptoms* that tell you how to resolve your particular symptoms. In those chapters, you will learn how the body gets out of balance in the first place and how to correct the imbalances that you have identified.

Using Your Results to Select Treatments in This Book

Now look back at your total scores for each of the four categories on the self-rating scale. Add together the totals from columns 1 and 2. Then add together the totals from columns 3 and 4. Compare the two new totals, one for your mild symptoms and the other for your more moderate to severe symptoms.

If your total for the first two columns is greater than for columns 3-4: You are probably in a relatively good state of health and balance. The tissues of your body are demonstrating their ability to tolerate the hormonal shifts at menopause relatively well. Your mild symptoms are probably caused by disturbed bodily rhythms, fatigue, excessive stress, weak digestion, or other disturbances in normal bodily functions. Chapter 3 will explain in detail how these imbalances develop, and Chapter 4 will show you how to correct them and thus help relieve your mild symptoms.

If your total for columns 3-4 is greater: Your symptoms indicate that your body is quite out of balance and your tissues are having trouble adjusting to midlife hormone shifts. This is probably due to an accumulation of wastes and toxins that are obstructing the delivery and interaction of your hormones with their target tissues and organs. In Chapter 5, you will be guided to pinpoint exactly what organs and tissues are blocked. Chapter 6 will show you how to design an individualized self-healing program to clear them.

If you circled items in column 4, the "severe" category: You'll find additional guidelines for specific disorders and diseases, such as osteoporosis, heart disease, and depression, in Chapters 7 through 11.

An Important Note

Although your results in the self-assessment scale will direct you to specific chapters in Part II of this book, I highly recommend that you also read the other chapters, even if they don't apply directly to your condition now. Key information and tips are found in each chapter, and you are likely to discover some that apply to you. The chapters in Part III on specific health concerns are packed with preventive information and helpful self-care tips for those health issues all women are concerned with at midlife: heart disease, osteoporosis, memory problems, and mood disorders. The final chapter provides a wealth of MAV prescriptions for your skin, a topic you will find useful for maintaining both inner and outer beauty, as you mature through and beyond midlife.

The Promise of Balanced Health

By now you understand how your body is programmed for perfect health, equipped with an incredibly sophisticated self-healing system that can respond to nearly every challenge, if that system can be maintained in good working order. Likewise, your body is programmed to glide through midlife and live a long, healthy life with little difficulty. This is the promise of a natural midlife transition, without drugs or hormones, and without rapid aging, brittle bones, and heart attacks in the years to come.

I hope this chapter has shown you this is not only possible but well within our reach. We have seen how the main causes of severe conditions, such as intolerable hot flashes, night sweats, osteoporosis, and heart disease, are not declining hormones but our lifestyle, superimposed on our genetic vulnerabilities. To heal them, you must address their underlying cause: the breakdown of the body's homeostatic and self-healing mechanisms. Only by strengthening the body's own inner intelligence will these mechanisms work effectively to keep you healthy.

ACHIEVING BALANCE

Table 2.1 How Balanced Are You?

For each of the symptoms listed on the left in Table 2.1, rate your level — balanced, mild, moderate, or severe — by circling the appropriate description in columns 1-4.

Midlife Symptoms	Balanced	Mild	Moderate	Severe
Hot Flashes	No hot flashes and no problems with body heat regulation	Mild or occasional warm flushes or hot flashes	Uncomfortable hot flashes occurring several times a day and/or night	Very disturbing hot flashes or sweats occurring many times a day and/or night
Vaginal Dryness	Normal lubrication	Mild or occasional dryness	Moderate dryness and/or discomfort during intercourse	Severe dryness and/or pain with intercourse
Insomnia or Sleep Difficulty	Sound sleep	Occasional trouble getting to sleep or going back to sleep after awakening (1-2 times a week)	Frequent awakenings during the night and/or trouble sleeping 3-4 times a week	Trouble sleeping on a nightly basis
Dry Skin	Normal skin moisture	Mild skin dryness	Moderate dryness with wrinkling in areas normally exposed to sun	Very dry skin with wrinkling and sagging in all areas
Weight Gain in Past Year	Weight stable or gain of up to 5 pounds	Gain of 6-10 pounds	Gain of 10-20 pounds	Gain of more than 20 pounds
Anxiety	Feel calm and settled most of the time	Occasionally feel anxious about things that did not previously cause anxiety	Often feel more anxious than in the past	Feel very anxious most of the time and/or have panic attacks
Mood Swings	Mood is stable or appropriate to life circumstances	Mild or occasional mood swings are noticeable	Fluctuations in mood are more pronounced and begin to affect relationships	Mood swings are very bothersome and interfere with work or family life
Headaches or Migraine	No headaches	Occasional mild tension headache (less than once a week)	Frequent mild to moderate headaches or infrequent debilitating headaches	Debilitating headaches occurring once a month or more

Table 2.1 How Balanced Are You? (continued)

Muscle Aches, Pains, or Stiffness	Muscles are comfortable	Mild or occasional aches or stiffness unrelated to exercise	Moderate aching and stiffness or easily fatigued or sore muscles	Pains in the muscles, tender spots, weakness or fibromyalgia diagnosis
Joint Pains	Joints are supple and without discomfort	Soreness or cracking in the joints that comes and goes	Recurring soreness or ache of moderate intensity in joint(s) (tendonitis/ bursitis episodes)	Persistent pain in the joint(s) or osteoarthritis diagnosis
Sexual Interest or Libido	Normal sex drive for you	Somewhat less interest than in the past	Much less interest	Sex drive has completely disappeared
Urination; Frequency and Continence	Normal urination pattern	Occasional urgency or more frequent urination	Increase in urinary frequency, noticeable sense of urgency, or occasional leakage	Leakage or sudden need to urinate on a regular basis
Urinary Tract Infections in Past Year	No UTI	No more than one UTI	Occasional UTIs (up to twice a year)	Frequent or persistent UTIs (more than twice a year)
Memory Problems or Forgetfulness	Good memory; no decline	Noticeable forgetting of names or other details	Frequent forgetting of names or details, especially those you should know	Difficulty remembering many things; need to write nearly everything down
Indigestion (Gas, Bloating, Heartburn)	Digestion is good, with no symptoms except rarely	Occasional (less than once a week)	Frequent (1-3 times a week)	Persistent (nearly every day)
Palpitations	Heartbeat is regular and without palpitations or skipped beats	Mild or infrequent palpitations	Frequent (more than twice a month) or anxiety-provoking palpitations	Occur almost daily or severe enough to take medication
Fatigue	Good energy, as in the past	Less energy than in the past	Tiredness or low energy at least half of the time	Constant feeling of fatigue
Depression	Mood generally good, upbeat	Occasionally feel depression or recurring lack of motivation	Often feel low, dissatisfied, more easily upset or crying	Feel seriously depressed for weeks at a time
TOTAL				

Part II

How to Restore Balance and Relieve Your Symptoms

3

THE WISDOM OF THE DOSHAS: UNDERSTANDING YOUR MILD MIDLIFE SYMPTOMS

One whose doshas are balanced, whose digestion is good, whose tissues and wastes are functioning normally, whose appetite is good, and whose body, mind, and senses remain filled with bliss, is called a healthy person.
— *the* Sushruta Samhita, *classical text of Ayurveda*

Maharishi Ayurveda tells us we are healthy and symptom-free when we are in balance — body, mind and spirit. In this chapter, I want to introduce you to three important forces responsible for balance — your doshas — and help you to identify which of your doshas is in need of balancing.

Disturbance in the doshas lies at the root of most midlife symptoms of mild intensity. Once you have determined which of your doshas is "off kilter," you will be able to correct your milder symptoms for a smooth symptom-free transition, as I explained to Anna in the story that follows.

Anna's Story: A Trouble-Free Flight

When Anna, a fifty-two-year-old blond, suntanned writer from California, first came to see me, she was still having her period every month. She had noticed that her perimenopausal symptoms, while not extreme enough to disrupt her life, had increased in the past five years to include occasional insomnia, a steady weight gain of a few pounds each year, and urgency (the tendency to leak small amounts of urine when under the stress of exercise).

Anna wanted some relief for her symptoms, but she also wanted to go through her menopause naturally. She related to me that she had visited her gynecologist recently, and after an examination was encouraged to start on a "natural" estrogen patch, along with a "natural" oral progesterone pill, even though she was not having any troublesome symptoms and preferred to go through it "naturally." Her doctor insisted, assuring her that these supplements would ease the upcoming transition. When Anna expressed some reluctance at taking medication, her gynecologist, a woman herself, warned her: "Just wait, and you'll know why you want estrogen replacement. You will want it soon, I'm sure — even if you don't want it now."

Anna's doctor explained how, in her view, going through menopause without estrogen was like jumping from an airplane without a parachute — Anna could bet on a rough descent. But with estrogen as her parachute, she told Anna, the descent would be smoother and the landing safe. Either way, she would arrive on the shores of menopause — but what did she want to find there, a rocky coast or a gentle beach?

Anna opted for the smooth ride and took the patch and pills, but after a few months, yielded to her better instincts (which warned her that anything that's not natural is sure to create side effects eventually). She abandoned the drugs in hopes of finding something more natural. Her search brought her to me and to the MAV approach for dealing with her menopausal symptoms.

After listening to the story, complete with her gynecologist's warnings, I assured Anna she wasn't doomed to a crash landing without taking HT, and that with proper guidance, she wouldn't even have to jump from the airplane at all. If you have a good pilot and a sound aircraft, I explained, there's no reason to abandon ship in the middle of the journey. Even without HT, you can arrive in comfort and set down smoothly.

Like Anna, all women must make the journey through this transition, but with a little preventative knowledge, it need not be a bumpy and uncomfortable ride. Just as with a cross-country flight, it helps to know what kinds of effects you'll be experiencing and how your body tends to react. For example, you might tend to get dehydrated from the dry cabin air, feel anxious during the flight, suffer from indigestion, or get sluggish and sleepy from the long hours of sitting. If you know what effects to expect, you can take measures to avoid them naturally: Drink lots of water during the flight, listen to calming music, and bring your own healthy snacks, so you don't have to eat airline food. Do these simple things and you will arrive feeling fresh and happy.

I explained to Anna that the same principles apply to the perimenopausal journey. You need to know what kinds of effects you might experience, and how your body will react to them. But unlike a plane trip, the menopausal journey is as unique to each individual woman's experience as is each woman. And this is where Maharishi Ayurveda is extremely useful.

How MAV Understands Your Mild Symptoms

Unlike Western medicine, with its one-size-fits-all, "cookie cutter" approach, MAV understands your symptoms in the context of your individual nature. We are each predisposed to respond to stress — whether it be a job promotion, a change in diet, or shifting hormones — in certain unique ways., Maharishi Ayurveda looks at your individual tendencies in order to customize your treatment. In doing so, the Ayurvedic picture takes into account not only your physical experience, but your mental and emotional experience, as well. In its most complete form, MAV takes into account your relationship with your immediate environment (food, house, family, city, etc.) and even your interaction with the entire cosmos (planets, sun, and moon), giving you a truly complete perspective of your health.

I explained to Anna the Ayurvedic *tridosha* theory, as I do for all of my new patients. Tridosha theory is the idea that there are three basic aspects that rule our tendencies and are responsible for our health. Most likely, you will begin to recognize your own tendencies — how you respond to influences occurring both inside and outside of your body. I will make it as simple as possible so you won't be tempted to skip it, because this orientation is key for you to derive the greatest benefit from the practical program in this and later chapters. Once you understand a few basic principles, you will be able to easily apply Ayurvedic medicine to correcting the imbalances that have caused your mild symptoms. The result will be a trouble-free flight through midlife and beyond.

YOUR DOSHAS

According to Ayurveda, there are three doshas (<u>doe</u>-shuhz), called *vata*, *pitta*, and *kapha*. You can think of the doshas as guiding physiological principles that keep all of your bodily functions balanced and healthy. Each dosha is present throughout your physiology, governing all activities of your body, mind, and emotions. Your doshas also are your body's "shock troops," mediating the first responses of your body to environmental stressors of all kind — climatic, dietary, physical, mental, and emotional.

The workings of the doshas are also seen in Nature *outside* your body, in the seasons of the year and times of the day — all of which interact with your physiology through your doshas. This comprehensive theory of the doshas provides us with a tremendous amount of prepackaged wisdom about how our bodies function both in health and disease. In fact, the fundamental approach of MAV is to restore and maintain balance within each of the three doshas, since they are the main determinants of our health.

The theory of the doshas is not intuitively obvious to most Western minds. We are used to our modern medical view of the body as a collection of bodily systems, each defined by the functions it performs. The digestive system helps us assimilate food, the cardiovascular system keeps blood pumping through our bodies, and the nervous system allows us to think and feel, to name a few. Each system is studied independently of the other, and treatments are offered by specialists trained in one and only one of the systems. There is no acknowledgement that these separated

Table 3-1 Dosha Functions and Qualities

DOSHA	FUNCTIONS	QUALITIES
Vata	**Controls:** Transportation Movement Flow Circulation Communication	Light, *like air or a feather* Dry, rough, *like plain popcorn* Cold, *like a cold wind* Moving, *always changing like the wind* Clear, non-sticky, *like polished granite* Coarse, brittle, *like dry hair* Quick, formless, *swift, and seen by its action only*
Pitta	**Controls:** Metabolism Digestion Transformation Energy production Enzymatic action	Hot, warm, *heat in any form* Sharp, *Biting or penetrating in quality like vinegar* Pungent, scorching, *like spices and irritating chemicals* Sour, *like citrus* Smelly, *like the scent of body odor or decaying substances* Liquid, *like stomach acids* Slightly oily, *slippery*
Kapha	**Controls:** Bodily substances Lubrication Fluids Strength and cohesion Bodily structures: cells, tissues, organs, muscles, bones, etc.	Heavy, *like stone, with gravity* Cold, *like ice, snow, cold drinks* Slow, *like an elephant* Sticky, viscous, *like gum or glue* Soft, *like a baby's skin* Oily, *like fried foods, butter* Sweet, *like sweet food or words* Stable, *steady, non-changing* Solid, dense, *like stone, dense like hard cheese*

systems might be in some way interconnected. Instead, our understanding of physiology is rooted in the machine model of separate parts, more suited to assembly line production and repair than to healing and maintaining the living, dynamic entity we refer to as the *body.*

In contrast, Maharishi Ayurveda looks at what is common to *all* the systems of the body instead of what is separate and distinct, and identifies three aspects that unify rather than divide our physiology. Each of these aspects, or doshas, can be seen to apply *across the board* to all our organs, tissues, and cells, giving us a view of the body as an interconnected whole rather than as disconnected parts.

The Wisdom of the Doshas

Because of their unifying abilities, the doshas can be used to identify and treat the root causes of your symptoms. We can use this wisdom of the doshas to access deeper, more powerful levels of your body's healing intelligence and to alleviate your menopausal symptoms naturally.

To begin to understand the wisdom of the doshas, consider how every system, organ, tissue, and cell in your body is involved in three common physiological functions: *motion, metabolism,* and *substance.* MAV says each of these basic activities is governed by a particular dosha. Vata governs all motion, pitta governs all metabolism, and kapha governs all substance. The three doshas are direct expressions of Nature's intelligence. They must function optimally at every level, cellular and system-wide, if we are to enjoy good health and well-being. Let's examine how these three fundamental functions are supported and guided by the three doshas.

Motion (Vata)

Motion, or flow, is occurring in all parts of your body at every moment. Nutrients flow into and wastes flow out of tiny passageways in the wall of every cell and even through tiny channels within the cell itself, much as water flows through a river and its tributaries. Larger channels of flow throughout the body — among them the arteries, veins, lymphatics, intestine, esophagus, and nerve pathways — all participate in this same activity of motion. Whether fluids, nerve impulses, or hormones, the activity of circulation is so important that if any part of your body is cut off from it, stagnation results and infection, cell death, and destruction of vital tissue quickly set in.

Movement through all your body's channels, as well as all motion relating to the body, is under the dosha *vata* (<u>vah</u>-tuh), which refers not only to motion itself but also to the guiding intelligence of Nature that coordinates all movement, flow, and circulation within your body. Each dosha has certain qualities. Vata is moving, changeable, quick, light, dry, rough, hard, cold, and fluctuating. Each dosha also has basic underlying, primordial elements arising from the unified field of quantum physics, linking it to the cosmos and all of creation. For vata, these elements are air and space.

In relation to the midlife transition, vata governs the secretion and delivery of your hormones (reproductive or otherwise) from their glands of origin to their organs of destination: your brain, vagina, skin, liver, bones, and so on. Vata also keeps your ever-cycling biological rhythms in balance and attuned to the cycles of day and night, the monthly cycle, and the changing of the seasons. Finally, vata dosha is primarily responsible for guiding the body's adjustment to change. As you can see, a healthy vata dosha is critical to a smooth midlife transition.

Metabolism (Pitta)

A second basic function happening at every level in your body is metabolism, the process of transforming the food you eat into energy. This is done largely through your digestive system, but metabolism goes on in each cell, organ, and tissue as your food is converted at smaller and smaller levels into energy. Different types of cells burn different fuels to make energy and keep functioning. For example, brain cells must have a continuous supply of glucose, while muscle cells need glycogen, glucose, and fatty acids to provide energy for movement. Every cell in your body must have a source of fuel for internal energy production. The sole purpose of digestion — breaking down your food into molecular "bite-size" pieces — is to supply nutrients to the cells so they can make the energy your body runs on.

This constant process of energy transformation, as well as all other transformations occurring throughout your body, is called *pitta* (pih-tuh, not pee-tuh, as in the Middle Eastern sandwich bread!). Pitta also governs all detoxification of chemicals and impurities, transformation of light into visual images, and emotional and intellectual "metabolism" of all our experiences. Pitta refers not only to these processes of metabolism but also to the underlying intelligence of Nature that keeps your metabolic functions performing properly, giving you energy and vitality. Pitta's qualities are warm or hot, pungent, energetic, slightly oily, sharp, and smelly. It correlates with the natural elements of fire and water.

During the perimenopause time, pitta is responsible for keeping your digestion strong, your metabolism balanced, and your weight normal in the face of changing hormones. It also guides the chemical reactions that occur within your cells after hormonal stimulation. Pitta (the only dosha with warmth) provides the heat of hot flashes.

Substance (Kapha)

Finally, your body has substance, including all the structural components that give it a form and framework at every level from the cells on up. Bones, muscles, fat, skin, organs, and fluids are all substances that are built, maintained, and repaired to give shape to your body. Substance is its most defining attribute, which is why we refer to that solid, physical specimen looking back from the mirror as our "body." Closer to the true picture, however, is the dynamic, flowing, and metabolizing physiology, a "work in progress," taking place right beneath our skin at this very moment and every moment, day and night, of our entire life.

Every cell, tissue, organ, and system in your body participates in this activity of building substance, either solid or fluid, to give the body shape and form. This makes substance the third unifying aspect of our physiology. Substance, and the underlying intelligence that guides its proper formation, is referred to in Ayurveda as *kapha* (<u>kuh</u>-fuh). Kapha qualities are heavy, slow, cold, damp, stable, soft, oily, sweet, sticky, and dense or solid. It is linked to the natural elements of earth and water.

After menopause, kapha dosha is responsible for keeping our bodily structure sound as we age. Being moist and unctuous, kapha is responsible for keeping your joints, skin, eyes, and vaginal tissues moist and lubricated. Kapha also provides strength, stability, and stamina — to your emotions and behavior, your immune system, and your body as a whole — helping to protect you from the aging process.

YOUR DOSHAS IN AND OUT OF BALANCE

You have a balanced *physiology* — a term I prefer to "body" to emphasize the dynamic internal state of biochemical reactions, communication, and flow going on constantly behind the static outer appearance — when all motion (vata), metabolism (pitta), and substances (kapha) in your body are functioning perfectly. Only when your doshas are balanced can they support and uphold your body's vital tissues.

What does it mean when a dosha is out of balance? Simply put, an unbalanced dosha is an aggravated dosha. An *increase* in the qualities associated with that dosha is manifesting somewhere in your physiology. For example, if your pitta is aggravated, you may experience excessive heat in your digestive process, resulting in heartburn. If vata is aggravated, you may have dry skin or vaginal dryness. If kapha is out of balance, you may have excessive mucus or feel lethargic. The way to bring a dosha back into balance and alleviate any symptoms is to pacify, or *decrease*, it by applying specific dosha-balancing measures.

According to the theory of the three doshas, if you know how any factor, including menopause, affects your doshas, you can apply dosha-balancing measures to remove your symptoms. Ayurveda helps you determine which dosha is out of balance by identifying your symptoms, which you can do for yourself in the quiz at the end of this chapter, and shows you how to correct your imbalance using natural methods based on two fundamental principles.

Two Healing Principles for Balancing Your Doshas

To explain how you can correct your dosha imbalances and treat your menopausal symptoms, I'd like to introduce you to two very simple healing principles of Ayurvedic medicine. The first is the principle of *similarity*: Like creates like. The second is the principle of *opposites*: Opposites restore balance.

The Principle of Similarity

The principle of similarity says that if one of your doshas gets out of balance (becomes aggravated), you will experience physical symptoms that directly reflect the qualities of that dosha. For example, if vata dosha gets out of balance and disturbs your skin, the symptom will be a dry and flaky rash, because dryness is a quality of vata. But if pitta dosha imbalance disturbs the skin, the rash will be hot, inflamed, and red, due to pitta's quality of heat. If kapha imbalance causes a rash, the skin will be cool and possibly oozing clear liquid, as kapha qualities are cold, moist, and damp. This direct relationship of dosha qualities to symptom qualities helps us determine which of the doshas is out of balance and then proceed to treat it.

This same principle is at work when you are exposed to outside influences, such as the weather. Remember, like creates like, so if the weather is cold, dry, and windy — qualities associated with vata dosha — then your vata is more easily aggravated and thrown out of balance. According to Ayurveda, vata dosha is responsible for your inner chill, the dryness of your skin, the dilating blood vessels turning your cheeks bright pink, and your hurried pace as you head for the warm indoors!

The principle of similarity can be helpful in predicting how you will respond to a particular environmental condition. For example, we know that in the winter, the air becomes very dry in our homes and workplaces when we turn on forced-air heating systems. This dry air causes a winter dry skin condition familiar to all of us who live in cold climates, a symptom that points to a vata imbalance.

Likewise, if you live in Hawaii, the warm, moist air of the islands hydrates your skin, adding moisture to your hair as well. And while some women may find the humidity causes "bad hair days," others welcome the velvety smooth, soft skin they experience year round due to the balanced kapha qualities of softness, moistness, and unctuousness. Thus, the principle of similarities works within your physiology, as well as in your environment, always expressing a reciprocal relationship of mutual qualities.

You can see that the principle of similarity is not unique to Ayurvedic medicine. It is at work in many of your everyday experiences — mentally and emotionally, as well as physically. Examples are flying in an airplane, staying up all night, having a heated discussion, breaking up with your boyfriend, grieving a parent's passing, giving birth, cranking on your computer, eating a gourmet meal, or virtually any other activity of life. Any of these experiences could provoke symptoms that reflect the qualities of the dosha that has become aggravated in your body.

Your Dominant Dosha(s). You may have a tendency to develop a stronger imbalance in one or two of your doshas, depending on your genetic makeup, your personality, your diet over the years, and other lifestyle habits. This leads to a condition of dosha dominance, which means a long-term tendency for imbalance in a particular dosha(s). And because like creates like, exposure to influences (whether inside or outside your body) with qualities similar to those of your dominant dosha will more easily throw that dosha out of balance.

For example, if your dominant dosha is pitta, then hot, spicy food or an overly warm room would probably aggravate your pitta very easily. You'd be wise to avoid eating at "tamale hot" Mexican restaurants to avoid experiencing irritability, hot flashes, and night sweats, to name just a few common pitta-dominant menopause symptoms.

To summarize, the principle of similarity tells us that if our doshas are balanced, then their specific qualities, such as the dryness of vata or the heaviness of kapha, won't cause symptoms or discomfort. However, if a particular dosha is increased by certain foods in your diet, the weather, your emotions, or other influences of like quality, that dosha will tend to get out of balance, leading to symptoms of a *similar* quality. For example, prolonged periods of cool, damp weather may aggravate chronic sinusitis, a kapha condition. Lots of raw, cold, and dry foods frequently aggravate irritable bowel syndrome, a largely vata-related condition.

The Principle of Opposites

The second important principle you need to know is the principle of *opposites*. While the influence of similar qualities increases (aggravates) a dosha, the influence of opposite qualities brings a dosha back into balance by decreasing (pacifying) it. The practice of applying opposite properties to balance a dosha is basic to all treatments of MAV.

The flight of northern "snowbirds" from Canada, New York, and other northern climes to the warm, sunny beaches of Florida to thaw out every spring is an example of how we naturally seek out balancing influences for our doshas. Every August, I see the reverse flow as my patients from Florida visit The Raj Ayurveda Health Center to escape the state's oppressive summer heat and balance their pitta with the cooling treatments of MAV.

One couple, Floridians Julia and John Martin, share the same strong pitta traits, including a tendency to get overheated and to develop acid indigestion and inflammatory disorders, such as skin rashes. Pitta-aggravating triggers abound in Florida, where the weather is warm year round and there's an abundance of pitta-increasing foods like citrus, fresh tomatoes, and seafood. Taking pitta-balancing treatments (see Chapter 4) on a regular basis has helped Julia overcome severe food intolerances and John overcome recurring skin rashes and joint inflammation.

We apply the principle of opposites every day of our lives. When your mouth feels dry, you drink some water to wet your mouth and remove the dryness. When you feel cold, you turn up the thermostat and warm up. If your stomach is empty and your cells devoid of nutrients, you fill up with nourishing foods. If you don't respond to the needs of your body in this simple manner, of course, you begin to feel uncomfortable. And if you continue to avoid your body's crescendoing cry, the consequences become much more serious. For example, life-threatening hypothermia can set in if you are exposed to such severe cold that your internal body temperature begins to drop.

Thirst, hunger, discomfort and the like are messages from your body's inner intelligence, aimed at alerting you to attend to some need your body has at that moment. The more knowledge and understanding you have in applying the appropriate remedies, the healthier you will be. Knowing about your doshas enables you to be much more precise in selecting the right foods and other measures to stay healthy and recover from any symptoms you may be having.

Let's see how this principle of opposites can help you lose weight, even if your body is telling you, "I'm hungry. Feed me anything, now!" Losing weight means reducing the substance of the body. You may have already figured out that that means reducing kapha, the dosha governing your body's structural components. (You might like to refer to the chart to refresh your memory about kapha's qualities.) Kapha is heavy, dense, solid, moist, sweet, smooth, oily, and cold.

So to balance your kapha and lose weight, you need a diet with less of a kapha quality: less oil, fewer dairy products, fewer cold foods and cold drinks, and very few sweets. Foods with qualities that oppose kapha — such as bitter, astringent, and pungent tastes, naturally low-fat and light foods (whole grains, vegetables, and legumes), and warm cooked meals generously spiked with piquant, warming spices (such as ginger, turmeric, and black pepper) — will pep up your sluggish metabolism and help you lose weight naturally. Staying active and getting lots of exercise is important to counteract the stableness of kapha, which tends to manifest as lethargy and inertia (the couch potato syndrome) when you are overweight.

Using These Healing Principles to Relieve Your Symptoms

Let's look at how the two healing principles work in relation to your mild menopause symptoms, such as hot flashes and vaginal dryness, and can help you to correct the imbalances at the root of these symptoms.

Let's start with the easier of the two symptoms to understand, vaginal dryness. Based on what you have learned about the different qualities that characterize the doshas, which one do you think is responsible for vaginal dryness?

The description of the symptom as "dry" is a giveaway. Only one dosha is dry, and that is vata, so an imbalance of vata dosha must be involved in the problem of vaginal dryness. In Chapter 4, I will explain why this symptom is so common at menopause and why it is more of a problem for some women than for others.

Now what dosha is responsible for hot flashes? If you have a vata-like, very quick mind, you may see "hot" and immediately think pitta! And you are right. However, pitta imbalance is only half the story.

The other cause of hot flashes is a vata imbalance. Vata, you may recall, governs all motion and circulation in the body, including the circulatory and the nervous systems, and has a fluctuating, unstable quality. Most physiologists attribute hot flashes to fluctuating temperature regulation by the part of your brain called the hypothalamus. When the hypothalamus becomes unstable, your body's temperature control fluctuates as if someone were standing at the thermostat in your room and turning it up, then down every few minutes. Your body responds by shunting blood to the surface of your body in an effort to dissipate heat quickly. The end result is sudden flushes of warmth, often followed by equally sudden overcooling.

This highly irregular, unstable pattern of temperature control reflects vata's quality of irregularity. The heat factor (pitta) of hot flashes is a secondary phenomenon. But vata is cold and pitta is hot. How are we going to balance both at the same time? Fortunately, it's not as complicated as it may seem. I'll give you a more detailed answer in Chapter 4, when I offer treatments for your symptoms. A clue is that Ayurveda always seeks to treat the primary cause first (without aggravating any secondary ones).

Stella's Story: Red Hot Pitta Pacified

Stella is a forty-seven-year-old administrator for a national scientific foundation based in Washington, D.C. I first met her there years earlier, when she came with her brilliant, but very ill husband, for treatment at my clinic. She remembered the help MAV had brought to her and her husband at the time, and was now back seeking a solution to a very severe and troublesome perimenopausal problem.

For the past four months, she explained, she had been experiencing extremely heavy bleeding with her monthly cycle — so heavy that she had fainted once due to blood loss and had to be taken to the emergency room. She became severely anemic, and as a result, her hair was falling out by the handful, and she felt stressed and exhausted. Hormonal treatments her doctor prescribed didn't work. Her gynecologist recommended the only other solution she knew — surgery to remove her uterus. Despite the fact that several of her friends had had the same problem and agreed with her doctor's opinion that surgery was the only option, Stella was determined to find an alternative, less invasive solution.

Upon evaluating Stella's state of balance, it was clear that red-hot pitta dosha was at the root of her heavy bleeding problem. Since her last visit, Stella had moved to New Mexico. I suspected her diet had changed to one typical of the region: lots of salsa, hot spices and Mexican food — all pitta-increasing foods. Indeed it had. In addition, she lived in an area of long, hot, and sunny days that also aggravate pitta. Her new life in the desert was increasing her pitta and throwing off her cycle off balance.

I explained all of this to Stella, who immediately committed to following a pitta-pacifying diet and lifestyle once she returned home. In the meantime, she underwent five days of treatment at The Raj. By the time she returned home, she felt calm, "chilled out" and balanced. However, it would be a few weeks before the true test of her treatment, her next period, arrived.

A couple months later I received the following good news from Stella:

"My first period after visiting you at The Raj was light. The following one was even lighter. My hair stopped falling out. Now I have entered my menopause without any symptoms. I feel great, energetic, happy and, best of all, I haven't had surgery."

Stella's story is not a unique one. With proper balance of pitta through diet, herbs, and other MAV treatments, nearly all my patients have been able to resolve their heavy bleeding problems without surgery. Hysterectomy is unnecessary when the wisdom of the doshas is understood and utilized to recreate balance and resolve symptoms naturally.

THE DOSHAS OVER TIME

Maharishi Ayurveda expands the tridosha theory to include not just your body but the hours in a day, the days of a year, and your entire life span. Thus, valuable information derived from the doshas can be applied throughout each day and across your life span to help you stay healthy through dosha-balancing habits and lifestyle routines.

Your Doshic Clock and Calendar

The doshic clock in Figure 3 shows how your day is divided. Each successive four-hour interval is dominated by one particular dosha. Starting at 2 A.M., the first

Figure 3.1 Your Doshic Clock

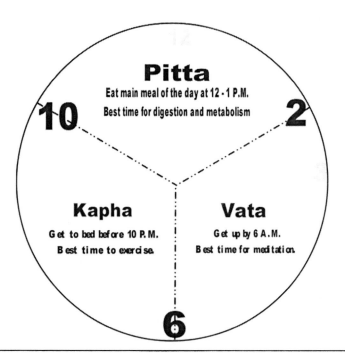

four hours of the morning are dominated by vata, your "active and alert" dosha. Getting up during this "vata time," by 6 A.M., can dramatically improve your alertness and efficiency during the day, provided you have had enough sleep.

Kapha dosha, the slow, heavy one, becomes strongest between 6 and 10 A.M. That means the longer you sleep past 6 A.M., the more sluggish, dull, and "brain dead" you will feel when you wake up. That dullness often tags along with you for the entire day. If you aren't riding the vata wave by 6 A.M., you will probably find it hard to get going and reach for a cup of coffee or tea to jump-start you for the day. Better than coffee is a brisk morning walk. From 6 to 10 A.M. is the best time of day to exercise, according to Ayurveda, because it counteracts any tendency toward the morning doldrums and helps fire up your metabolic rate for the whole day.

By 10 A.M., mental sharpness rises as pitta kicks in, stoking the digestive fires for a roaring appetite by lunchtime. During this pitta-dominated time of 10 A.M. to 2 P.M., your metabolic "fire" is best able to digest and burn your food. Accordingly, Ayurveda recommends that lunch be your heaviest meal. The high-burning flames of midday pitta help us to understand why research shows that eating the majority of your calories earlier in the day is best for losing weight.

This cycle of four-hour-long dosha periods repeats itself from 2 P.M. to 2 A.M. starting with vata during the afternoon, kapha during the evening hours, and finally pitta spanning the two hours before and two hours after midnight.

The Three Seasons

According to Ayurveda, there are three dominant seasons, not four. These three seasons are distinguished by weather patterns and climatic changes that correspond to the qualities of the three doshas. Knowing the dosha effects of the three seasons will guide you in keeping your doshas balanced regardless of the weather and help you to stay healthy all year-round.

In the northern hemisphere, *kapha season* is in the spring, from March through June, when everything is sprouting, growing, and blossoming. Growth and substance dominate, along with melting snows and a tendency for rainy, damp weather, all of which tend to increase kapha within us. More phlegm and mucus, allergies, and sinus congestion are common, not to mention spring fever, that lazy, soft, lethargic feeling we welcome after the harshness, dryness, and biting cold of winter.

Spring flows into summer, bringing with it the heat of *pitta season*, which runs from July through October. Bright, intensely sunny, hot, and humid days bake out the leftover winter chill from deep in our bodies. But by late July, we are looking for shade and refreshing ourselves with pitta-quenching summer fruits like watermelon, grapes, and pears. Many women experience more hot flashes and irritability in the summer heat as pitta heats up their minds and bodies. By October, we welcome the relief of cooler nights, the frost on the pumpkins, and the brisk morning air, which chills out our pitta and reminds us that winter is just around the corner.

November through February are the cold, dry, and windy months of *vata season*, when dry skin, dry eyes, vaginal dryness, and a tendency toward worry or depression are common. Yet these tendencies can be counteracted with vata-balancing measures, including more warm cooked foods, more oils in the diet (pure and organic, of course), a regular routine, and an early bedtime.

The Doshas Across Your Life Span

Tridosha theory describes three distinct stages of life, each lasting about one-third of a total lifetime. Given an average life span of seventy-five years, these three stages can be divided into periods of roughly twenty-five years. Each one is dominated, as you may have guessed, by a different dosha: kapha (up to age twenty-five), pitta (ages twenty-six through fifty), and vata (from age fifty-one on).

From this, it doesn't take a lot of math to figure out that at around age fifty-one, around the average age of menopause for women today, the second stage of life is changing to the third stage. In Ayurvedic terms, our bodies are undergoing a shift from the stage of life dominated by pitta to the stage dominated by vata.

These life stages and their presiding doshas influence our bodies in a long-term, general way. Their influence provides a backdrop to the more transitory influences on our doshas from circadian, seasonal, climatic, dietary, psychosocial, and other passing factors in our lives. Being aware of these natural shifts in our doshas can help us to anticipate and prevent the development of symptoms.

When we are children, the predominance of the stable, heavy, moist kapha dosha gives us tremendous resilience, strength, growth, and vitality. Yet during this time, we can be vulnerable to kapha imbalances, such as respiratory congestion and ear infections. In teenage years, the influence of the pitta stage begins to become apparent: hormones kick in, skin breaks out, and adolescent rebellion begins.

During the second stage of life, we use pitta energy to fuel our ambitions and drive to accomplish the bulk of our life's work in the material world and in our family life. Pitta imbalances like skin problems, ulcers, migraines, and premenstrual syndrome (PMS) irritability are not uncommon during this time.

By age forty, the vata stage begins to show up. Hormone cycles become less regular and more fluctuating, skin dryness and wrinkles become more apparent (in both sexes), the hair thins for many women as well as men, and our strong, kapha muscle mass is replaced by flaccid body fat if we are not exercising regularly.

These natural tendencies of each dosha life stage are not, however, written in stone. For example, the length of each stage can vary. In fact, Ayurveda defines a normal life span as well over one hundred years, not the seventy-five or so years we may currently hope to survive (or outlive!) in good health. What is set is the sequential flow from one stage to another. What is not set is the need for imbalance at any stage. Knowledge of the three Ayurvedic stages of life does not bestow a sentence of weakness or deterioration upon us. On the contrary, it gives us a framework in which to understand the natural changes in our bodies as we pass through life and, best of all, gives us practical, effective ways to counteract these effects to reduce the aging process and help us maintain good health throughout life.

The Pitta-Vata Shift

Let's look at what the change from pitta stage to vata stage means for your health and for your menopause. Ayurveda tells us that menopause is the distinguishing event that marks a woman's transition from the pitta-dominated to the vata-dominated stage of life. We know that any change can cause at least some stress or a lot of upheaval, depending on how adaptable we are — or the system in question is. In Ayurvedic terms, change means movement, a moving or flow to the next stage. Movement and flow mean, as you might recall, that vata dosha is involved. Change always involves, and tends to increase, vata dosha. By the principle of similarity, *like increases like.*

The most common dosha to have out of balance at menopause, simply because there is change going on, is vata. More dryness, fluctuating hormone levels, unstable temperature control, unstable mood, and forgetfulness can all be understood in terms of vata disturbance. Often a variety of symptoms in one woman can be understood and *treated* by the balancing of just one underlying dosha that is responsible for them all.

Another principle of the doshic life-stage shift that is relevant to menopause arises from the fact that a transition implies going *from* somewhere as well as arriving at someplace new. For example, when you arrive in California from Boston in January, your body temporarily "remembers" the time of day as three hours later, the weather as icy cold, and your favorite foods and everything else that was your life in Boston. It is adapted and habituated to this style of functioning. For your body to adapt to California, the old must be transformed, which can be a temporarily disrupting experience. You may feel jet-lagged or lethargic or have trouble sleeping for a night or two.

Similarly, when you shift from the pitta stage of life to vata, not only may vata get disturbed, but your pitta dosha may also lose its point of reference. Some women have in a sense "accumulated" the hot effects of pitta through the years and have more pitta symptoms at menopause, making this the second most common dosha to be disturbed. Such symptoms may include irritability, anger, hyperacidity, feeling overheated, heavy menstrual bleeding, skin problems, migraines, bleeding hemorrhoids, and frequent urinary tract infections.

PINPOINTING YOUR IMBALANCES: A SELF-ASSESSMENT QUIZ

By now I hope you're curious to learn which of your own doshas may be out of balance and at the root of your personal symptoms. Once you have determined that by taking this quiz (on the following page), you will be ready to design your own customized treatment program following the instructions I will provide in Chapter 4.

Understanding Your Results

Add up the checks you made for each dosha. The one that received the highest score is the dosha you most need to balance.

If your score was highest for vata, your vata dosha is mainly responsible for your menopause symptoms. Follow the recommendations for vata balancing in Chapter 4.

If your score was highest for pitta, your pitta dosha is mainly responsible for your menopause symptoms. Follow the recommendations for pitta balancing in Chapter 4.

If your score was highest for kapha, your kapha dosha is mainly responsible for your menopause symptoms. Follow the recommendations for kapha balancing in Chapter 4.

Quiz: Which Dosha Is Causing Your Symptoms?

Put a check by each symptom that applies to you.

Vata Imbalance

- ✓ Vaginal dryness
- ✓ Anxiety
- ✓ Mood swings
- ✓ Dry skin
- ✓ Constipation
- ✓ Hot flashes
- ✓ Feeling cold or cooler than normal when not flashing
- ✓ Forgetfulness
- ____ Crying spells
- ____ Tension headache
- ✓ Joint or muscle aches
- ____ Irregular cycles
- ✓ Urinary urgency or frequency
- ____ Heart palpitations
- ✓ Fluctuating blood pressure
- ✓ Insomnia
- ✓ Joint or muscle aches

13 TOTAL

Pitta Imbalance

- ✓ Hot flashes
- ____ Feeling warmer than usual when not flashing
- ____ Heavy bleeding
- ____ More days of heavy flow than usual
- ____ Migraine headaches
- ✓ Anger or irritability
- ____ Increased bowel movements or loose stools
- ____ Skin rash or acne
- ✓ Unpleasant body odor
- ____ Urinary tract infections
- ✓ Night sweats or sweating during the day

4 TOTAL

Kapha Imbalance

- ____ Excessive weight gain
- ____ Fluid retention
- ____ Breast swelling or fullness
- ____ Abdominal heaviness
- ✓ Stiffness in the body
- ✓ Lethargy
- ✓ Lazy or unmotivated feeling
- ✓ Elevated cholesterol
- ✓ Yeast infections

5 TOTAL

If two of your dosha scores were much higher than the third, first follow the recommendations for the dosha you scored highest in. For finer tuning, also read the special recommendations for dosha combinations (vata-pitta, vata-kapha, or pitta-kapha) and adjust your self-care approach accordingly.

If your scores were equal (or within 2 points) for any two doshas, follow the guidelines in Chapter 4 as follows:

Vata and pitta equal: Follow the "Three Key Tips" for vata and the "Eat Your Way to Balance" diet for pitta.

Vata and kapha equal: Follow the "Three Key Tips" for vata and the "Eat Your Way to Balance" diet for kapha.

Pitta and kapha equal: Follow the "Three Key Tips" for pitta and the "Eat Your Way to Balance" diet, also for pitta.

THE RELEVANCE OF DOSHA THEORY TODAY

I frequently marvel at how much power we gain for both prevention and healing simply by becoming aware of the three doshas and their healing principles of similarity and opposites. Interestingly, whenever modern medicine has managed over the decades to figure out the dietary or lifestyle causes for a particular health condition (for example, heart disease, peptic ulcers, acne rosacea, and migraines), its recommendations exactly match the dietary and lifestyle factors identified for these disorders in the ancient Ayurvedic texts. In fact, the Ayurvedic prescriptions are even more detailed; they explain individual variations and subtypes of the particular conditions that modern medicine has not yet spelled out. And, of course, rather than isolating the lifestyle, dietary, and individual triggers for just a few disorders (like the Western approach), Maharishi Ayurveda identifies these elements in every condition and applies this knowledge to healing the patient.

By now you are getting the idea of how the tridosha concept of Ayurveda can help you to understand your physical symptoms in relation to the imbalances that caused them and how you can design specific treatments to bring back a state of balance for greater health. You will quickly become conversant in these concepts simply by reading this book and getting a little practice in applying the principles to your menopausal health as you go along. If you are like most of my patients, you will be amazed at how quickly and easily you begin to see results as you gradually adjust your lifestyle to one that is more balancing for you and your doshas.

What can you do when these imbalances are already manifested? It's not too late to correct them in a truly natural and lasting way, the subject of the next chapter.

* 4 *

Creating Balance for Relief of Your Mild Symptoms

Health results from the natural, balanced state of the doshas. Therefore, the wise try to keep them in their balanced state.
— *the* Charaka Samhita

In this chapter, we will address balancing your doshas by looking at the larger factors in your life, such as lifestyle and diet. It's in these areas that Ayurveda tells us we can find the causes that disturb the doshas and create your mild symptoms. Because your doshas react to everything in your daily living — what you eat, when you went to bed, and even what you are thinking and feeling — you can be sure that any doshic imbalance you experience reflects some aspect of your life that is likewise out of balance. When you address this "big picture" of dosha imbalance, you will often experience the spontaneous improvement or resolution of symptoms without having to address each symptom separately.

Keys For Balancing Your Doshas

General recommendations for balancing each of your three doshas, including lifestyle, diet, and self-care, are summarized in Table 4.1, "Three Keys for Balancing Each of Your Doshas." Following these recommendations will give you a secure foundation for making progress with all of your menopause symptoms, as well as

Table 4.1: Three Keys for Balancing Each of Your Doshas: Lifestyle, Diet, and Self-Care

VATA	PITTA	KAPHA
Lifestyle. *Establish a regular routine,* including regular early bedtime, getting-up time, and mealtimes. Staying rested is key for you. **Diet.** *Eat mainly warm, cooked, wholesome foods* at each meal. Reserve salads and raw vegetables for side dishes. Carefully avoid cold drinks, iced desserts, and other cold foods. **Self-Care.** *Calm your nerves and soothe dry skin with a self-massage* each day with warm olive oil.	**Lifestyle.** *Chill out your nervous system* by avoiding TV, computer, and telephone after 9 P.M. Turn your light out by 10 P.M. for a cooler, more restful night. **Diet.** *Never skip or delay your meals.* Eat lunch by 12:30 P.M. and dinner by 7 P.M. Avoid processed foods, junk foods, cheese, yogurt, red meat, hot spices, alcohol, caffeine, vinegar, sugary desserts, and fried foods. Eat organic, wholesome foods with lots of fresh vegetables and sweet, juicy fruits. Drink plenty of fresh, pure water. **Self-care.** *Take the pitta cleanse* (see page 76).	**Lifestyle.** *Arise early every morning.* 6 to 10 A.M. is kapha time, so avoid sluggishness by rising by 6 A.M. **Diet.** *Indulge your sensual, nourishing kapha nature with delicious home-cooked meals.* Eat plenty of legumes, whole grains like barley, and cooked vegetables. Spice generously with thyme, basil, mint, oregano, cumin, turmeric, fresh ginger, and black pepper. Avoid red meat, dairy, cold drinks, and sugar. **Self-Care.** *Exercise, exercise, exercise.*

strengthening your body's inner intelligence so it can work for you as it was intended to.

As I stated in Chapter 3, dosha imbalance by itself does not cause disease. Therefore, these recommendations for balancing your doshas are aimed at resolving milder symptoms, not deeper imbalances. If your symptoms do not improve substantially within three to four weeks after you begin applying them in your daily life, please go on to Chapters 5 and 6. There you will find how to tailor your own personalized self-care program to help correct the deeper imbalances that are responsible for your more persistent symptoms.

Your everyday general diet plays an important role in keeping your doshas in balance. This chapter gives you specific diets for balancing each of your doshas, but first I am including a general healing meal plan that applies to all imbalances. Following the diet principles in this general meal plan is key to gaining the benefits of the dosha-specific diets given later in this chapter.

Now let's look at each of your doshas (vata, pitta, and kapha) and how to treat your symptoms by balancing each one.

CREATING BALANCE

Healing Meal Plan for All Imbalances

Breakfast: Do not skip breakfast. Even if you are not hungry, at least have a stewed or baked apple or pear with raisins (see recipe later in this chapter in "The Pitta Cleanse") to start your day. This provides easily digestible nutrition and helps increase your appetite for lunch. If you are hungry, also have a bowl of cooked whole-grain cereal. If you have a strong appetite and tend to get hungry well before lunchtime, make your cereal with milk or soy milk and add ground nuts for extra protein.

Lunch: Lunch should be your main meal of the day. It's the only meal where you may eat any nonvegetarian foods (such as meat, poultry, fish, or seafood) and curdled foods such as cheese, cottage cheese, or yogurt. Include whole grains, freshly cooked vegetables, and a concentrated source of protein (lentils, chickpeas, or other legume; tofu or other soy; fresh cheese; nuts/seeds; nonvegetarian entree; etc.). Your lunch should consist mainly of cooked foods, though you may have a small amount of salad on the side if you wish.

Afternoon Snack: Have fresh fruit, dried fruits, nuts, unleavened crackers, boiled warm milk or soy milk, or rice cakes.

Dinner: Favor light, easy-to-digest foods such as cooked grains, cooked vegetables, and soups, including legume soups such as lentils. Avoid nonvegetarian foods (i.e., poultry, meat, fish) and cheese at the evening meal.

Bedtime Snack (if hungry): Try warm milk or soy milk boiled with a pinch of cinnamon, cardamom, or ginger, or hot cereal made with plenty of water.

DRY AND MOVING VATA: "QUEEN OF THE DOSHAS"

Vata, as you may recall from Chapter 3, is responsible for regulating all change, activity, and movement in mind and body, including all cycles and biorhythms. If vata is balanced, your internal clock will be regular and cyclic, and all changes and transitions within your physiology will be smooth. You will fall asleep easily and wake up feeling clear and alert. Your hunger will come at mealtimes, and you will feel satisfied between meals. Your menstrual cycle will come on time, the flow will last its usual time, and no bleeding will occur in between cycles. At menopause, your cycles will gracefully disappear, with no troublesome or disturbing symptoms.

This scenario may sound like a dream to you, but according to Maharishi Ayurveda, this natural, normal functioning is our birthright. If you are not experiencing this regular, easy state of health, look to the irregular habits, both personal and cultural, that have thrown your vata out of kilter.

If your vata is unbalanced, you are more likely to experience the kinds of menopause symptoms that exhibit the qualities of vata dosha: dryness, moving, and change. The dry quality of vata can lead to more vaginal dryness, dry skin, and constipation. Vata's stimulating effect on your nerves may contribute to feelings of anxiety, sleeping problems, heart palpitations, and tension headaches. Its irregular and

Tips on Food Selection and Preparation for All Dosha Types

General: Cook your own food as often as you can. Select fresh, in-season fruits and vegetables and certified organic foods whenever possible. Avoid genetically engineered foods, as Nature's intelligence has been altered in them at a very fundamental level. (See Resources Appendix for a Web site address giving updates on which foods to avoid.)

Vegetables: Cook in a small amount of water after sautéing with spices and a little olive oil, or steam and then add sautéed spices.

Oils: Use only extra-virgin, cold-pressed, organic oils, since refined oils promote inflammation and are damaging to the body. They often contain trans-fatty acids, pesticides, and other toxic residues from the refining process.

Spices: Spice your food at each meal. This helps your digestion, reduces gas, adds phytoestrogen, detox, and antioxidant support, helps balance your doshas and, of course, makes your food taste delicious. After steaming the vegetables, you may add the prescribed oil or ghee sautéed with spices. To prepare, heat 1 to 2 teaspoons of oil/ghee over medium-low heat. First add any seeds (like cumin) and fry gently until golden brown. Then add any of the powdered spices listed above. Pour this mixture over the vegetables, adding fresh herbs such as parsley or cilantro and salt at the very end.

Sugar and salt: Minimize sugar and salt.

Fruit: Soak dried fruits in water overnight or until they are soft. Eat sweet, juicy fruits as between-meal snacks.

Grains: Cook your grains with ½ to 1 teaspoon of ghee or olive oil per serving to balance their inherently drying effect on the body.

Nuts and seeds: Keep them natural, without added oil or salt. Ideally soak overnight in water and eat them, or cook with the softened nuts for better digestion and more balancing effect on vata and pitta doshas. Alternatively, bake or toast them until lightly browned.

Legumes: Soak the dried beans, peas, or dahl overnight or all day in room-temperature water. Pour off the water and use fresh water to cook them in. This makes the beans less gas producing and also saves you cooking time.

Dairy: Milk should be organic and ideally unhomogenized; bring to a boil and drink while still warm. Add a pinch of cardamom or cinnamon to help digestion and to reduce any tendency for sinus congestion from milk drinking. To ensure good digestion of the milk, never drink milk with a full meal, or anything that is salty or sour, including most fruits. Generally, it is best to drink milk on its own or with sweet dried fruits (raisins, dates), cereals, breads, or cooked grains. Cheese, yogurt, sour cream, and anything curdled (including soy cheese, rice cheese, and soy yogurt) should be eaten at lunchtime only. Curdled foods are too heavy to digest properly in the evening or at breakfast. Do not eat cheeses or yogurt with fruit to avoid dosha-imbalancing effects.

Nonvegetarian foods: Items should be freshly cooked, warm, and not processed or fried.

fluctuating qualities can cause mood swings, increased frequency or urgency of urination, and irregular menstrual cycles (such as more than one period in a month, spotting between cycles, or skipped periods). For one of my patients, Karen, vata imbalance meant digestive problems, as well as hot flashes and insomnia.

Karen's Story: Adjusting to Vata

Karen is an intelligent, fit, and trim forty-nine-year-old homemaker and mother of three who first came to see me for help with hot flashes and to discuss issues relating to her perimenopause. Because of her extensive familiarity with natural health approaches and her lifelong approach to maintaining good health in both mind and body, Karen thought perhaps she could handle menopause on her own with diet and exercise. However, what she had always done to maintain health — keeping a "healthy diet" and working out one to two hours daily — was no longer working. Her hot flashes and sleep problems persisted in spite of her efforts.

To make matters worse, she began to experience constipation for the first time in her life, as well as annoying, uncomfortable bloating and flatulence on a daily basis. Since she had always had good digestion and elimination, Karen was perplexed by these symptoms and frustrated that she was unable to overcome them naturally.

I explained to Karen that although these might seem like four different symptoms — hot flashes, insomnia, flatulence, and constipation — by Ayurvedic evaluation, all four were due to the same underlying imbalance in vata dosha. With some simple changes, she could balance her vata, improve her digestion and elimination, and get rid of her hot flashes and insomnia as well.

A review of Karen's diet revealed that for breakfast she drank a cold smoothie with protein powder, juice, banana, and yogurt. Sometimes she had an apple for a midmorning snack. Lunch was late, after her workout at about 2 P.M., and usually consisted of a large Caesar salad with raw tofu and garbanzo beans, an iced tea, and a few crackers on the side. Dinner was her largest meal and tended to be late in the evening, often not until 8 P.M., when her husband got home from work or she went out with friends.

I suggested we try a different approach. While her good exercise habits and diet were healthy by normal standards and had been suitable during her pitta phase of life (when digestion is characteristically strong), at perimenopause (the start of the vata life phase), so much exercise and raw, cold food were aggravating her vata dosha and overwhelming her digestive capacity. Food that she was used to thinking of as healthy and wholesome had become difficult to digest, especially when improperly prepared and consumed at the wrong time of day. To improve her digestion and elimination, she would have to modify her diet and exercise habits in a way that balanced vata dosha.

Karen's two-week treatment program included shifting her meals to earlier times, eating more warm, cooked foods with vata-balancing spices, avoiding raw foods and caffeine, and favoring warm drinks instead of iced beverages. I encouraged her to go to bed earlier to improve her sleep and gave her a gentle cleansing herbal program to help relieve her constipation more quickly.

At her checkup two weeks later, Karen was elated. Although she had had to work at adjusting her schedule and cooking habits, she was extremely pleased that her hot flashes were completely gone and she was sleeping through the night nearly every night. Her constipation and flatulence had both disappeared. At a follow-up consultation months later, Karen's improvements were holding steady and she was enjoying life without any of the troublesome symptoms that had caused her to seek help.

Calming Your Vata

You may have noticed when you were taking the quiz to measure your dosha balance in Chapter 3 that there were many more symptoms listed for vata imbalance than for pitta or kapha. This is because during the menopausal transition there is a natural increase in your vata imbalance, due partly to menopause being a time of *change* or transition in and of itself, as we discussed earlier. Another reason is that you are beginning a new stage of life, a stage dominated by vata. The occurrence of both of these factors simultaneously increases the likelihood of vata imbalance at this time.

Traditional texts of Ayurveda tell us that, in general, vata is more easily disturbed than the other two doshas. Given that any activity or sensory stimulation, especially stressful kinds, tend to aggravate vata, it is no wonder that in our day and age vata is the dosha most commonly out of balance. Fortunately, while vata is easier to get out of balance than the other two doshas, it is also quickest to respond to healing interventions. The single most important therapeutic measure for balancing all of the functions of vata in your body is *regularity*, which refers not only to timely elimination but also to the timing of your meals, your bedtime, and the time you rise each morning.

To balance vata, follow the three key recommendations listed below.

Key #1: Establish a Regular Daily Routine

Keeping a regular routine of early bedtime, waking time, and mealtime aligns all of your biorhythms into a harmonious and coordinated flow. A variety of scientific studies attest to the fact that such regularity dramatically affects the inner rhythms of your hormones, blood pressure, and even body temperature.

For example, you normally secrete ten to twenty times more cortisol, the hormone that helps cope with stress, early in the morning just before waking. (No surprise; it's like your body makes its own cup of coffee to help you face the day!) Night workers, however, who regularly sleep during the daytime, secrete their highest levels of cortisol in the late afternoon or early evening, before they get up. The body adjusts its internal schedule of hormone function according to your daily routine.

The bottom line is that a *regular routine* balances your vata dosha more powerfully than any other intervention. And since vata is the leading, or "Queen," dosha according to Ayurveda, keeping it balanced goes a long way toward balancing your pitta and kapha, too. You can think of vata as the conductor dosha, orchestrating all of your physiological processes. As vata goes, so go the other doshas.

Some Tips for Achieving a Regular Routine. Keeping a regular routine is second nature to some people, but for others, getting up, eating, and going to bed on a regular schedule are barely conceivable. In my practice, I've found that those women who need a regular routine the most are often the very ones for whom regularity does not come easily. You might guess that such women tend by nature to have the unstable, changeable, always-moving vata qualities in abundance. They may be artistic, vivacious, spontaneous, enthusiastic, and concerned that an early bedtime — or even a regular one — would cramp their lively social life.

Yet the good news is that the same women who are inclined toward an irregular schedule are most likely to benefit immensely and immediately when they make the effort to adopt a regular routine. Chronic, annoying health problems such as anxiety, sleep problems, constipation, gas and bloating, and mood swings tend to improve rapidly when they adopt a more regular routine. An additional benefit is that these vata-dominated women more often feel their naturally vibrant and energetic selves and less often feel moody, tired, or insecure.

I have found that no single approach to establishing a regular routine works for every person — it is a highly individual matter. Some people are all-or-nothing types who do best by deciding when they will start their new routine and then rearranging their schedule to do it all at once. Others find it more helpful to establish a regular routine one step at a time.

If you are a one-step-at-a-time person, I suggest you first establish one "anchor time" each day — a regular bedtime, waking time, or mealtime — whichever is easiest for you. Always make a point of having that particular meal on schedule, or arrange your evenings so you can get to bed by a certain regular time. Focus on anchoring that one event at a particular time of day for one, two, or three weeks, until it becomes easy and automatic. Then add a second anchor time in your schedule, and later a third and a fourth. Eventually, your every meal, bedtime, and waking time will each have its own stable place in the soothing, vata-balancing rhythm of your day.

A few tips on bedtime are in order, as this tends to be the most challenging habit for people to change. Begin with a very doable time. For example, if you are in the habit of going to bed at 1 A.M., but you know you could get to bed by midnight, start with that change. Gradually move your bedtime earlier by half-hour or even fifteen-minute intervals. Allow a few weeks to pass after each change for the new time to become automatic and effortless. Make 9:45 P.M. your eventual goal.

In three to six months, I believe you will find that your mood and energy during the day and the quality of your sleep have improved dramatically. The change to an earlier bedtime is one of the best-kept secrets for not only feeling better and sleeping better but looking younger. Don't be surprised when soon after you try it, a co-worker, friend, or your husband greets you with an admiring remark such as, "You look really good today. Did you lose weight or something?"

Key #2: Eat Mainly Warm, Cooked, Wholesome Foods

Besides a regular schedule for meals, the most vata-balancing principle of diet is to favor warm, cooked foods. Reserve salads and raw vegetables for on the side and take care to avoid cold drinks, iced desserts, and other cold foods.

Remember how Karen's constipation, gas, bloating, insomnia, and hot flashes, all disappeared within a few weeks after she changed her diet and schedule to balance her vata? Karen's main diet during the day consisted of a cold smoothie for breakfast; raw vegetables, salads, and ice-cold caffeinated tea for lunch; and crunchy raw apples for snacks. All of these foods are cold, crisp, and/or rough — properties that aggravate vata.

To balance her vata through her diet, Karen changed to all warm, cooked foods: cooked whole-grain cereal with soy milk and a stewed apple for breakfast; vegetables, grains, and protein for lunch; and a warm, cooked meal in the evening. She also began eating lunch and dinner earlier. Almost immediately, her indigestion symptoms of gas, bloating, and constipation (signs of out-of-balance vata) were completely resolved.

Adjust your daily eating habits to balance your vata by following the dietary guidelines in the sidebar "Eat Your Way to Balance: Vata." (For more information on products, including spices, oils, and specific dosha-balancing herbal preparations mentioned in this chapter, see the Resources Appendix.)

Key #3: *Calm Your Nerves and Soothe Your Skin with Self-Massage*

Fundamental to self-care in Ayurveda is the regular practice of a self-massage called *abhyanga* (ahb-<u>yung</u>-guh.) Specific oils (olive, coconut, almond, and sesame) are selected according to your skin type and which dosha you wish to balance. Since vata governs your nerves and circulation, which are both very prominent in the skin, massage is always balancing for vata dosha. Also, since oil is described as the most vata-pacifying substance — being unctuous, heavy, soothing, soft, and warming — massaging with oil is especially soothing for vata.

Your skin is one of the main sites where estrogen is formed in your body after menopause. Although I have never seen research on this, it may well be that the abhyanga enhances production of estrogen by your skin cells, helping your body make up for less hormone production by your ovaries. The Ayurvedic texts also state that abhyanga helps to prevent osteoporosis and increases bone strength.

For those of you who have irregular schedules, dry skin, vaginal dryness, and hot flashes; exercise frequently; or tend to be anxious in your mood, an oil massage daily (or as often as possible) will be especially beneficial. These conditions add an extra "vata load" to your life, and you will find that taking a few minutes each morning to do a self-massage with oil will help counteract the spaciness, dryness, anxiety, stiffness, aches, and pains that can come from vata rising in your body and mind. My patients often comment on how relaxing they find their morning self-massage with oil and report that its calming effects last throughout the day.

An extra bonus for vigorous exercisers (or anyone over forty, for that matter) is the effect of a daily oil massage to prevent injuries to the muscles, tendons, and joints. The classical Ayurvedic text, the *Charaka Samhita*, tells us that one who does

Eat Your Way to Balance: *VATA*

General Dietary Tips for Vata

• Favor warm, cooked foods and warm beverages. Avoid cold drinks, iced beverages and desserts, cold food and frozen desserts like ice cream and frozen yogurt.

• Choose soft, unctuous foods like cooked grains, cooked vegetables, cooked cereals, and soups over dry, crunchy foods.

• Avoid raw vegetables except occasionally in small amounts.

• Be sure to eat enough, especially if you are underweight, and include healthy oils such as olive oil, wheat-germ oil, and nuts and seeds in your daily diet.

• Eat in a settled environment. Avoid eating while reading, watching TV, doing business, talking on the phone, driving a car, or standing up.

• Avoid carbonated beverages and stimulants such as caffeine, caffeinated beverages, and chocolate.

• If you are not a vegetarian, favor chicken, turkey, fish, seafood, and eggs. Avoid beef, lamb, pork, and other red meats.

Food Items That Balance Vata

• **Vegetables**: Favor asparagus, zucchini, fennel, carrots, tomatoes, artichokes, cucumbers, yellow squash, okra, tiny eggplants, broccoli, spinach, and red or green chard. In small portions, occasionally: snow peas, peas, winter squashes, sweet potatoes. Strictly avoid salads, raw vegetables (except freshly juiced into vegetable juice), potatoes, cauliflower, brussels sprouts, and cabbage.

• **Oils:** Use olive oil or sunflower oil.

• **Spices:** Use cumin, ginger, mustard seeds, celery seeds, fenugreek, hing (asafetida), fresh garlic, basil, parsley, cinnamon, cardamom, cloves, anise, fennel, black pepper, salt, black salt, lemon juice, tamarind, and turmeric in small amounts. Avoid onions and hot spices, such as chilies, cayenne, salsa, and red peppers.

• **Salt:** Use rock salt or sea salt.

• **Sugar**: You may use date sugar, rock sugar, or raw, whole cane sugar in small quantities.

• **Fruits**: Choose sweet grapes, plums, cherries, kiwi, peaches, apricots, mangoes, papaya, dates, pineapples, berries, oranges, or grapefruit. Strictly avoid bananas, raw apples, and raw pears. Soften raisins, figs, prunes, dried pineapple, and dried papaya by soaking in water before eating, for better digestion.

• **Grains:** Choose couscous, bulgur wheat, quinoa, amaranth, rice (basmati, Texmati, or jasmine), pasta.

• **High-protein foods:**
  • Use mung bean soup (split or whole) and red, green, or brown lentils. In general, avoid large dried beans such as pinto beans, black beans, and chickpeas.
  • Eat cooked tofu (sauté in oil and spices, or steam), tempeh, and other soy products.
  • Use all nuts and seeds except peanuts.
  • If you are not a vegetarian, choose organic chicken, turkey, fish, and eggs.

• **Dairy products**: Try boiled warm milk, yogurt (not mixed with fruit), and lassi (a freshly made drink of one part fresh yogurt diluted with three parts water, with a pinch of cumin and a pinch of salt added). Cottage cheese, fresh mozzarella, panir (a traditional Ayurvedic fresh, homemade cheese), ricotta cheese, and goat cheese are fine, but avoid any hard cheeses.

How to Give Yourself Abhyanga

Perform your abhyanga each day before your bath, ideally in the morning. Warm up your oil by setting a small squeeze bottle of it in hot water, in the sink or a small container. When it's warm, you are ready to begin. Sit on an old towel in the middle of your bathroom. You will use the flat of your hands, not your fingertips, for the entire massage, which is essentially an application and rubbing in of the oil. Squeeze out one or two teaspoons onto the palms of your hands, rub together, and then rub your hands against your scalp gently to apply the oil thoroughly. (Skip this step on days when you do not wish to wash your hair.) Then gradually work downward: doing neck, shoulders, arms, abdomen, breasts, back, legs, and feet — one side and then the other for each body area. Use long strokes over the long bones, circular motions over your joints, a large clockwise circle over your abdomen, and circular motions around your breasts. Grasp and pull gently as you slide your grip along the length of each finger from knuckle to end of the fingernails and off. Your abhyanga should take about twenty minutes, but it is better to do a shorter one than to skip it entirely. (For more tips on abhyanga, see the Resources Appendix for Web site addresses.)

abhyanga regularly will not injure as easily and, if injured, will heal more quickly. I have certainly found that to be the case for my patients and for me as well. I am confident that anyone who does an abhyanga daily is very unlikely to ever develop chronic tendonitis, carpal tunnel syndrome, fibromyalgia, or other chronic pain problems.

Recent research has shown that sesame oil (the oil of choice for musculoskeletal aches and pains) has anti-inflammatory properties as well as antibacterial and anticancer effects on the skin. Massaging the body with sesame oil quickly improves circulation and promotes healing of the tissues so that bothersome chronic inflammatory conditions just don't have a chance to set in. Doing the massage on a daily basis keeps your muscles and tendons more lubricated and pliable, so they're less likely to injure in the first place.

Using different oils for the massage can bring about specific results. If you feel hot all the time or are having many hot flashes, for example, use coconut oil, which has tremendous cooling properties. (See Veronica's story below, in which she attributes the disappearance of her hot flashes in part to her coconut-oil massages.) Also, if you are prone to red, inflamed rashes on your skin, you will find coconut oil the most soothing (paradoxically, sesame oil can increase inflammation, due to its purification effects.) If dryness is your main problem, use olive or almond oil. Do expend the extra effort and cost to get *organic* oils for your massage. They are less irritating to the skin and do not introduce dangerous chemical residues or trans-fatty acids into your body.

RED-HOT PITTA

The most salient quality of pitta is heat. Think of your pitta as your internal combustion engine, burning the food you eat as fuel to keep your body's metabolism running. Pitta is also responsible for how you "metabolize" mental and emotional experiences in your heart and mind. If your pitta is balanced, your digestion and metabolism will be strong, your energy will be high, your weight will be perfect, your complexion will be radiant, and your thinking and emotions will be steady and positive.

If you scored high on the pitta scale in Chapter 3, you are more likely to experience symptoms that are related to the qualities of pitta dosha, such as heat. Your internal "thermostat" may run excessively hot, and you may be prone to more hot flashes and easy sweating. An overheated pitta can also affect your mind and emotions, causing irritability, impatience, and a quick temper. When my patient Veronica's pitta dosha was out of balance, she had nightly hot flashes and disturbed sleep.

Veronica's Story: A Case of Persistent Hot Flashes

Veronica is a forty-eight-year-old, fair-skinned, freckled redhead from South Africa who came to see me at The Raj Ayurveda Health Center for Maharishi Rejuvenation Treatment (described in Chapter 10) and for a consultation regarding her hot flashes. She told me that for the past eight months she had been suffering from eight or nine hot flashes a day. They occurred mainly during the night, disturbing her sleep. Veronica had been educating herself about herbal approaches to menopause and had tried several products without getting much relief.

Her evaluation revealed that an imbalance of pitta dosha, the hot metabolism principle, was at the root of her hot flashes. Some of the herbs she was taking were better at balancing vata and had a heating effect that was making her flashes worse. I advised Veronica to stop taking her current herbs, begin a pitta-balancing diet and routine, and give herself a daily oil massage with cooling, herbalized coconut oil. I also recommended that she take a cooling herbal formula with pearl calcium, which is used in Ayurveda to reduce pitta and is said to have a special balancing effect on the hypothalamus.

I received an e-mail from Veronica a few weeks later: "You prescribed a complete pitta pacifying regime, but because I was traveling, I was only able to apply the cooling massage oil (coconut based) and take the pearl supplement. The flushes disappeared within two days and I have not had a single one since then. I am adding the other remedies now, but it is almost not necessary. Thank you for your help."

Chill Out Your Pitta

While vata is the most likely dosha to become disturbed at midlife and after, pitta follows closely behind. Menopause marks the passage into the phase of life dominated by vata and away from a twenty-five to thirty-year phase dominated by pitta. According to MAV, hot pitta qualities tend to build up in the body during those years and can result in annoying adult acne, skin rashes, inflammation of joints and tendons, or heartburn. Just about any "itis" (which is Latin for "inflammation") you can think of is due to pitta imbalance and is common at this transitional junction of pitta and vata phases of life.

Around the midlife transition, you may also find you feel hotter in general during the day than you did just a few years ago, or in comparison to others around you, and you may be more prone to hot flashes and night sweats, especially if your vata is also "flying high." A combination of unbalanced pitta and vata is most conducive to hot flashes. Think of what happens when a gust of wind (vata) hits your campfire (pitta.) The flames suddenly flare up and the heat of the fire increases.

The solution lies in quelling the fire while at the same time protecting its flames from the ravages of the wind. We need to balance both vata and pitta to overcome the tendency toward hot flashes as well as to deal with the host of other combined vata- and pitta-related symptoms you may have identified in the Chapter 2 self-rating scale, "How Balanced Are You?"

To balance your heat, follow the three keys recommended below.

Key #1: Chill Out Your Nervous System

Like all the doshas, pitta can be seen at work both in the physical body and at the level of the mind and emotions. Factors affecting either pathway can lead to pitta imbalance and fortunately both pathways can also be accessed to restore pitta balance.

Your mind's abilities to discriminate, plan, reason, analyze, and take initiative all fall into the domain of your hot pitta dosha. It is also intimately involved in activities that require any kind of visual processing, such as reading, writing, and watching TV. You can get your heat out of balance when you overuse these capacities to work long hours on a computer. (Irritated, bloodshot eyes are a telling sign of aggravated pitta.) The intense visual stimulation and discrimination required to work at a computer screen tend to increase heat in your brain and nervous system.

Balanced pitta creates mental clarity, a focused mind, and energy to accomplish what you need to do. But unbalanced pitta can create frustration, impatience, irritability, and anger. Many women find that being mentally and emotionally on edge is a setup for increased hot flashes and can trigger them directly. In fact, anger disrupts your neurochemistry so powerfully that it has been shown to be as potent a trigger for heart attacks as sudden, strenuous exercise. Habitual or chronic anger aggravates pitta, and when we find ourselves stuck in anger or irritability, we can expect there is an ongoing imbalance in pitta as well.

We can further disturb our heat balance by allowing our drive and ambition to finish a project or achieve a goal make us skip meals and stay up all night, physiological triggers that wreck havoc with our pitta functions of digestion and metabolism, not to mention our overall health. The result is often a pitta-style emotional response of irritability and reduced capacity for handling stress the next day.

This kind of vicious cycle sets you up for an ever-increasing heat imbalance. Women prone to workaholism (who tend to be high in pitta by nature) learn over and over that trying too hard to get ahead can get them out of balance and make them vulnerable to health setbacks that defeat their achievements in the long run.

The first rule for mentally and emotionally balancing pitta is to keep your goals and ambitions in balance. Don't expect too much too quickly; that sets you up for frustration, disappointment, and anger. Avoid working under pressure by managing your time and having structures in your life (calendar, datebook) that help you complete your work with time left over to relax. Learn not to bite off more than you can chew and say no to an overload of either work or social activities. Above all, maintain your regular routine: mealtimes, bedtime, and rising time. This will help prevent pitta aggravation and keep your vata balanced as well.

Paying attention to your doshic clock can help you to keep your hot pitta symptoms under control, especially hot flashes. Research shows that hot flashes follow a daily pattern, peaking in most women in the late evening hours around 10 P.M., when body temperature is also still near its daily high. This hot flash peak coincides with the start of pitta time, the four-hour period of day during which your hot dosha is more active in your body.

This simultaneity is no coincidence. Thousands of years ago, Ayurveda described daily doshic and physiological rhythms and their relation to the rhythms of Nature, as we discussed in Chapter 3. It has used them to promote health and healing ever since. Indeed, today's growing body of scientific research on chronobiology verifies many of Ayurveda's principles of time.

To balance pitta effects during the evening hours, when body temperature is high and hot flashes are more easily triggered, it is important to develop cooling evening habits. This means both mentally and physically chilling out in the hours leading up to 10 P.M. Some tips on how to do this follow.

Chill Mentally. Many professional women tell me that the evening is the only time they have to do household chores, catch up on phone calls and e-mail, spend time with their families, and do everything else that they don't have time for during the workday. Consequently, many of them are running at full steam, trying to fit everything in well past the time pitta rises at 10 P.M. It is no surprise to me that these women frequently complain of trouble getting to sleep and a tendency to wake up during the night (with or without hot flashes), and not be able to get back to sleep. It is much better to go to bed early and then arise earlier than usual, if necessary, to catch up on unfinished tasks.

Chill Physically. If you are in the habit of bathing in the evening, make sure that your bathwater is not much warmer than body temperature. Keep your home and bedroom cool, especially at bedtime and during the night. Good ventilation, a fan, and even a slightly open window in winter can be helpful. Avoid hot drinks and alcohol in the evening. A cool drink or a light snack before bed may also satisfy your pitta, quelling hunger and thirst (both pitta aggravators), throughout the night.

Key #2: Never Skip or Delay Your Meals

A number of my patients have noticed that their hot flashes occur more often when they are hungry or late for a meal. There is a good reason for this. Normally, acids and enzymes are secreted on a regular schedule, following the stomach's circadian rhythm. This digestive readiness is greatest around noon, in harmony with the sun being at its peak of heat and light-giving energy for the day. If you delay eating until 2 or 3 P.M. to catch a bite between meetings or classes, you miss putting food in your stomach at the time it is most primed to digest a meal.

The result, Ayurveda tells us, is that the pitta energy of digestion, without having any food to work on, in effect works on your *insides*, promoting inflammation and an overall increase in internal pitta, or heat. We will discuss in a later chapter the long-term effects of this type of eating on your digestive capacity. For now it is sufficient to know that delaying your meal, especially at midday when pitta is naturally strongest within your body and outside in Nature, leads to an increase of pitta in your body, dangerously throwing that dosha off.

Skipping lunch also tends to aggravate your mental and emotional heat. You have probably learned that it's never good idea to bring up certain issues (complaints, financial problems, or requests for money, to name a few) to your spouse, your boss, or a certain friend before he or she has eaten lunch. You may have found that people are much more amenable to just about anything after a good meal. A sour disposition and an empty stomach seem to go hand and hand, a combination that is predicted by Ayurvedic dosha theory.

What to Eat to Cool Down. Keeping in mind the popular saying, "you are what you eat" and the ancient Ayurvedic principle of similarity, "like increases like," you might guess that consuming a lot of hot drinks and hot, spicy foods would increase your inner heat and trigger hot flashes. That is certainly the experience of many women.

In Ayurveda, foods and drinks that increase heat in the body are referred to as pitta aggravating, and those that reduce heat are referred to as pitta pacifying. If you scored high on the pitta scale in the Chapter 3 quiz, "Which Dosha Is Causing Your Symptoms?", your diet should be pitta pacifying, or heat reducing.

In the Vedic approach, there are two basic kinds of heat. *Thermal* heat is the kind that feels warm to the touch, like hot tea or a hot casserole. *Chemical* heat is created by caustic substances, such as acids. When such substances come into contact with the body's tissue in excess (if, say, acid is spilled on the skin), the resulting burn can be even more serious than a burn from fire. This awareness of chemical heat tells us that in addition to avoiding hot liquids, such as tea, coffee, and soups, to balance pitta you should also avoid excessively acidic, sharp, hot, spicy foods or otherwise pungent flavors that might "burn" the tissues of your body.

You may recall that pitta governs the functions of digestion and of metabolism. All the action of hydrochloric acid in the stomach and the breaking down of food by pancreatic enzymes in your intestines is accomplished by a kind of chemical soup that Ayurveda associates with pitta. During these processes, hot, acidic, pitta-type waste products can build up in your tissues, especially in the small intestine, liver, and blood. This buildup can lead to pitta problems elsewhere in the body, such as inflammation of the skin, breakouts and rashes, heartburn, body odor, urinary tract infections, loose stools, and increased hot flashes and sweating.

To counteract these effects, a pitta-pacifying diet emphasizes foods that are innately cooling to the body, not just thermally but also chemically. These foods help to eliminate the unhealthy buildup of excess acids and other toxic byproducts of metabolism by promoting their elimination through the kidneys, liver, and bowel.

Focus on consuming plenty of juicy, sweet, and nonacidic vegetables and fruits, as well as spices with gentle diuretic effects, such as coriander and cilantro. Eat pure, fresh, organic foods as much as possible. To help put out any fires that may spring up, be sure to drink plenty of fresh, pure water every day.

For further tips on how to adjust your diet to balance your pitta, refer to the sidebar "Eat Your Way to Balance: Pitta."

Key #3: Cool Out with a Pitta Cleanse

In the first year or two after your periods stop, I recommend you do a three-day pitta cleanse at regular intervals, at least once each season (four times a year) or as often as once a month. Some good reasons for this recommendation follow.

Cleansing After Menstruation Has Ceased. Ayurveda views the loss of blood during the menstrual cycle as more than merely the aftereffect of the lack of fertilization of the ova. Rather, MAV sees menstruation as an advantageous mechanism by which a woman's body is cleansed of accumulated toxins, which are eliminated through the blood that is lost. When this monthly cleansing ceases at menopause, it is especially important for women to undergo periodic gentle cleansing, such as the pitta cleanse described here, or the more thorough and deep cleansing of Maharishi Rejuvenation Treatment, or *panchakarma*. These cleansing approaches provide alternate routes for toxins to leave the body and help the body adjust to the lack of the purifying monthly menstrual flow.

One leading researcher on the role of the menstrual cycle in human evolution, biologist Margie Profet of the University of California at Berkeley, theorized in a landmark paper that the purpose of the menstrual flow is to purify the genital tract. She noted that menstrual blood contains more white blood cells (fighters of infection

Eat Your Way to Balance: PITTA

General Dietary Tips for Pitta

· Eat your meals on time. Never skip or delay your meals.

· Drink plenty of plain, pure water every day; room temperature is best.

· Favor sweet juicy fruits such as melons, pears, apples, grapes, and plums. Minimize citrus, strawberries, peaches, and any sour-tasting fruit.

· Avoid toxins, drugs, and stimulants such as alcohol, recreational chemicals, and caffeine. Also avoid pesticides and artificial flavorings, colorings, and preservatives.

· Avoid hot, spicy foods, sour or acidic tastes (including vinegar-containing foods, salad dressings and condiments, and pickled foods), refined sugar, and greasy or fried foods.

Food Items That Balance Pitta

• **Vegetables:** Favor all green leafy cooked vegetables (except spinach), and broccoli, okra, lettuce, and brussels sprouts. Also eat winter squashes (acorn, butternut, hubbard), summer squashes, zucchini, fennel, cucumber, asparagus, artichokes, carrots, green beans, cauliflower, cabbage, peas, snow peas, lettuce, parsley, cilantro, bok choy, sweet corn, and sweet potato (in small amounts cooked with other vegetables or soup). Avoid tomatoes, green and red peppers, eggplant, and spinach.

• **Fruits.** All fruit should be sweet in taste, not sour. Favor melons, cantaloupe, honeydew, sweet grapes, dark grapes, avocado, coconut, apples, pears, persimmons, pomegranates, sweet mangoes, black plums, raisins, and dates. Avoid citrus fruits, kiwi, banana, and any sour-tasting fruit.

• **Oils.** Use ghee (best for pitta balancing) or olive oil.

• **Spices.** Use coriander, anise, fennel, cardamom, and turmeric, as well as fresh green cilantro, parsley, rosemary, and basil leaves. Avoid chilies, hot peppers, cayenne, asafetida (hing), garlic, ginger powder, and such condiments as mustard, ketchup, and soy sauce.

• **Salt.** Use in small quantities, preferably rock salt or sea salt.

• **Sugar.** You may use date sugar, rock sugar or raw, whole cane sugar in small quantities.

• **Grains:** Consume couscous, bulgur wheat, quinoa, amaranth, rice (basmati, Texmati, or jasmine), barley, and pasta.

• **High-protein foods.** Favor mung-bean soup (split or whole) and red, green, or brown lentils. All other dried peas or beans are fine if indigestion does not result. Sauté tofu in olive oil and spices, or steam. Avoid fermented soy products like tempeh and soy sauce.

• **Nuts/seeds.** Eat pumpkin seeds and almonds (blanched is best) unprocessed, without added oil or salt. Limit quantities, as all nuts and seeds increase pitta somewhat.

• **Nonvegetarian.** If you crave animal products, stick to chicken, turkey, and egg whites.

• **Dairy products:** Try organic boiled milk or lassi (a freshly made drink of one part fresh yogurt diluted with three parts water). Cottage cheese, fresh mozzarella, panir (a homemade soft cheese,) ricotta cheese, and goat cheese are all right in small amounts. Avoid yogurt (except as lassi) and all aged or sharp cheeses.

and scavengers of wastes) than the blood flowing through our veins and arteries, which indicates the enhanced cleansing power of the menstrual flow.

Ayurveda goes one step further in viewing the monthly blood loss as a means of purifying the body as a whole. This matches the experience of many women I have talked to who report that in the days just before their period, they often feel bloated, sluggish, and physically and emotionally toxic. Yet after their period, they feel fresh and light, as though the body has cleansed and renewed itself on a deep level.

Earthly, Motherly Kapha

Recall that your kapha dosha is responsible for all structures, fluids, materials, and substances of your body. It holds your body together, binding all the parts into a cohesive whole. Kapha is a nurturing dosha, like a mother who with her loving embrace nourishes, soothes, and heals her offspring. Think of an Italian mother serving dinner to her family and you will have grasped the essence of the role of kapha in the body. Kapha nourishes, sustains, and supports our tissues. During the midlife transition, a balanced kapha dosha gives your body, mind, and emotions extra stability and strength — just what you need to withstand the ups and downs of your vata and pitta doshas and glide through the transition smoothly.

If you scored high in the kapha rating scale in Chapter 3, you may very well have an abundance of the generous, nurturing kapha instincts. However, you also have an excess of kapha in your system, giving you sluggish metabolism and a tendency to be lethargic and slow to move, physically and mentally. My patient Grace's kapha imbalance symptoms included depression, lethargy, and weight gain.

Grace's Story: From HT to Maharishi Ayurveda

Grace is a sixty-year-old lawyer with a high-powered position in a federal agency. She greeted me at our first meeting with a firm, businesslike handshake but a warm, inviting smile. She was delighted to be seeing a physician trained in Maharishi Ayurveda and to be back for more Ayurvedic treatment, she told me, because her past experience with MAV had been so positive.

Grace told me that until she began her first MAV treatment, nine months earlier, she had felt "terrible" for several years. She said the start of menopause in 1994 was the beginning of the first ill health she had ever experienced. Fortunately, she had never experienced any really bothersome symptoms of the menopause transition itself. She didn't remember ever having hot flashes.

What she did have was depression, insomnia, weight gain, and a feeling of heaviness, sluggishness, and lethargy. Grace had been the primary breadwinner in the family since her

The Three-Day Pitta Cleanse

Plan your cleansing for at least a three-day period. It is usually best for working women to starting on Friday evening. You may repeat the cleanse once a month until symptoms are gone, and then do it once a season for prevention. Alternatively, you may follow the cleansing program every day for up to a week each month until your symptoms are gone.

Follow the "Healing Meal Plan for All Imbalances" at the beginning of this chapter, with selected grains and vegetables (organic if possible) from the "Eat Your Way to Balance: Pitta" diet. Begin your cleanse with your evening meal on the first day, followed the next morning by a pitta detox cocktail (recipe below) before breakfast. Aloe vera juice and lime juice work especially well to cleanse your liver and digestive system as well as balancing your hormonal system and nourishing your reproductive organs.

Pitta Detox Cocktail. Choose from the two versions below, depending on your elimination habits. Drink on an empty stomach before breakfast.

1. *Lime elixir* is especially good for women who have loose stools or several bowel movements each day. Preparation: Bring one cup of pure water (filtered or spring water) to a boil. Let cool down to drinkable temperature. Add juice of an entire small lime or half of a large lime.

2. *Aloe elixir* is better for women who have only one bowel movement daily and tend toward constipation or those who have a tendency toward heartburn. Drink one-half cup aloe vera juice (*not* the gel, which is much stronger, and *not* whole-leaf aloe, which is not recommended by Ayurveda).

After drinking your pitta detox cocktail, eat a baked or stewed apple or pear. Put the whole apple or pear in the oven and bake at 350 degrees for about 30 minutes or until soft. For best results, insert three whole cloves around the circumference of the apple or pear before cooking. Remove from the oven and allow it to cool before eating. To stew, simmer one sliced apple or pear in two cups of water with three whole cloves for about thirty minutes or until soft. Remove from water and allow it to cool before eating. Follow this with eight prunes that have been soaked overnight or stewed with your apple or pear. If you are still hungry, complete your breakfast with one to two cups of hot, cooked whole-grain cereal, seasoned with cinnamon or cardamom.

---

lawyer husband had switched to a more fulfilling but much lower-paid teaching career several years before, so she didn't have much time to indulge herself in either self-pity or self-care. She had tried HT but felt immediate worsening of her symptoms and stopped it after two months. That didn't leave her with much else to try other than antidepressants, which she decided against. In her characteristically stoic and optimistic way, she decided to "push on," keep working hard, and hope a solution would present itself.

It wasn't until her teenage son developed learning difficulties and depression that Grace began to explore natural medicine. She learned of MAV through her reading and brought her son to see me in Washington, D.C. He gained so much from his MAV program that she began to think, "Maybe this could help me, too!"

With her demanding work schedule and family life, she felt the best way to get started was to immerse herself in a week-long intensive treatment program at one of the in-residence Maharishi Ayurveda Health Centers.

"It was a life-transforming experience," she told me. She found the organic vegetarian food so delicious that she felt inspired to follow her MAV doctor's recommendations for a similar diet after she returned home. She restarted her practice of Transcendental Meditation, which she had learned long ago and found valuable but had gotten away from due to her busy schedule. She also discovered the benefits of yoga asanas and incorporated regular yoga practice into her schedule.

Grace credits these changes in her lifestyle for a 180-degree turnaround in her health. Over six months, she lost 30 pounds without trying and quickly began to feel light and energetic again. The depression lifted and has not returned.

"The cooking, the TM, the yoga, it's all worth the time," she told me. "I feel so much better."

Caring for Your Kapha

Fortunately, the one dosha that does not seem to go wild at menopause is your kapha dosha. Not that kapha, your heavy, structural dosha, never gets out of balance in middle age — it does, as clearly evidenced by middle-aged spread — but the process is usually slower and more under your control. Kapha imbalance also plays a role in high cholesterol, fibroids and other growths, and diabetes.

Since kapha is associated with the heavier, more substantial elements of water and earth and with your sense of taste and smell, what you eat and drink is critical to balancing your kapha.

Following are three key recommendations for helping you to balance your earthy kapha dosha.

Key #1: Arise Early Every Morning

In Chapter 2, we saw how MAV breaks the day into six four-hour periods, each ruled by an alternating dosha in a repeated cycle. The time you awaken in the morning and the particular dosha that rules that time period can make a big difference in your day.

From 2 to 6 A.M. is vata time, with qualities that are light, quick, moving. From 6 to 10 A.M. is kapha time, associated with the qualities dull, heavy, and sluggish. Ayurveda tells us that the quality associated with the start of an action affects the quality of the whole action. This can be summarized by the aphorism "Well begun is half done." If you start your day during vata time, you'll be more alert — light, quick, and moving — for the entire day. If you start between 6 and 10 A.M., your day will have the quality of kapha — heavy, dull, and sluggish.

This information can help you to have more energy and be more productive. The longer you sleep in during kapha time, the longer kapha accumulates, making your eyes puffy, your sinuses congested, your joints stiff, and your thinking foggy. If you don't get out of bed until 9 A.M., the urge to reach for your morning coffee is hard to resist. To overcome this tendency and get yourself up during vata time, go to bed earlier the night before. Fall asleep no later than 10 P.M. Then getting up at 6 A.M. (or 7 at the latest) will be easy, and you'll see the difference it makes in what you get done during the day.

Key #2: Indulge Your Sensual, Nourishing Kapha Nature with Delicious Home-Cooked Meals

The saying goes that you are what you eat. And certainly your body renews itself each day from the materials obtained through your diet. By the principle of similarity, if you eat heavy, dense, fatty foods, you are more likely to have a heavy, dense, fatty body — one overloaded with too much kapha, too much substance.

Unfortunately, many women whose bodies easily accumulate a lot of kapha are irresistibly drawn to overeating by rich, delicious flavors and enticing aromas. Their true hunger level often takes a backseat to the sensual pleasure of eating, and they habitually eat more than their bodies really need.

The good news is that women with kapha tendencies can usually be satisfied by a wide variety of foods, as long as they taste wonderful. They can be just as happy eating a well-spiced, low-calorie, vegetarian Mexican meal as they would be eating a fat-packed 12-ounce cut of roast beef with a baked potato, butter, and sour cream. The key is to find or prepare flavorful, interesting, and luscious meals using food ingredients and preparation techniques that are kapha balancing.

For people with a kapha imbalance, the American Heart Association's mandate to increase the amount of foods naturally rich in fiber and decrease foods naturally high in fat (such as dairy and meats) could not be more relevant. These dietary principles, of course, are healthy for everyone; however, they are essential for those with kapha imbalance. For details, see the sidebar "Eat Your Way to Balance: Kapha."

Key #3: Exercise, Exercise, Exercise

The main objective in balancing kapha is to keep your metabolism lively. Kapha is slow moving and tends toward sluggishness and inertia, so staying active is of paramount importance. The latest research on fitness and health indicates that at least thirty minutes of moderate-intensity exercise nearly every day is needed for protection against a wide variety of diseases. More exercise is better.

If you are trying to lose weight and you scored high on the kapha scale, you will probably need more exercise to lose weight at the rate you'd like. However, even thirty minutes a day will go a long way toward helping you speed up your metabolism, shed excess fluid, reduce stiffness and sluggishness, improve your mood and energy, and lower your cholesterol.

CREATING BALANCE

Eat Your Way to Balance: KAPHA

General Dietary Tips for Kapha

• A vegetarian diet rich in legumes like lentils and dahls, whole grains like barley, rye, and millet, and lots of cooked vegetables is very helpful in maintaining a healthy weight and good digestion. Eat also fruits, nuts, seeds, and wholesome fresh ingredients. Strictly avoid red meat.

• Spice your food generously with thyme, basil, mint, oregano, cumin, turmeric, fresh ginger, and black pepper (easy on the latter two if hot flashes are an issue).

• Eat your main meal at noon and a lighter meal early in the evening, by 7 P.M.

• Prepare your food at home as much as possible. Try to limit restaurant meals to no more than once or twice a week.

• Avoid refined sweets (cakes, cookies, candy, etc.). Avoid sugar, excess fat, and cold drinks.

• Minimize dairy products.

• Avoid the "energy sappers": leftovers and canned, bottled, frozen, and processed foods.

Food Items That Balance Kapha

• **Vegetables.** Eat one cup of green, leafy cooked vegetables every day. Eat fewer potatoes, beets, sweet potatoes, and other root vegetables.

• **Fruits.** Eat apples, pears, persimmon, papaya, guava, pomegranates, cranberries, and figs. Avoid bananas, avocado, coconut, citrus, and any sour-tasting fruit.

• **Oils.** All oils and fats are inherently kapha increasing and should be used sparingly. Use olive oil and do not overheat it.

• **Spices.** Use all spices except salt, especially ginger, black pepper, mustard seeds, turmeric, cinnamon, and cloves. Use fresh green herbs in quantity, especially oregano, sage, thyme, mint, and basil.

• **Salt.** Use sparingly, preferably as rock salt (such as the brand "Real Salt").

• **Sugar.** Avoid sugar. You may use a very small amount of rock sugar or raw honey in small quantity. Do not cook with honey or heat it above 110 degrees. (Rock sugar is available in Indian grocery stores.)

• **Grains**: Barley is the best grain for you, followed by millet, buckwheat, rye, oats, and kashi. Couscous, bulgur wheat, or quinoa is fine several times a week. Limit rice and pasta to once or twice a week. Use only basmati, jasmine, or Texmati rice. Avoid yeast and leavened breads and crackers. Chapatis, rice cakes, or tortillas, and crackers made without yeast or baking soda are fine. Toast chapatis or tortillas or dry-fry them in a skillet before eating.

• **High-protein foods:** All dried beans and peas are acceptable. Avoid any legumes that give you digestive symptoms, such as flatulence.

• **Soy:** Tofu is fine if sautéed with plenty of spices. Avoid processed soy products such as tempeh, textured soy protein, and soy burgers. Soy milk is also fine.

• **Nuts/seeds.** Small portions of unsalted sunflower, sesame and pumpkin seeds, pecans, and walnuts without added oils are all right. Nuts are inherently kapha increasing, so they should be consumed in small amounts only (no more than eight to ten per day). Avoid nut butters.

• **Dairy Products.** Choose organic skim milk; boil with a pinch of ginger and turmeric and drink warm.

• **Nonvegetarian.** Chicken is acceptable, but have it only if you strongly desire it. A vegetarian diet is recommended.

IF YOU HAVE MORE SERIOUS SYMPTOMS

The recommendations I have given in this chapter should be sufficient to resolve your symptoms if they scored as "mild" in the Chapter 2 quiz. However, if your symptoms persist or are more severe than those covered in this chapter, you will find further help in the information and recommendations given in Chapters 5 and 6.

* 5 *

Your Metabolism: Key To Resolving Your More Serious Symptoms

Healthy tissues bestow happiness and vitality. Polluted tissues bring misery and disease.
— *the* Kashyapa Samhita

You have seen how your mild midlife symptoms result from your doshas being out of balance and can be easily resolved when you take steps to restore balance. More serious symptoms, however (such as persistent hot flashes, chronic insomnia, or excessive weight gain) are signs of deeper imbalances that will persist to set the stage for later disease if left untreated.

What Causes Your More Serious Symptoms?

A classic textbook of Ayurvedic medicine, the *Charaka Samhita*, states that a simple imbalance of your doshas is not enough to cause serious health problems. For more troublesome symptoms and disease to manifest, the actual tissues of your body — your bones, muscles, fat, organs, skin, and blood — must be affected in some way.

Modern medical theory and the ancient texts alike acknowledge that for disease to be present, your tissues and their organs must be seriously disturbed. But modern medicine tends to ignore the causes leading up to that disturbance. Instead, most doctors merely offer the current range of symptomatic treatments, such as anti-inflammatory drugs or painkillers, and state apologetically that they don't know what has caused your fibromyalgia, colitis, or other disorder.

In this chapter, we will look through the lens of Maharishi Ayurveda to see the causes of your more serious symptoms before embarking on a program to correct and eliminate them in Chapter 6. You may have identified some of your more troublesome symptoms on the self-rating scale in Chapter 2, "How Balanced Are You?" My patient Victoria's experience shows how your serious symptoms can be due to underlying causes that are treatable with MAV.

Victoria's Secret: The Mistaken Menu

I was surprised when Victoria came to my office for a consultation about her midlife symptoms. I knew her as an accomplished wellness-oriented psychotherapist who is highly respected in her community. She impressed me as one of those dynamic, together individuals who seem able to do it all, including staying healthy and happy despite a very busy lifestyle. However, Victoria told me she had recently been feeling very tired and sluggish and had begun to have severe hot flashes, night sweats that disturbed her sleep, and annoying mood swings — a classic triad of menopausal symptoms. To make matters worse, a benign thyroid nodule she'd had for several years started to get larger.

Victoria knew something was wrong in her body, and she was desperate for some relief. She had tried a high-soy diet and several over-the-counter herbal products for hot flashes but without much success. She wanted relief for her menopausal symptoms, but she wanted it naturally, without hormone therapy.

Given the wellness orientation of her practice, I assumed Victoria had been following some kind of healthy regimen herself. Yet here she was in my office, describing her rather severe menopause problems. I was perplexed. Something didn't quite add up.

I began my inquiry by asking Victoria whether the past few years had been particularly stressful. She admitted that in the past five years, she had been burning the candle at both ends, growing her practice and taking care of her school-age children. She'd let her exercise program slide and hadn't been as careful with her diet as in previous years. There had been extra stress in her family with the passing away of her husband's parents and, as she described it, "just a lot to deal with."

I proceeded to the next step of diagnosis, an examination of Victoria's pulse in order to determine the overall state of balance in her body. Reading the pulse is traditionally one of the most important aspects of the physical exam in MAV. It gives a direct way to determine the state of balance of the doshas and the tissues, as well as the strength of digestion.

In contrast to the dynamism and drive that she radiated outwardly, Victoria's pulse felt heavy, thick, and dull. This reading alerted me that something deeper than a simple dosha imbalance was responsible for her symptoms.

I followed up on Victoria's comment about her diet. The pulse of someone whose diet consists largely of vegetables, grains, and fruits, with minimal animal products, normally has a light, clear, and lively quality, a sign that there is little or no toxic buildup in the body. This was clearly not the case for Victoria.

"My diet was pretty good until recently," Victoria said. "About a year ago, I decided to try a popular low-carb diet to drop a few of the pounds I had put on from not exercising. I lost 9 pounds, but after six months of eating mainly meat and cheese, with very few carbohydrates, the truth is I wasn't feeling very good. Just recently, I started back on my usual healthier, more balanced diet."

Mystery solved! Victoria's pulse was certainly demonstrating that you are what you eat. Now that she had filled in the missing pieces, I could see how she'd set herself up for the moderate to severe menopausal symptoms she was experiencing. Five years earlier she had begun eating on the run, staying up late at night, and exercising less frequently, if at all. Then, in the past year, she'd followed an unbalanced diet consisting largely of animal products like meat and cheese. The cumulative effect of her erratic lifestyle and food choices that challenged digestion was showing up in her pulse reading as dullness, heaviness, and lethargy.

I explained to Victoria that right before menopause is not a good time to be eating heavy, hard-to-digest foods. Digestion slows with age, and foods like meat and cheese can cause sluggishness and blockages that make it harder for the body to adapt to the changing hormone levels of menopause.

A month later, I was pleased to hear from Victoria that she had followed the diet and herbal recommendations I had prescribed and was feeling much better. Her mood swings had disappeared, her hot flashes and sleep had improved by 90 percent, and she had even lost a few pounds without feeling hungry or deprived.

"I feel lighter and more balanced," she reported. "And I am especially happy to report that the thyroid nodule is reduced."

THE DRAMA OF AMA

If you have moderate to severe symptoms — frequent hot flashes, insomnia, joint pains, painful vaginal dryness, extreme mood swings or other symptoms — then it's possible that you, like Victoria, have blockages that are causing your symptoms. According to MAV, these blockages are the result of *ama* (<u>ah</u>-muh), or metabolic wastes and toxins that have built up in your tissues.(Although ama has a very precise definition in Ayurvedic medicine, for ease of understanding, I will use the terms "waste," "cellular waste," "impurities," and "ama" interchangeably in the following discussion.) This accumulated cellular waste can cause a myriad of symptoms, including gas and bloating, joint pains, chronic sinus congestion, night sweats, excessive fatigue, constipation, stiffness, muscle soreness, and "brain fog." If not corrected, ama in your tissues eventually leads to full-blown disease in the areas where it has accumulated the most.

When I first describe to my patients how impurities may be causing their symptoms, many of them nod their heads appreciatively. It confirms what they have known instinctively — that their bodies were loaded down with wastes, a toxic overload of "garbage." They have sensed that this condition was at the root of their health problems. This inner perception is highly motivating, and I find that patients

Some Common Signs of Being Waste-Full

Here are some common signs that ama has accumulated in your tissues.

- You wake up tired even after a good night's sleep.
- You feel lethargic.
- Your tongue is coated.
- You don't feel real hunger, even when you haven't eaten for several hours.
- You have generalized aches and pains.
- You lack mental clarity and energy.
- You feel a sense of heaviness in the abdomen, arms, or legs; or the body as a whole.
- You feel weary and unenthusiastic.
- You experience frequent indigestion, such as gas, bloating, or heartburn.
- You feel blocked anywhere in the body, including constipation, sinus congestion, and difficulty breathing.

with this bodily insight are, without exception, willing and eager to do whatever it takes to eliminate the ama from their bodies and regain their natural inner lightness and vitality, even if it means making major diet and lifestyle changes.

Your Seven Tissues

According to the Ayurvedic understanding, seven fundamental tissues, called *dhatus* (<u>dha</u>-tooz) make up your body (see the sidebar "Your Seven Tissues"). Loosely translated, these seven tissues correspond in modern physiology to plasma, blood, muscle, fat, bone, bone marrow, and sperm/ova. When ama builds up in any particular tissue, you can expect symptoms and even disease. For example, if impurities build up in your blood, heavy menstrual bleeding is likely. When ama builds up in the smooth muscle tissue of your uterus, it can trigger the growth of uterine fibroids. Toxins in your fat tissues contribute to cellulite, weight gain, diabetes, high cholesterol, and heart disease. Cellular waste in your joints can lead to joint pain and arthritis. In summary, ama accumulating anywhere in the body can lead to any number of diseases.

Your tissues, like the doshas, are intelligent. Although I will be using the terms "tissue" and "dhatu" interchangeably, the term "dhatu" refers not only to a particular tissue, but also to the underlying intelligence that structures and supports that tissue. By understanding the full intelligent activity of your tissues, we gain access to a deeper, more complete healing approach than would otherwise be possible.

Your Seven Tissues
1. **Plasma** or *Rasa* (<u>ruh</u>-suh): the clear part of the blood (serum or plasma)
2. **Blood** or *Rakta* (<u>ruhk</u>-tuh): red blood cells and bile
3. **Muscle** or *Mamsa* (<u>mahn</u>-suh): muscle tissue
4. **Fat** or *Meda* (<u>may</u>-duh): fat, hormone, and carbohydrate metabolism
5. **Bone** or *Asthi* (<u>uh</u>-sthee): bone, cartilage, hair, and nail tissues
6. **Bone Marrow and Central Nervous System** or *Majja* (<u>muh</u>-juh): nerves, immune cells, and bone marrow
7. **Reproductive essence** or *Shukra* (<u>shoo</u>-kruh): ova or sperm

The Tier of Your Tissues

The Ayurvedic understanding sees your seven tissues as functioning *interdependently*, each affecting the others, in a sequence from plasma all the way to the reproductive essence. Underlying their relationship is *agni*, the power of digestion and metabolism, which weaves the tissues and their functioning together to form an intelligently orchestrated dance of metabolic give and take.

The tier of your tissues starts with digestion, when the food you eat is transformed in your stomach and intestines into a rich nutrient "soup." The soup is absorbed across the intestinal lining into your bloodstream and passes through your liver, where it is further metabolized. Ready to feed your cells, the soup (now the first tissue, or blood plasma) enters the bloodstream and is carried to the various tissues of your body, starting with the blood (your second tissue or red blood cells).

MAV describes how your tissues receive their nourishment in an orderly lineup, each one taking its turn in a cascade of delivery. Because each of the seven tissues has its own enzymes and metabolic processes — its own agni — each tissue in essence "cooks" for the next tissue waiting in line. If any tissue's metabolism is weak and can't cook, it fails to nourish itself and then passes on the poorly cooked inedible mix (ama) to the next tissues down the line. Waste-like ama then accumulates in your tissues, interfering with the functioning of each tissue in predictable ways and leading to specific symptoms and problems that are described in the Ayurvedic medical texts. (See Chapter 6 for further details.)

Your Symptoms and the Tissue Cascade

A simple example of how interruptions in the tier of your tissues can cause symptoms is iron-deficiency anemia, a common problem for perimenopausal women who have heavy bleeding with their periods. If your digestion is weak, your blood may not be able to absorb adequate iron from your diet to meet your body's needs. This means your blood plasma (rasa) will be deficient in iron, which is essential to the health of the next tissue in line, the red blood cells (rakta). Without enough iron, your red blood cells will be smaller than normal and therefore carry less oxygen. The next tissue down the line, your muscles (mamsa), will be undersupplied with oxygen and become easily fatigued. This is how weak blood (rasa and rakta) translates to tired muscles (mamsa), less exercise tolerance and stamina, and a generally run-down condition.

A quiz at the end of this chapter will help you identify where waste-like ama may be causing problems in your body. Then you will be ready to design your own individualized therapeutic approach using the specific diet, herb, and lifestyle recommendations given in Chapter 6 for clearing ama from your body and restoring optimal health to your cells and organs.

Ama, Your Hormones, and Your Health

When your digestion fails to break down your food completely, larger than normal food particles are permitted to enter your bloodstream and circulate to your tissues. These misshapen, oversized ama particles travel through progressively smaller and smaller channels on their way to your tissues until they lodge in narrow passageways and get stuck. A blockage of this nature can occur in any of your body's organs and tissues, cutting off channels that would otherwise carry nutrients and *hormones* into your cells. This blocking of hormone delivery and nutrients is an important way in which ama leads to more extreme symptoms of menopause and to degenerative conditions in later life. Your hormones cannot reach or bind with the appropriate cells. This is why soy products and sometimes even HT itself does not relieve a woman's hot flashes or other menopausal symptoms. The soy or hormone molecules just never connect with the cells that need them. In such cases, the cleansing approaches outlined in this chapter and Chapter 6, and the deeper cleansing treatments of MAV, such as Maharishi Rejuvenation Treatment (MRT) described in Chapter 10, are necessary.

DIGESTION AND YOUR SYMPTOMS

All disease occurs due to imbalance in digestion.

— *the* Charaka Samhita

Whether or not your body makes good nutrition or makes ama from your food depends on how strong your digestion is. In fact, the power of your digestion, known as *agni* (<u>ugh</u>-nee) in MAV, is the single most important determinant of your health and longevity. According to MAV, good digestion and metabolism is absolutely essential for a long, healthy life. Loosely translated, agni means fire and refers to the powerful transformative energy that breaks down and converts your food into energy to fuel your body's trillion cells. More than simply the absence of gas, bloating, heartburn, constipation, diarrhea, and other bothersome maladies of the digestive system, your agni is a superintelligent maestro conducting all digestive and metabolic processes throughout your entire body.

Remember Victoria, who ate a diet of meat and cheese just before menopause? The reason those foods caused ama buildup in her system was that her digestion, weakened by stress and irregular habits, could not provide the firepower to digest them. Digestion and metabolism is governed by pitta dosha, which rules all chemical reactions in your body. A well-stoked agni "fire" runs your body efficiently, keeping the buildup of toxic waste and debris — ama — at bay. A dampened digestive fire, like a campfire on a rainy day, is unable to burn its fuel — your food — completely. It leaves partially digested food materials and metabolic byproducts to collect in your tissues.

Weak digestive power is also responsible for an overall decline in our assimilation as we get older. Studies on aging indicate that after the age of forty or fifty, absorption of nutrients is reduced, leading to chronic vitamin and mineral deficiencies that play an important role in chronic health problems that tend to arise in our later years. Scientific understanding is beginning to elucidate why Ayurveda puts so much emphasis on creating and maintaining ideal digestion.

Your Digestion and The Midlife Transition

During the midlife years, your digestion is particularly vulnerable to weakness. Vata dosha in particular tends to become disturbed and can aggravate your digestive fire (like wind blowing on a fire), leading to ups and downs in your digestion. Sometimes your digestion works well, but other times you don't digest your food completely and suffer from heartburn, bloating, and excess wind in your intestines.

If your digestion is consistently disturbed, and ama-type wastes clog your tissues as you transit through menopause, you will be especially prone to severe hot flashes and night sweats, excessive weight gain, and even high cholesterol. If these symptoms aren't corrected, you may be more prone to develop high blood pressure, diabetes, or heart disease down the line.

In fact, any metabolic imbalances you have are likely to be unmasked when the beneficial effect of estrogen on your tissues is withdrawn at menopause. If you have been eating well and exercising, the decline in your estrogen level at midlife is less likely to result in troublesome symptoms or the gain of many unwanted pounds. In this case, you're entering midlife with a strong and healthy agni, which brings fire to your digestion and helps it withstand the transition without becoming upset or weakened.

Your Digestive Fire: A Victim of Modern Lifestyle

In our culture, turning forty is unofficially viewed as a pivotal moment in our life span — after forty it's all "downhill." We expect to gradually lose our figures (if we haven't already!), gain weight, and suffer a general, gradual decline in our health. But this does not have to happen. Ballooning weight, high blood sugar and cholesterol, and elevated blood pressure is not programmed into our genes. Indeed research has found that over 80 percent of diabetes and heart disease, the major weight-related diseases, are completely preventable through lifestyle alone. And many women do maintain their high school weight, attractive figures and vitality throughout their lives. What could be their secret?

Ask them and they will probably tell you that they eat regular meals, a balanced diet and go easy on the sweets and alcohol. In short, they have avoided the usual chronic lifestyle mistakes that lead to weight gain in midlife.

We have seen how late nights, dinners on the run, lack of exercise, midnight pizza sprees, and constant stress over several decades can throw your doshas out of whack. Since each dosha has a role to play in digestion, imbalance in any one of them can lead to weakened digestion, ama formation and slowing of your fat metabolism as ama clogs your fat tissue. Why do metabolism, digestion, and assimilation weaken after forty? Cumulative dosha "abuse" is the simple answer.

How to Strengthen Your Metabolism Based on Your Digestive Type

Disturbance in any of the three doshas can be responsible for weakening your digestion and metabolism, each dosha leading to a different symptom complex. However, the end result is the same — metabolism imbalance and weight problems. The three main digestive types are described below, along with recommendations for balancing each and restoring good metabolism.

Vata, your airy dosha, "fans the flames" and can cause symptoms of gas and bloating when aggravated. To balance your vata digestion, be sure to eat sitting down, in a relaxed environment, and favor warm, cooked foods and warm drinks. Avoid eating while you read or drive a car, and right before or after exercise.

Pitta provides the digestive "firepower" and can cause heartburn, excessive thirst, sourness, and acid reflux when aggravated. To balance your pitta digestion, be sure to eat a wholesome, cooked, balanced meal at lunchtime. Never skip or delay your meals, avoid consuming spicy or acidic foods and avoid alcohol in excess.

Kapha governs the secretion of liquid to aid digestion. When it is aggravated, your food sits in your stomach and digestion and metabolism slow down, leaving you feeling tired and sluggish. If you have kapha digestion, you will be more prone to

> ### Hot Flashes and Metabolic Waste
>
> One of my vaidya mentors explained hot flashes in this way: When your channels are clogged with wastes, the heat (pitta) from metabolism builds up in your tissues. You experience as flashing the sudden surges of heat and flushing as the body tries to dissipate the buildup quickly. A similar phenomenon occurs when you have a heater on and all the windows and doors are closed. To cool down the room, first you must turn down the heater (as in pacifying pitta), but you also need to throw open the windows and doors (as in clearing the tissues of channel-obstructing ama) so the heat can flow out. He prescribes a pure, simple cleansing diet, herbs and Maharishi Rejuvenation Treatment to clear the ama and resolve symptoms quickly.

quick weight gain, and are most in need of regular exercise. To fire up your sluggish digestion and metabolism, always have your main meal at noon, avoid eating heavy meals late at night and avoid cold, frozen or leftover foods. Favor low-glycemic vegetables and legumes, eat fewer grains, and avoid sugar.

Modern Medicine Meets Ama

Modern medicine is no stranger to ama. Although it doesn't have a general term for it, medical science recognizes specific types of illness caused by accumulated metabolic wastes. It knows ama as excess cholesterol, free radicals, trans-fatty acids, uric acid, and homocysteine, among others. Atherosclerosis (blockage of the arteries due to disturbances in cholesterol metabolism), gallstones (from sludgy, ama-laden bile), gouty arthritis (due to excess uric acid from faulty protein metabolism), or kidney stones (from the buildup of calcium or oxalic acid) are all diseases that result from the buildup of ama. According to MAV theory, not only these, but nearly every chronic disorder involves accumulation of some form of ama somewhere in the body.

At its worst, ama can stimulate an immune reaction against it, resulting in inflammation, a condition known as "pitta-charged" or "toxic" ama (*ama visha* in Ayurvedic terminology.) Indeed, the latest medical theory credits *inflammation* as the key underlying factor in many chronic diseases, including heart disease and cancer. What modern medicine does *not* address is what *causes* the inflammation to begin with. Rather than a chance confused immune response, Ayurveda understands inflammation as the body's healing response at work trying to eliminate the toxic ama that underlies it. Clear out the toxins, Ayurveda advises, and the inflammation will resolve without anti-inflammatories, steroids or other drugs and their harmful side effects. Given another hundred years, modern medicine will surely have some natural, side effect-free answers to chronic inflammation. These will probably closely resemble the Ayurvedic ones we know today, or may even be adopted directly from the Ayurvedic tradition. Fortunately, we can shortcut decades of research on inflammation, toxins, and waste and begin to utilize solutions today by looking more closely at the MAV healing approach to your metabolism, digestion, and problems resulting from them, including weight gain.

Your Metabolism and Your Weight

The most common metabolic imbalance for women at midlife and later is disturbance in meda (*may*-duh), the tissue governing your fat, hormone, and carbohydrate metabolism. Since all your body's hormones interact on the level of meda, it is not surprising that as your hormones begin to fluctuate and then drop off sharply, your fat and carbohydrate metabolism may go a bit haywire also.

Disturbed fat metabolism helps to explain why you may be gaining weight from midlife on "for no reason." You may not even be eating more, but still, year by year, the scale creeps up. According to Ayurveda, your fat tissue has accumulated ama and therefore no longer metabolizes well. The next consequence can be that your fat cells stop responding to insulin — elevated blood sugar, triglycerides, and eventually diabetes can be the end result. Since meda is connected to the kidneys, hypertension is also predicted from meda imbalance.

Modern medicine has recently identified this complex of imbalances predicted long ago in MAV, and termed it "the metabolic syndrome." (Linguistically speaking, these syndromes stem from identical origins, with "metabolic" utilizing the Sanskrit root "meda." Perhaps we should call it the "meda-bolic syndrome"!) Nearly 25 percent of Americans currently have the metabolic syndrome, with 40 percent over the age of sixty having the condition. Both modern medicine and Ayurveda recognize this pattern of imbalance as a risk factor for clogging of the arteries, heart disease and stroke — end-stage expressions of the ama problem.

In my opinion, the metabolic syndrome and the current craze for low-carbohydrate diets are both born of decades of refined carbohydrate-abuse by our culture. It was time for the pendulum to swing back to the other extreme. As a result of gorging ourselves day after day, year after year, on white breads, sugary sodas, snacks, sweets, and excess alcohol, over one-quarter of our population has ama-clogged meda and can no longer metabolize carbohydrates properly. While low-carb diets may give a short-term weight loss advantage by bypassing this metabolic blockade, research shows that after one year, other, more balanced diets give comparable results. Like Victoria, avoiding carbs can induce a quick weight loss, but after a few weeks on the diet, people usually start to feel heavy, clogged, and unwell — the logical consequence of an ama-enhancing diet devoid of antioxidant-rich, fresh fruits, vegetables, and whole grains and high in hormone and antibiotic-laden fatty animal products.

Metabolic Syndrome

If you have at least three of the following conditions, you meet the criteria for the metabolic syndrome, and a significant meda imbalance: overweight primarily in your "middle," (with a waistline measuring over 35 inches), high triglycerides (fasting greater than 150), mildly elevated blood sugar (110-125 fasting), borderline hypertension (greater than 130/85), and a "good" cholesterol reading of less than 50.

Be sure to follow the guidelines for kapha reduction in Chapter 4, for weight loss given below, and for clearing your fat tissue of ama provided in Chapter 6. With this program, you will be well on your way to reversing this serious metabolic imbalance.

If you have the metabolic syndrome, or wish to prevent it, it is not necessary to adopt a meat and cheese diet. I have found that a vegetarian or primarily vegetarian diet, without sugar, white rice, white flour, and other refined carbohydrates, is equally effective as a low-carb diet for quick weight loss. And rather than feeling dull and clogged after several weeks on the diet, my patients feel lighter, clearer, and more energetic. A number of their other health problems beginning to disappear, as well. For long-term health, there is just no substitute for a wholesome, balanced diet.

TWO COMMON PITFALLS TO WEIGHT LOSS AND HOW TO OVERCOME THEM

Weight Plateaus While Dieting

Some patients have come to me for help with weight loss after months of dieting without successful weight loss. They truly are consuming fewer calories than before, but are not losing any weight. Slow metabolism due to ama in the fat tissue is invariably the cause. While scientists insist that weight loss is as simple as "calories in less than calories out," my patients' experience tells otherwise. At some point, just how well the body handles those calories is a factor, and that is determined by how much ama is present. Fortunately, overcoming this problem is the norm for my patients. With meda-busting techniques such as toxin-dissolving herbs, boiled hot water, and a pure, simple, kapha-reducing home-cooked diet, most begin to lose significant weight within a month.

Cravings

Cravings are another big problem for many people who wish to lose weight. What causes cravings? You guessed it — ama, and a diet that is not balanced. When your cells don't receive the nourishment they need, they feel starved and send out false hunger signals even if you have just finished eating a full meal. This sets you up for a vicious cycle of overeating, increased ama, and more cravings.

One of the most powerful techniques for overcoming cravings is to eat a wholesome, home-cooked diet for a week, using the guidelines of the Healing Meal Plan in Chapter 4. Eating fresh, organic, homemade food from the Healing Meal Plan along with drinking plain boiled hot water frequently during the day (see below for instructions) nearly always results in the elimination of cravings within just a few days. Resist the temptation to cook on the weekend and freeze for the week, as eating leftovers leads to ama. Furthermore, microwaving — our nation's favorite way to heat up leftovers — has been shown to destroy over 90 percent of the antioxidants present in vegetables.

Another reason for cravings is a diet that is not completely balanced. One criterion of a balanced diet according to Ayurveda is that it contains each of six fundamental tastes, ideally at each meal. The six tastes are: sweet (fruit, whole grains and certain vegetables preferred over sugar), sour (lemon, orange), and salty, bitter (as in green leafy vegetables), astringent (drying and "pucker" inducing foods such as dried beans, pomegranate and cranberry), and pungent (hot spicy, as in ginger and black pepper). The Smart Spice mix in the next chapter will provide you with a convenient way to get all six tastes in each meal. Carry it with you to restaurants and use it in your cooking, along with a squeeze of lemon or lime, to ensure you get a balance of all six tastes in your diet.

The Role of Exercise

Your fat metabolism is intimately connected to your muscle metabolism, according to both modern medicine and ancient Ayurvedic medicine. From midlife on, women (and men too) tend to lose lean muscle mass, especially if they do not exercise regularly. Even while at rest, muscle tissue burns more calories in a day than an equivalent amount of fat tissue. Therefore, loss of muscle tissue with age and sedentary lifestyle results in a tendency to put on weight even though you may be eating the same number of calories as earlier in your life. Fortunately, this loss of muscle tissue can be largely prevented by exercise and strength training. Keeping your muscle metabolism strong through regular exercise ensures that more of what you eat gets burned by your muscles, with fewer calories being stored as fat. It also helps prevent the formation of ama in your fat tissue, the source of weight that doesn't want to come off, even with dieting.

YOUR METABOLISM

The Healing Miracle of Hot Water

One of my most esteemed Ayurvedic physician mentors first came to America in 1989. Upon arrival at the airport, he got his first glimpse of the population that he would be treating, and immediately became concerned about the magnitude of the task before him.

"When I took my first close look at the people in the new country where I would be consulting, I saw fatigued faces, uneven complexions, puffy and overweight bodies — *so much ama*, I thought. How can I ever help these people when they have this much ama?"

Fortunately, the memory of an ancient healing technique he learned from his grandfather, also a great vaidya, popped into his mind. "*Hot water!* I thought. Plain, hot, boiled water has the necessary power to melt this ama and gradually remove it from their bodies."

Sips of hot water throughout the day became the foundation of my mentor's advice for those with chronic health problems. Around the world today, thousands of individuals, including many in my practice, have benefited from this simple, but miraculous, prescription from a great vaidya and his grandfather.

A groundbreaking study published in Consumer Reports magazine in May 2002 reported that the best diet may be no diet at all. The study of more than 32,000 dieters found that an overwhelming majority of "successful losers" who lost at least 10 percent of their starting weight credited exercise — not food deprivation — as their top strategy. Eighty-three percent of the "superlosers" — those who maintained their weight loss for five years or more — said they lost weight without the help of commercial diet plans or programs. Rather, they were successful through generally improving their diet, exercising, and being persistent with their lifestyle changes. This study shows that picking a strategy you can live with in the long run (one that involves both a healthier diet and more exercise) is the key to successful weight loss.

Further studies indicate that it is easier to stick to an exercise program if you do it with others. Having an exercise partner, such as a friend or spouse, significantly increases your ability to stick with your chosen exercise. It also helps to find something you really enjoy doing. Whether it is golf, Pilates, yoga, brisk walking, tennis, bicycling, dancing, skiing or some other activity, it is very helpful to develop a passion or healthy addiction for it. If you feel better after you do the exercise (and you will!), if you find an exercise you love, and you have a companion or group to exercise with, chances are you will be successful. Keep in mind that the critical factor in weight loss and exercise is to adopt a balanced approach that you find appealing, and be *persistent!*

Sharon's Story: Hot Water Triumphs

Sharon, a forty-year-old mother of two, had been obese for over fifteen years. At barely 5 feet and 210 pounds, she was nearly 100 pounds over her ideal weight. Although Sharon was not particularly interested in changing her lifestyle, she came to me on the urging of a friend, in hopes that I might be able to help her with her weight. She confided a sweet story. Her thin and wiry nine-year-old daughter had learned in school a few days before that being overweight was dangerous to one's health. She ran home after school and shared this new knowledge with her mother, pleading with her to lose some weight.

I spent over thirty minutes educating Sharon about how to improve her metabolism, reduce ama, and lose weight using a variety of Ayurvedic techniques such as a lighter evening meal, eating more fresh vegetables, cooking with spices, and so forth. She left filled with new ideas, however I sensed that she was not completely convinced that it would be worth the effort.

A couple of months later, I ran into Sharon. She looked different. I realized that she seemed to have lost some weight. "Sharon," I asked, "did you lose some weight?" "A little," she said. Actually, she then admitted, it was about 30 pounds. Curious, I asked her what had been working for her, hoping that something I told her might have been helpful. She confessed, "I really didn't like most of the things you told me to do, but there was one thing I did — the hot water." She went on to say that the first few days of hot water, instead of her usual giant slurpee drinks, were a bit rough, with some gurgling, and discomfort in her abdomen. She stuck with it though and after a week or so the symptoms passed and she "just started losing weight." She thanked me for inquiring, as it reminded her to get back to her hot water.

About six months later, I ran into Sharon again — this time without recognizing her at first. She was wearing pigtails and was so trim that I thought she was someone ten years younger. "Sharon," I exclaimed, you have *really* lost weight." "A little," she offered. "No, a *lot*, I insisted." "Ninety pounds," she admitted with a smile. This time her daughter was standing next to her. "What a wonderful gift you have given each other. Keep up the good work!" They have, and Sharon continues to look and feel great two years later.

Three Sure-Fire Diet Tips for Losing Weight and Keeping It Off

1. Drink boiled hot water frequently throughout the day.

Sipping hot water throughout the day improves your metabolism, digestion, and assimilation and helps cleanse the body of blockages and impurities. It also is a great aid for reducing food cravings between meals.

For best results, take at least a few sips of hot water every 30 minutes throughout the entire day, until 7 or 8 P.M. If you move about a lot during the day, purchase a stainless steel thermos and carry it with you. If you sit at a desk most of the day, you may find a cup-sized hot plate or cup-warmer handy. You can pour your hot water in the cup, put it on the warmer and sip it throughout the day as you work.

The most effective water is pure, reputable spring water that has been boiled for about ten minutes. Boiling water for ten minutes reduces its heavy kapha quality (you will usually see a fine powder at the bottom of the pan that consists of precipitated materials from the water) and energizes the water with boiling action (vata) and heat (pitta). The end result is a water that is balancing for all three doshas, and optimal in clearing ama and improving digestion and metabolism. Drinking water from your hot water dispenser at work is better than not drinking any at all, but is not as effective as boiled water.

2. Eat a warm, cooked main meal at noon and a lighter, vegetarian evening meal.

You may recall from the dosha clock in Chapter 3 that digestion and metabolism are strongest at noon. Therefore, lunch should be the main meal of the day. Research confirms that the same number of calories consumed late in the day leads to weight gain, but if eaten earlier in the day does not.

Your lunch should consist of warm, cooked foods with a wide variety of tastes and dishes. Warm food is more easily digested and assimilated. Cold foods suppress digestion (recall your high school chemistry — cold temperature suppresses chemical reactions, and the process of digestion is chemistry!) The result of regular meals of cold foods is indigestion, the accumulation of ama, and weight gain.

A good, balanced lunch also helps you feel less hungry in the evening, making it easier to stick to that all-important *light* evening meal of cooked vegetables, whole cooked grains and soups — without meat or cheese — for optimal digestibility, weight loss and metabolism.

3. Avoid leftovers.

Maharishi Ayurveda holds that putting food in the refrigerator after it has been cooked seriously deteriorates the quality and digestibility of the food. Indeed, research has found that certain foods including wheat and potatoes, form an indigestible starch called "retrograde starch" when cooked and then refrigerated. This indigestible starch causes gas and ama formation in the intestines, a recipe for blocked metabolism and weight gain.

The essence of Ayurvedic food preparation is summarized in the following Ayurvedic axiom: **"Eat fresh food, freshly prepared."**

Because of the time demands of our lives, and logistics of shopping and cooking, this simple recommendation may be difficult to achieve all the time. However, every step in this direction will help with your weight and overall health.

A convenient way to get a home-cooked, nearly fresh meal of pure, wholesome ingredients for lunch each day is to cook barley and lentils (a good fat-busting combination) overnight in a crock pot. In the morning, add chopped vegetables and cook for another half-hour or so while you get ready for work. Before leaving, add some spices sautéed in olive oil (try cumin, black pepper, fresh ginger root, coriander, turmeric and salt to taste). Put in a wide-mouth thermos and bring for lunch. Add some rye crackers (another fat busting grain according to Ayurveda), and fresh fruit for a well-balanced, pure, and nutritious lunch.

Waste and Your Bodily Wastes

It may seem redundant to speak of waste, or ama, in your body's *wastes*. We normally think of urine, stool, and sweat, called *malas* (<u>muh</u>-luhs) in Ayurvedic medicine, as wastes by their very nature. However, MAV considers bodily waste products a normal and neutral part of the body and sees them as either pure (healthy), or impure (unhealthy and containing ama).

Impure waste products, like unhealthy tissues, are the result of ama buildup. Impure wastes create symptoms in the tissues and organs in which they reside, such as urinary tract infections, irritable bowel syndrome, and constipation.

When the bodily wastes are pure and eliminated in proper quantities, the body is endowed with extra strength. When they are impure, or of excess or deficient quantity, the body is drained of strength and vitality. The Ayurvedic expression "No mala, no *bala* (strength)" speaks to this. Think of how after a bout of diarrhea from an intestinal flu, your body is virtually devoid of stool and you are left feeling weak and drained.

For good health, your three bodily wastes should be of proper quantity and quality. Their elimination from your body should be normal, timely, and unobstructed. If not, symptoms or even disease will eventually result. Tips on how to improve the purity and health of your urine, stool, and sweat will be given in Chapter 6.

Urine. Pure and healthy urine is light-colored and does not have a strong smell. It is passed easily without undue urgency, frequency, or irritation. And it is devoid of bacteria. When urine is impure, it becomes a fertile medium for bacterial growth and may result in a full-blown urinary tract infection (UTI), complete with frequent urination, pain, burning, and fever.

UTIs are common for some women around menopause and are often blamed on lowered estrogen levels. It's true that changes in hormonal levels can cause changes in your genitourinary tissues, setting you up for UTIs. One such change is the shrinking of the tissue around the urethra (where urine leaves the body) that typically occurs with reduced estrogen levels, thinning the barrier that keeps bacteria outside the bladder. Another change is that the pH (acid balance) of the vagina and the flora in the urogenital area may shift, causing friendly bacteria to die off and allowing the unfriendly kind to flourish.

However, frequent UTIs are not an inevitable consequence of menopause, nor are reduced estrogen levels their only cause. Repeated or persistent infection usually signals the presence of ama or other impurities in the urine itself or the bladder or surrounding tissues. A buildup of ama can act as a kind of fertilizer that helps bacteria take hold and multiply, leading to full-blown infections. Despite the hormonal shifts of menopause, if you prevent ama and maintain proper diet and drinking habits, UTIs should be a rare or nonexistent event.

Stool. Healthy bowel movements, according to Ayurveda, occur once or twice a day, ideally in the early morning upon arising and possibly again later in the day. Pure, healthy stool should resemble the size, shape, and consistency of a ripe banana and should float in water and have no foul smell. Healthy stool depends on the type of diet you eat, the health of your colon (which must include a proper balance of "friendly" bacteria), and the quality of digestion taking place upstream in your stomach and small intestine. Improper digestion and assimilation of food before it reaches the colon will disturb the formation of healthy stool.

Sweat. Your sweat is intimately connected to the health of your fat tissue. According to MAV, sweat is a natural excretion route for toxins from your fat tissue. Ama in your fat tissue will lead to disturbances such as body odor, excessive or insufficient sweating, and infections of the sweat glands.

THE HEALING NECTAR OF OJAS

You have seen how faulty digestion and metabolism can cause your menopausal symptoms. Now consider for a moment what it would be like if your digestion and metabolism were functioning perfectly. Everything you ate would be transformed into ama-free energy for use by your body, and you would experience a vibrantly alert and blissful state of mind and emotions, the result of having created what MAV calls *ojas* (o-juhs).

Ojas is described in MAV as the most refined and subtle essence of the physical body. When fully activated, ojas is the "bliss factor" that goes beyond good health to keep you fully immune and strengthened against all disease. Ojas connects mind and matter, consciousness, and physiology; as such, it is as much one as the other. Most importantly, ojas is the "superfluid slide" that links the underlying intelligence of Nature to its expressions in your mind and body.

Modern medicine has not yet identified any one substance that correlates to ojas, but you can understand ojas by how it functions in your body. Think of ojas as the opposite of ama. Where ama is a waste product of incomplete digestion that leads to clogging toxicity, ojas is a supremely refined, health-giving elixir resulting from perfect digestion, which permeates every cell with life-giving energy. Where ama blocks the connection between any two organs, tissues, or cells in the body, ojas connects and integrates those separate parts into a whole. Where ama blocks the expression of the body's intelligence, ojas enhances it.

Ojas is responsible for keeping all the cells of your body functioning coherently together, much as the conductor of a symphony orchestra keeps all the instrumentalists playing as a coordinated whole, in perfect harmony. The unified rhythm, beat, flow, and melodies of the human physiology are kept in synchrony and balance through the power of ojas. When your ojas is enlivened, you have a healthy glow on your face, and the light in your eyes burns brightly. Your hormones are communicating the right messages, at the right times, in the right amounts to your cells and DNA. When ojas is high due to ama-free digestion and metabolism, menopause symptoms are minimal and your body adjusts easily to its inner shift in hormones.

Optimum ojas is the key to perfect health, as well as to balanced and blissful emotions and even the full unfolding of inner spiritual development. Ojas promotes longevity and is an internally generated antidote to aging. When ojas is fully enlivened, your mental and physical stress and strain, the basis of sickness and suffering, are eliminated, and you are destined to live a long life free of disease. It has been said that the whole of Ayurveda is aimed at maximizing the production and maintenance of ojas. For specifics, see the sidebar "Signs You Are Becoming Ojas-Full."

Self-Assessment: Where Oh Where Has My Ama Gone?

To become ojas-full and enjoy perfect health during a symptomless menopause and beyond, you must rid your body of ama. Since every woman accumulates ama in a different pattern, you need to design an individualized program to help cleanse it from your tissues. The first step is to identify areas in your body — tissues, organs, bodily wastes — where impurities have built up and are causing blockage. Locating these sites is important because the symptoms you experience are due to disturbances in specific body areas, those most burdened with ama.

With the help of the two self-assessment quizzes that follow, one for your tissues and one for your bodily wastes, you can pinpoint exactly where ama has

Signs You Are Becoming Ojas-Full
· You feel fresh, rested, even blissful upon awakening in the morning. · Your skin has a healthy glow. · Your tongue is pink and clear. · Your body feels lighter. · Aches and pains are disappearing. · You do not feel bloated or heavy in your abdomen. · You feel energetic during the day. · You feel enthusiastic. · Your mind is clear. · People say, "Have you lost weight?" or "What are you doing? You look so good!"

accumulated in your body. Precise prescriptions from the Ayurvedic texts will help you reverse the symptoms of disrupted tissues and bodily wastes and restore clear passageways in your body for adequate hormone delivery, tissue nourishment, and normalization of weight. Take the quiz below and use your results to create your own personal treatment plan in Chapter 6.

Quiz: Which Tissues Are Waste-Full?

Look at the list of symptoms for each tissue and check off the ones you are experiencing. When you are finished, total the number of symptoms for each tissue category. Then arrive at a grand total for all categories and write it on the line at the end of the quiz.

What to Do Next

If you scored 3 or higher in any tissue category, follow the guidelines given for that tissue(s) in Chapter 6.

If you scored 2 or higher in any tissue category, eliminate any causative factors listed in the guidelines for those tissues, also in Chapter 6. This will help you to prevent problems in this area in future years.

If your grand total was 14 or higher, or you have persistent symptoms not yet addressed by a physician, please see your family doctor for a checkup, including a complete history and physical as well as bloodwork. Your midlife symptoms may be complicated by another condition, such as hypothyroidism, arthritis, or an autoimmune disorder that also needs treatment and attention.

THE AGELESS WOMAN

Quiz: Which Tissues Are Waste-Full?

1. **BLOOD PLASMA (RASA).** The clear, serum portion of the blood.
   - ✓ Very dry skin
   - ✓ Premature graying of the hair or wrinkling of the skin at an early age
   - ✓ Mild or occasional vaginal dryness
   - ✓ Excess mucus or respiratory congestion
   - ✓ A feeling of weakness and tiredness, lack of stamina, fluctuating energy levels
   - ___ Ovarian cyst now or in the past (fluid-filled only)
   - ___ Breast cysts (fluid-filled only)
   - **5** TOTAL

2. **RED BLOOD CELLS (RAKTA).** Red blood cells and bile.
   - ✓ Severe hot flashes or frequent feeling of excessive heat
   - ___ Very heavy bleeding or "flooding"
   - ___ Frequent or chronic skin rashes, acne, pustules, hives
   - ___ Gallstones now or in the past (or have had gallbladder removed)
   - ___ Bleeding hemorrhoids
   - ✓ Constant or problematic thirst
   - **2** TOTAL

3. **MUSCLES (MAMSA).** Muscle tissue.
   - ___ Constant muscle aches or pains, or easily fatigued muscles
   - ✓ Chronically swollen tonsils or lymph glands in the neck
   - ✓ Itchy ear canals or eczema of ear canal or excess ear wax
   - ___ Fibroids of the uterus (now or in the past)
   - ___ Fibrous or glandular lumps in the breasts
   - ___ Severely dry, cracking lips
   - **2** TOTAL

4. **FAT AND HORMONES (MEDA).** Fat, hormone, and carbohydrate metabolism.
   - ✓ Weight gain (at least 10 pounds overweight), or inability to lose weight even on low-calorie diet
   - ___ High blood sugar (diabetes)
   - ___ High cholesterol
   - ✓ Chronic or frequent problem with malodorous sweat or body odor
   - ___ Fatty cysts under the skin or scalp or in the breasts
   - ✓ Thyroid disorder (diagnosed by a physician, including abnormal blood tests)
   - ✓ Frequent night sweat or sweats during the day associated with hot flashes
   - **(13)** TOTAL

YOUR METABOLISM

Quiz: Which Tissues Are Waste-Full?

5. BONES (ASTHI). Bone, cartilage, hair, and nail tissues.
   - ✓ Low bone density (osteopenia) or osteoporosis
   - ✓ Hair breaking a lot (many split ends) or hair very dry and lacking luster
   - ✓ Problems with your teeth (breaking easily, many cavities, etc.)
   - ✓ Nails breaking frequently
   - ✓ Constant joint pains or arthritic condition
   - ✓ Deep pains in the bones
   - **6** TOTAL

6. BONE MARROW (MAJJA). Central nervous system tissue and immune system.
   - ✓ Frequent or recurring infections
   - ___ Excess secretions of the eyes
   - ✓ Dryness of skin on upper eyelids
   - ✓ Constant spacey and distractible feeling, inability to focus or concentrate
   - ___ Pain in the tendons, easily injured tendons, or recurrent tendonitis
   - ___ Frequent feeling of faintness or dizziness
   - **3** TOTAL

7. REPRODUCTIVE ESSENCE (SUKRA). The ovum (egg) and its supportive tissues.
   - ✓ Absence of libido (no sex drive)
   - ✓ Severe vaginal dryness
   - ✓ Overall lack of sexual attractiveness
   - ✓ Dull, unclear eyes
   - ___ History of more than one miscarriage
   - ___ Infertility
   - **4** TOTAL

36 **27** GRAND TOTAL for all symptoms in all categories

Now take the next quiz for your bodily wastes:

Quiz: Which Wastes (Malas) Are Impure?

URINE

___ Frequent urinary tract infections

___ Frequent urinary burning

_✓_ Bladder discomfort without infections

___ Strong smell to urine

___ Dark yellow urine even when you are drinking plenty of water

_1_ TOTAL

STOOL

_✓_ Heavy stool that drops to the bottom of the toilet bowl

_✓_ Very loose stool, diarrhea, or stool accompanied by mucus

_✓_ Stool very hard, in small balls, difficult to pass or not eliminated every day

___ Undigested food visible in the stool

___ Stool always very foul smelling

_3_ TOTAL

(If you have blood in your stool, or black stools, see your physician immediately for further evaluation.)

SWEAT

___ Sweat irritates your skin or provokes rashes or infected sweat glands

_✓_ Sweat smells bad

_✓_ Unpleasant body odor

_✓_ Too much sweat

___ No sweat, even when you are very hot

_3_ TOTAL

What to Do Next

If you scored 1 or above in the urine section, follow the guidelines for purifying your urine in Chapter 6.

If you scored 1 or above in the stool section, follow the guidelines for purifying your stool in Chapter 6.

If you scored 1 or above in the sweat section, follow the guidelines for clearing the fat tissue (meda) in Chapter 6.

Design Your Own Individual Program

Now that you have determined which of your tissues and bodily wastes are causing your moderate to severe symptoms, you are ready to design your own individual program to rid your body of obstructing waste and impurities. The next chapter provides specific recommendations tailored to your own symptoms to help you make the channels and passageways of your body open and clear for vital nourishment and happier hormones. Eliminating ama will reduce your symptoms and ensure your continued vitality and health for life.

☆ 6 ☆

Purification for Relief of Your More Serious Symptoms

Perfection in health requires purity of the channels and gaps.
— *the* Charaka Samhita

We have seen how ama builds up in your body, blocking the interaction of nutrients and hormones with your tissues and causing your more serious and troublesome midlife symptoms. In this chapter, you will learn how to rid your body of this hormone-blocking, disease-causing waste, clearing it from all your internal passageways down to the microscopic levels where it lodges within your cells. With your personalized program, tailor-made for cleansing and purifying those specific tissues and bodily wastes that give rise to your individual symptoms, you can begin to turn around stubborn midlife problems and feel healthier and younger once again.

Designing Your Individualized Self-Treatment Program

If you suffer from troublesome symptoms that have not resolved with simple lifestyle and dosha-balancing measures, then more powerful techniques to cleanse and remove ama from your body are in order. You can design your own two-part deep cleansing program with the information provided in this chapter. First, the section titled "Foundation Program: Three Steps to an Ama-Free Body" consists of a personalized herbal water recipe, a spice mixture, and a mixture of balancing grains. Second, the "Correcting Specific Tissue and Waste Imbalances" section provides lifestyle and diet tips for clearing your tissues and bodily wastes of ama, as determined by your results in the Chapter 5 quiz. This guide also identifies which diet and lifestyle factors cause imbalances in which particular tissues so you can avoid those causative factors and protect your body in the future. If you are not a do-it-yourself type, or you feel you need extra help in handling your midlife symptoms with Maharishi Ayurveda, or you simply want a professional opinion, it is always valuable to consult with a MAV-trained health-care practitioner for a personal evaluation and pulse assessment. See the Resources for information on how to consult with a MAV practitioner near you or on the Web.

Research on the Foundation Program

Several years ago, I tested a standardized version of this program with twenty-seven women between the ages of forty-five and sixty-five who had a variety of midlife symptoms, as well as increased bone turnover, a risk factor for weak bones and fractures later in life. The program included a wise water, power grains (including organic soy granules), smart spices, daily oil massage, and two herbal products for bone health. The basic premise of this pilot study was that imbalanced doshas, ama, and weak digestion lie at the root of midlife symptoms and bone loss, not lack of estrogen. By creating inner balance, both bone health and other symptoms should improve. The results were very encouraging. On average, the participants experienced significant reductions in hot flashes, heart palpitations, insomnia, and excitability. In addition, their bone turnover rate showed a trend towards normalization.

Many of the participants also reported overall improvements in digestion, physical strength and stamina, energy and mood. Claudine's experience is typical of the women who participated in this study: "During the study, I simply felt better, more nourished; my body felt more satisfied. I also felt much more relaxed and less strained in my life. I've continued with the program after the study was over because it made me feel so good!"

FOUNDATION PROGRAM: THREE STEPS TO A PURE BODY

The foundation program is your ticket to new found vitality through ama-free living. By following the simple three-step approach, you will begin to cleanse toxic buildup from your cells and tissues to restore full energy and maximize your remaining hormone power. The phytoestrogen-rich foods, spices, and herbs you are eating will also help balance your hormones and enhance assimilation of valuable nutrients. The result should be a substantial decrease in your symptoms and, in the long term, protection against the degenerative diseases that can accompany menopause and old age.

The foundation program has three steps:

- First, throughout the day, drink your own personalized herbal *wise water*, formulated specifically to address your symptoms. Wise water is key to clearing stubborn, deeper deposits of ama from the tissues and helping to clear wastes and toxins from your body via the kidneys and liver. Water carries the healing power of the herbs deep into the inner recesses of your tissues. The herbs and spices in this water provide phytoestrogen support at the same time that they cleanse the channels in the cells and tissues thoroughly and gently.

- Second, eat a personalized *smart spice* mixture. You can sauté this mixture in olive oil or ghee and drizzle it on vegetables, or add it as seasoning to your soups or legumes, or simply sprinkle on top of whatever you are eating, even in a restaurant. This mixture supplies phytoestrogens, helps with digestion, stimulates metabolism (without overstimulating your body as diet pills do), and helps your body burn up the accumulated ama in your tissues.

- Third, every day eat a mixture of *power grains*, including whole barley, rye, millet, and two ancient grains recently reintroduced to our modern diet, *quinoa* (<u>keen</u>-wah) and *amaranth* (am-uh-<u>ranth</u>). This mixture provides a healthy mix of naturally occurring vitamins, minerals, and plant hormones. It also provides high-quality protein in an easily digestible form that won't block your body's channels the way meat or cheese products do. It is perfect for an evening meal, together with a lentil soup and vegetables.

This basic three-step foundation program should be followed for at least three months. Even though improvements may come quickly, keep in mind that the ama and imbalances have usually been around a long time. In order to make lasting improvements and to overcome resistant symptoms, it's best to continue your three key healing components for at least ninety days. After that, you may continue the entire program as long as you feel good with it and are enjoying benefits. However, it is a good idea to retake the quiz at the end of Chapter 5 every three months and readjust your wise water recipe to match your evolving needs.

You are now ready to design your own individual foundation program with the help of my directions and recommendations. First, a word of caution about the herbs and spices you will be using in your recipes and formulations.

An Important Note on Safety and Tolerability: What to Expect

The herbs and spices used in the herbal water and the spice mixture are well tolerated by the great majority of individuals. The risk of adverse reaction is especially low in these recipes because they are used in very small amounts and are diluted in a relatively large amount of water or cooked with food. This diluted delivery system allows the herbs and spices to penetrate to the target tissue where they are needed, but makes them gentle on the rest of the body.

In treating literally hundreds of patients with herbal water and spice mixtures over a number of years, I do not recall any patient ever having an allergic reaction to any of the herbs or spices. On the other hand, allergic reactions to anything new are always possible. If you know you are allergic to some ingredient, obviously you should just leave it out.

If you are a particularly sensitive type and your personalized wise water recipe contains some herbs or spices that you are unfamiliar with, start with only the basic three spices: cumin, coriander, and fennel. After a few days, add one ingredient new to you, in a smaller amount than recommended. If that goes well, increase it gradually to full dose. Then begin to add a second unfamiliar ingredient at a small dose. Continue similarly until your herbal water recipe is complete.

Sometimes mild, transient discomforts may occur as a result of the cleansing process in action, especially in the first week or two you use herbal water and personalized spice mixture. If you feel any minor discomforts, such as increased bowel movements, mild headache, restless sleep, or intestinal gas, stop for a couple of days until things settle down and then start again at half dose. If serious symptoms occur while you are following this program, see your doctor right away. They are most likely not related to this program and should *not* be ignored.

If you have any serious health problems or are on blood thinners or other prescription medications, be sure to check with your physician before following this or any other herbal or supplement program. Never discontinue prescription medications without consulting your physician.

If you are taking a lot of over-the-counter medications or vitamins, herbs, and food supplements, try to reduce those supplements before beginning this program. It is also best to begin to reduce the main offenders in your diet (alcohol, red meat, fried foods, excessive sweets, or processed foods). Purifying your diet directly supports the process of cleansing your body. Remember that your liver must process all the ama and toxins that will be released as you cleanse your tissues. If your liver is already trying to process other medications, supplements, and herbs, as well as hard-to-digest foods, then you may overload it and will not get optimal results from this program. Keep in mind that you are trying to improve your body's inner balance through enlivening and supporting your body's inner intelligence. Hitting it with a multitude of isolated chemical signals, whether "natural" or not, is likely to do more harm than good.

Step One: Drink Your Personalized Herbal Wise Water

The first and most important step in getting started is to formulate your own personalized recipe for your wise water according to the directions that follow. Your wise water will include specific herbs and spices chosen to cleanse the tissues you identified in the Chapter 5 quiz as causing your symptoms. Once you have formulated your recipe, make and drink your wise water every day to start the process of relieving your symptoms. Please follow the instructions carefully regarding both the *content* of the herbs in your herbal mixture and the *preparation* of the water itself. Every detail has a reason, and deviating from the prescription will reduce its effectiveness.

Preparing Your Wise Water

Your wise water must be made fresh each day. Use only whole seeds or tea-cut size pieces of the ingredients (except manjistha, which is a powder). For dried flowers, use only organic, food-grade flowers and only the petals, without stems or leaves.

Boil one and a half quarts of plain, pure water for five minutes. Pour into a thermal container, preferably one that is portable and has a glass or stainless steel (not plastic) lining. Then add your recommended herbs. *Don't* boil the herbs in the water, or the delicate bioactive ingredients, including aromatic components, will evaporate. Tighten the lid on the thermal flask and allow the mixture to steep for at least fifteen minutes before drinking.

Formulating Your Wise Water Recipe

Your personalized recipe starts with a base of the following three herbs: cumin, coriander, and fennel. Use ¼ tsp. of each. (Please use measuring spoons for accuracy.) *Cumin* helps you absorb and use nutrients; *coriander* helps eliminate toxic chemicals and wastes through your kidneys; and *fennel* helps reduce gas and bloating and normalizes your digestion (agni).

Add to this base the *specific* herbs and spices prescribed for your individual tissue and waste imbalances, and your specific menopausal symptoms you identified in the Chapter 5 quiz. (i.e., add the ingredients listed for any tissue that you scored a "3" or higher in the Chapter 5 quiz.) In the section that follows, *Personalized Wise Water Ingredients*, these specific herbs and spices are listed for each tissue and bodily waste.

Write It Out

See Table 6.1 for a sample of this recipe worksheet. Divide a piece of paper into two columns, labeled "My Tissues/Wastes" on the left, and "My Wise Water" on the right. Refer back to your Chapter 5 quiz results. In the left-hand column, write the name of each tissue and waste you scored high in. You might write, for example, *blood plasma, fat and hormones,* and *urine.*

Next, in the right-hand column, write down the three basic ingredients I have already given you — cumin, coriander, and fennel — and their amounts, a quarter teaspoon each. If you have prominent hot flashes, mood swings or irritability, add ingredients recommended for your symptoms listed under *Specific Midlife Symptoms* in the following section, *Personalized Wise Water Ingredients.*

Finally, look again in that section for specific tissue and waste imbalance recommendations. For each tissue or waste you have listed on your sheet, write in the right-hand column the herbs and amounts for balancing it. For example, for blood plasma write: *ajwan seeds, 1/8 tsp.* For fat and hormones, and for urine, add the herbs mentioned for those tissues. *If an herb or spice appears in your recommendations more than once, simply include it in the largest amount specified (i.e., do not triple the amount if it is recommended for three separate tissues).*

Personalized Wise Water Ingredients

The following herbal ingredients are for use according to your specific tissue and bodily waste imbalances, as well as any specific midlife symptoms you may be experiencing.

In the following lists, find those tissues and bodily wastes that your Chapter 5 quiz results revealed are the source of your ama blockage and resulting symptoms. Add the specific ingredients listed for those tissues to your personalized wise water recipe. (The Resources section tells you where to buy various ingredients.)

Specific Tissue Imbalance

- **Blood Plasma (Rasa):** Add 1/8 tsp. of *ajwan seeds* (Since ajwan seeds are somewhat heating, reduce or skip this ingredient if you are having lots of hot flashes.)

- **Red blood cells (Rakta):** Add ¼ tsp. of *manjistha* (powder or leaves of tea-cut size).

- **Muscle (Mamsa):** Add 1/8 tsp. Indian sarsaparilla.

- **Fat and Hormones (Meda):** Add 1/8 tsp. black cardamom seeds or 3 green pods of whole cardamom.

- **Bone (Asthi):** Add ¼ tsp. marshmallow root (the herb, *not* the white puffy marshmallow sweets from your grocery store!).

Table 6.1 Sample Recipe Worksheet for Your Personalized Wise Water

My Tissues/Wastes	My Personalized Wise Water
Basic Formula for everyone:	Cumin seeds ¼ tsp. Coriander seeds ¼ tsp. Fennel seeds ¼ tsp.
Blood Plasma	Ajwan seeds 1/8 tsp.
Fat and Hormones	Cardamom 1/8 tsp. black seeds or 3 whole green pods
Urine	10 crushed pumpkin seeds Increase coriander seeds (see above) to ½ tsp.

- **Bone Marrow (Majja)**: Add ¼ tsp. bala root.

- **Reproductive Essence (Shukra):** Add ¼ tsp. Indian asparagus root.

Specific Bodily Waste Imbalance:

- **Stool:** Add 2 leaves of fresh mint (crush slightly with your fingers before adding).

- **Urine:** Increase coriander to ½ tsp. Add 10 crushed pumpkin seeds.

- **Sweat:** Include 1/8 tsp. Indian sarsaparilla root.

Specific Midlife Symptoms:

If you have any of the following specific symptoms of menopause, add the following herbs or spices as indicated, for extra balancing power.

- **Troublesome hot flashes**: Add 1 tsp. organic rose petals to your basic recipe, and ½ tsp. Indian asparagus root (*shatavari*.)

- **Mood swings**: If easy crying and feeling emotionally sensitive is your main symptom, add ¼ tsp. Indian, Chinese, or Egyptian hibiscus flowers to your basic formula. (Note: Do not use Western/American hibiscus as it can have an aggravating effect on menopausal symptoms.) If anger or irritability is your main symptom, add 2 dried rosebuds or 1 tsp. of dried rose petals (organic or food grade only). You may use both types of flowers in your wise water if needed.

- **Vaginal Dryness**: Include 1 ½ tsp. marshmallow root in your Wise Water.

- **Lack of libido**: Include ½ tsp. of Indian asparagus root. (*Shatavari*, the traditional name for this plant means "one hundred husbands!")

Instructions for Drinking

Drink your wise water throughout the day until about 6 P.M. (After that it may promote nighttime urination that can disturb your sleep.) Pour ½ to 1 cup of it into a glass and allow to cool to lukewarm or room temperature before drinking. Most thermal containers have a screw-on lid that pours when partially opened. This automatically strains most of the herbs. Otherwise, you may want to place the herbs in a stainless-steel tea ball before you put them in the water or pour the water through a tea strainer before drinking.

Please simply drink the liquid portion. Do not eat the herbs themselves. The water-soluble fraction of the herbs is therapeutic, but the other components of the whole herb may be aggravating to your body. You may drink plain water and other beverages during the day according to your thirst and desire, but be sure to drink all your wise water by the end of the day.

Clean your thermal flask with a bottle brush after each use to remove any residue that may build up inside.

Step Two: Add "Smart Spices" to Your Daily Food

Many spices are potent aids to digestion and elimination, helping to prevent ama formation and aiding its removal, and are phytoestrogenic as well. Others, like turmeric, are *antioxidants and detoxifiers* that fight the spread of free radicals and other toxins. Some, such as ginger, are *probiotics*, which promote healthy bacteria in the gut for strengthened immunity. Others support the immune system, reduce inflammation and heat in the body, are natural pain relievers, and help calm the nerves. In fact, nearly every spice listed in this chapter has been shown by scientific research to have not only one, but *many* of these effects, all delivered in the form of one tiny, completely natural spice package.

Unfortunately, those of us eating Western diets have largely missed out on this tremendous built-in source of antioxidants, phytoestrogens, probiotics, and the like. Our Western-style diet is nearly devoid of spices, compared to Indian and Asian

The Wondrous Gift Of Wise Water

The healing hot water technique that I described in Chapter 5 works well for nearly any health condition in anyone. However, there are a few notable exceptions. If you suffer from heartburn, acid indigestion, or any serious inflammatory condition, hot drinks are best avoided. Also, as any perimenopausal woman knows, hot drinks of any kind are likely to trigger a hot flash. Despite its great applicability for so many chronic conditions, plain hot water, the first gift of "wise water" to America, unfortunately did not provide a solution to many of my patients' perimenopausal problems.

Fortunately, I have since had the opportunity to work extensively with another distinguished vaidya, who taught me about an herbalized water that was universally beneficial and safe in all conditions, and can clear ama without heating up the body.

This "wise water" acts like a gentle sustained-release formula, delivering phytoestrogen effect and the supportive action of accompanying herbs throughout the day. In the case of menopause, it can deliver hormone-balancing effects at the same time that it gently clears out cellular wastes that may otherwise block the action of the hormone on the tissues.

Under his guidance, I began to apply this program. The results have been extremely rewarding. I have found the wise water and the other recommendations in this chapter very helpful in effectively treating a variety of midlife symptoms, including hot flashes, without creating side effects.

cooking. Fortunately, it is not necessary to change your entire cooking style to begin to gain the benefits of these intelligent, health-giving spices. To accommodate those who must eat in restaurants, and to make spicing your food at home a breeze, make up your own portable spice mixture from the recipe and instructions provided below. (See Box: SMART SPICE MIXTURE RECIPE.)

This mixture is called "smart" because it will automatically provide whatever your body needs — it will purify and detoxify, normalize heat, stimulate digestion, help elimination, reduce gas and bloating, and provide antioxidant protection.

These spices are usually readily available in supermarkets, Indian grocery stores, and most health food stores. Ideally, use organic spices (try your whole food grocers first) to prevent contaminating your wise water and smart spice mix with harmful pesticides.

Preparing Your Smart Spice Mixture

Mix together the cumin, coriander, and fennel seeds, and the turmeric powder. Grind into a fairly fine powder in a spice grinder or clean coffee grinder. Stir your spice mixture in a dry pan over medium heat until lightly browned (about two minutes) to bring out their full flavor and beneficial effect. Cool and then store the mixture in an airtight portable container and keep in a cool place away from direct sunlight. Make this spice mix fresh every couple of weeks to derive the greatest effect from the spices. (You may buy the spices already in powder form, but they won't be nearly as effective or have as lively and delicious a flavor as those you grind fresh

Smart Spice Mixture Recipe

10 Tbsp. fennel seeds

6 Tbsp. coriander seeds

6 Tbsp. cumin seeds

2 Tbsp. turmeric powder

yourself.) Also, resist the temptation to skip the step in which you lightly brown the spices in a pan. Eating some raw spices, especially turmeric, can be unhealthy for the liver and other parts of the body.

Using Your Smart Spice Mixture

All spices contain a wide variety of beneficial components. A particular spice's components are either *water soluble* (available for use by your body when dissolved in water), while other components are *lipid soluble* (available when carried by fats or oils). To get the full benefit of both water-soluble and lipid-soluble components of your spices, include both of the following methods of cooking with your spices each day.

For benefit of water-soluble components: Mix ½ tsp. of your spice mixture in with soups; while cooking, add ½ tsp. of your spice mix to grains that are cooked in water, such as rice; sprinkle over vegetables while steaming; or at least sprinkle on steaming hot vegetables at the table.

For benefit of lipid-soluble components: Measure ½ tsp. of your spice mixture in 2 to 3 tsp. of olive oil or melted *ghee* (clarified butter, available in most health food and gourmet stores; see Resources for the address of the Web site that contains this recipe), and heat at medium temperature until an aroma is apparent, about one to two minutes. Then add vegetables for a stir-fry, or drizzle the mixture over your cooked rice, grains, vegetables, or other dishes just before serving.

When eating out and unable to cook, put a portion of your mixture in an airtight container and carry with you in your purse or brief case. Sprinkle ½ to 1 tsp. of your mixture on your vegetables, sandwich, grains, pasta, or other dishes at both lunch and dinner.

Step Three: Add Power Grains to Your Daily Diet

Now you are ready for the final step in the foundation program, adding powerful grains to your daily diet. Grains are from the class of foods known as *carbohydrates*. As athletes know, carbohydrates are a dependable source of long-term endurance and energy. However, they are not all created equal. Many of the carbs we eat in our typical American diet — white bread, commercial cereals, baked goods — are highly refined and devoid of vitamins, minerals, and fiber. The refining process strips whole grains of their inherent cholesterol-lowering, cancer-reducing, blood sugar-balancing, and probiotic effects.

Whole power grains, complete with their outer husk and nutrient-rich inner germ, provide slow-release energy along with naturally packaged vitamins, minerals, and protein. They deliver steady, dependable energy throughout the day, helping to prevent that dip many of us experience as the afternoon wears on.

Gathering Your Power Grains

To begin to gain the benefit of your power grains, make a trip to your local whole-foods market to stock up on quinoa, amaranth, millet, rye, barley, bulgur, wheat, whole-wheat couscous, and buckwheat. All of these grains have phytoestrogenic effects and are rich in minerals and protein. The first four are particularly high in minerals and protein and are considered especially healthful by Vedic medicine. You may want to add organic, non-genetically modified (non-GMO) soy granules (available in many whole-food stores) for complete protein balancing and added phytoestrogen action.

Preparing Your Power Grains

Place 2 cups of water in a saucepan and bring to a boil. Add 1 tsp. of ghee or olive oil and ½ cup of grain. Use any one grain at a time, or mix two or more for variety and to equalize texture and flavors. (For example, amaranth can be heavy and sticky when cooked alone, so you may wish to mix it with an equal amount of quinoa.) Boil for 10 minutes and then reduce heat. Simmer until the grain is tender, usually about 15 or 20 minutes longer (except for whole rye, which takes up to 40 minutes to cook). Adding the teaspoon of oil is important to prevent grains inherent drying effect of on the body and intestines, which is particularly unwelcome at and after menopause. You may add your spice mixture to your grains as you cook them or sauté your spices in oil and drizzle over the grains at serving.

Eating Power Grains Daily

Include at least one serving of power grains in your diet each day, for breakfast, lunch, or dinner. Using a crockpot overnight or during the day while you are at work can make grain preparation easy and convenient.

Many women have told me they especially like these power grain combinations: 1) For lunch or dinner, equal amounts of couscous, quinoa, and amaranth, or just quinoa and amaranth; 2) for breakfast, equal amounts of quinoa,

---

An Important Note on the Availability and Quality Control of Your Herbs and Spices.

Most of the herbs and spices used in both the personalized herbal water and the personalized spice mixture are readily available in herb shops, health food and whole foods stores, as well as Indian grocery stores. However, quality control, particularly for any imported herbs, is not very reliable and varies enormously from company to company. One of the most prominent wholesalers of herbs in this country, for example, does not test its imported herbs for heavy metal contamination, a *must* for herbs coming from the Far East, including India.

For these reasons, I recommend that you use only certified organic spices, which are grown and processed according to stringent quality control standards. Fortunately, organic spices are now available in most whole foods stores. For the recommended Ayurvedic herb ingredients, refer to the Resources for a dependable source, Maharishi Ayurveda Products International (MAPI). MAPI upholds the highest standards in ensuring purity and authenticity of all its products, and that is an important reason why I have used their products exclusively for over fifteen years.

In addition, under the guidance of the Council of Vaidyas of Maharishi Ayurveda (a group of eighty Ayurvedic physician consultants), a specific formula called "Hot Flash Relief" has been created in accordance with principles outlined in the ancient texts to help reduce hot flashes without creating side effects. I have found this product to be helpful to the majority of my patients with hot flashes, whose symptoms usually improve within the first month of use. This formula is now available for women who need additional help with stubborn hot flashes, and for those who desire the simplicity of a pre-made formula.

---

couscous, and oats, or quinoa and oatmeal, cooked in milk or water with a little ghee and 1/8 tsp. cinnamon or cardamom powder.

CORRECTING SPECIFIC TISSUE AND WASTE IMBALANCES

In this section, you will learn what lifestyle habits and dietary factors have led to the buildup of ama in your particular tissues and wastes. With this awareness, you will be able to avoid these causes while you are doing the foundation program and on into the future. Once your channels have been cleared, your body must be strengthened to help prevent the buildup of ama in your most vulnerable areas. This section also gives tips for strengthening and nourishing each of your affected tissues and wastes through diet and lifestyle.

Cleansing Your Tissues

Your symptoms tell you which tissues are clogged with nutrient and hormone-blocking ama. But what causes ama to build up in those particular tissues more than in others? Check the results of the Chapter 5 quiz to see which of your tissues showed the most buildup of ama. Then find those tissues below to identify the causative factors that make you vulnerable to disturbance in each area.

The symptoms for each tissue disturbance should clear up gradually as you stick to the three-step foundation program and eliminate the causative factors. Basic recipe hints are given here. For more detailed recipes, check the Web sites listed in the Resources.

1. Blood Plasma (Rasa)

Rasa is the clear, plasma portion of your blood that carries nutrients absorbed from your intestines to your entire body. There is a special connection between rasa and the skin, mucous membranes, breasts, uterus, and ovaries.

Factors That Cause Rasa Disturbance. Rasa is most easily disturbed by factors that affect the overall strength of your digestion, such as fasting, eating meals at irregular times, not drinking enough water, eating a lot of dry foods (chips, crackers, popcorn, dry cereals), consuming too much salt, skipping or delaying meals (especially when you're hungry), eating when you're *not* hungry or before your previous meal is fully digested, and overeating. Rasa can also be disturbed by staying up late at night, not getting enough sleep, breathing shallowly and holding your breath when stressed, and by mental stress, worry, and fear. Avoid these causative factors to help rebalance your rasa.

Lifestyle and Dietary Tips. To rebalance rasa, rehydrate your body with plenty of pure water, juicy fruits, and vegetables. These help to build up and nourish the clear part of your blood as well as purifying it. To resolve rasa symptoms, eat one or two sweet juicy fruits every day, drink plenty of pure, room-temperature water, slow down, relax more, and get more sleep, and give yourself an abhyanga oil massage each day (see Chapter 4).

2. Red Blood Cells (Rakta)

Rakta refers to the red blood cells and bile, which is composed largely of the breakdown products of red blood cells.

Factors That Cause Rakta Disturbance. Rakta is most easily disturbed by the types of foods you eat and your emotional life. Very acidic foods (tomatoes, fermented foods), very alkaline foods (leavened with baking soda), and toxins (alcohol, nicotine, drugs, chemicals) aggravate rakta, as does frequent anger or frustration. If your rakta is disturbed, avoid fasting; hot, spicy, or very salty foods; vinegar (including condiments and salad dressings); caffeine; any unnatural food additives or contaminants (like artificial coloring or flavors); preservatives; MSG; and pesticides. Also avoid alcoholic beverages, recreational drugs (including marijuana), fermented foods (including sourdough breads and soy sauce), and aged cheeses (including Parmesan and Feta). Avoid exposure to toxins (including many household cleaning products), over-the-counter painkillers, allergy medicines, and as many prescription drugs as possible. To help maintain your bliss, avoid violence, watching violent movies or news shows, and going to bed late (after 10 P.M.).

Lifestyle and Dietary Tips. To purify and balance rakta, follow a diet of more neutral tastes (not excessively spicy, sour, or salty) with plenty of pure water and organic fruits and vegetables. Also, cultivate a more forgiving and tolerant state of mind through meditation and plenty of cooling outdoor exercise (not tennis in the hot sun!). (Details on how to balance your emotions are given in Chapter 10.) To resolve rakta symptoms, never skip or delay your meals; eat one or two sweet, juicy fruits each day (pears, apples, grapes, and melons are especially good); eat plenty of squashes, zucchini, cucumbers, fresh cilantro, and beets; include rose-petal jam or rosewater in your daily diet (try a teaspoon of rose-petal jam on toast or two teaspoons of rosewater in lassi or warm milk); drink a quarter cup of aloe vera juice daily; drink fresh, organic carrot juice once or twice a week (add a dash of black pepper, or juice with two thin slices of fresh ginger root for ama-free digestion); eat some raisins each day (soak in warm water until soft, or cook with hot cereal, stewed fruit, or vegetables for better digestion).

3. Muscles (Mamsa)

Mamsa refers to the muscle tissue in your body, which includes your uterus, blood vessels, glands, bladder, bowels, and heart.

Factors That Cause Mamsa Disturbance. Mamsa is most easily disturbed by factors that promote the formation of dense, sticky, and clogging ama from your food. That includes foods that are old, left over, or otherwise not fresh, and foods that are cold, dense, rich, or heavy (such as many cheeses, deli foods, and ice cream). Leftover or impure meats (nonorganic meat or fowl, for example) are especially disturbing to your body's muscle tissue. Since these foods are made of muscle themselves, they tend to affect your body's muscles directly, providing either good protein nourishment or toxic substances to your muscle and glandular tissues. If mamsa is disturbed, avoid overeating and eating deep-fried foods, cold foods (salads, ice cream, cheese, frozen yogurt, yogurt, deli sandwiches), and cold drinks right out of the refrigerator or iced beverages. Avoid eating nonorganic, leftover, or processed meat, poultry, or fish, and avoid eating meat or cheese later in the day (after 2 P.M.). Get plenty of physical exercise.

Lifestyle and Dietary Tips. To balance and purify mamsa, pursue activities that tone and strengthen your muscles and increase circulation to them, such as yoga, stretching, exercise, and a daily oil massage. Also, follow a lighter, preferably vegetarian diet. Eat *amla* berry preserves (available in Indian grocery stores) or take amla berry tablets (one tablet twice a day with meals). Amla berry helps the body make healthy muscle tissue, according to Ayurveda. Eat one or two dates per day and one-half to one cup cooked buckwheat at least once a week. Strictly avoid red meat, pork, and cheese.

4. Fat and Hormones (Meda)

Meda refers to the fat tissue, hormones, and carbohydrate metabolism and is involved in regulating the metabolism of the entire body. The liver, fat tissue, pancreas, thyroid, and brain play especially important roles in meda.

Factors That Cause Meda Disturbance. Meda is most easily disturbed by factors that clog up and slow down your metabolism, such as eating too much fat or sugar, not exercising enough, eating too many calories, and eating too much in the evening. If your meda is disturbed, avoid eating refined carbohydrates (sweets, cookies, cakes, chips, crackers, etc.), french fries and any other deep-fried foods, curdled foods (cheese, yogurt) in the evening, and heavy foods like meat or cheese or creamy, rich foods on a regular basis. Avoid cooking with impure oils such as nonorganic, refined vegetable oils, lard, or genetically modified canola oil, eating late at night (after 8 P.M.), and consuming excess fat. Avoid drugs and medications that disturb sugar metabolism (such as corticosteroids), pesticides, and any fat-soluble chemical toxins.

Lifestyle and Dietary Tips. To resolve meda symptoms, get more exercise, increase the amount of fiber you eat, cut out refined sugar and white flour entirely, reduce fat and oils in your diet, eat organic foods as much as possible, and use only organic, unrefined olive oil or up to two teaspoons of ghee daily. (Always sauté your olive oil/ghee in spices as described earlier in this chapter.) The following foods are especially good for you: bran, whole cooked grains (especially barley and quinoa), green, leafy vegetables (chard, kale, spinach, and broccoli), and legumes (lentils, dahls, dried beans, and peas). Eat them every day.

5. Bones (Asthi)

Asthi refers to your bone tissue and what MAV calls its metabolic "relatives," your cartilage, hair, teeth, and nails, where symptoms of poor asthi nourishment may appear.

Factors That Cause Asthi Disturbance. Asthi is most easily disturbed by factors that aggravate vata dosha, such as late nights, mental stress, and irregular meals. If asthi is disturbed, avoid impure (lead-contaminated) calcium supplements; mercury and other toxins; smoking; hormonal imbalances (including reproductive, thyroid, and adrenal hormones); certain medications and drugs known to cause bone loss (including seizure medications and corticosteroids); and mental stress. (Major depression increases your risk of osteoporosis.) Get enough nutrition, especially calcium, magnesium, zinc, iron, and vitamin D, and enough exercise.

Lifestyle and Dietary Tips. To keep your bones strong, you need adequate dietary calcium and vitamin D. However, you also need good digestion and assimilation to allow these nutrients to be absorbed. MAV says that asthi requires balanced vata dosha for good health. (Details on how to support your bone health are found in Chapter 8.) To resolve asthi symptoms, eat calcium-rich foods, including sesame seeds, tahini, broccoli, blanched almonds, kale, and fresh asparagus whenever it's available. Take a twenty- to thirty-minute morning walk in the rising sun, preferably without sunscreen (vitamin D production through the skin is more effective than a supplement, some studies indicate) and give yourself a daily oil massage (see Chapter 4).

6. Bone Marrow (Majja)

Majja includes not only your bone marrow, the main production site for your red blood cells and immune cells, but also your immune system, brain, and central nervous system.

Factors That Cause Majja Disturbance. Imbalance in majja can mean that your immune system is not functioning optimally. "Adrenal exhaustion," inability to handle stress, and chronic lack of stamina are common symptoms of majja weakness. Get a complete checkup from your medical doctor if your majja tested out of balance in the Chapter 5 quiz. If majja is disturbed, avoid eating unnatural, unwholesome foods (like junk food, processed food, fake fats, genetically engineered food, food not ripened on the tree or vine, and food grown with pesticides). Also avoid drugs that suppress bone marrow function (including corticosteroids); mercury, lead, and other toxins that impair immune function; and alcohol and other recreational drugs. Reduce your mental stress. Consume foods rich in calcium, magnesium, and vitamins B6 and B12. Get plenty of sunlight to ensure adequate vitamin D intake.

Lifestyle and Dietary Tips. It's very important that you get more rest, do gentle but regular exercise, a daily oil massage, and eat very healthy and pure, wholesome foods to help restore your immune strength and the strength and resilience of your nervous system. To resolve majja symptoms, avoid junk food and processed foods, eat organic foods as much as possible, and include asparagus in your diet (aim for two or three times per week). Eat nurturing foods like date milkshakes (add two medjool dates to 1 ½ cups organic milk and bring to a boil, let cool to warm, blend in blender, and drink) and rice pudding (cooked fresh at home with organic milk, basmati rice, raisins, chopped nuts, a few threads of saffron, and organic raw sugar to taste). Include walnuts, pecans, and blanched almonds in your daily diet, and eat mangoes when they are in season.

7. Reproductive Essence (Shukra)

Shukra relates to the reproductive essence of the body, specifically the eggs in females and the sperm in males but more generally the vagina, uterus, and ovaries. Shukra is also closely related to immune function and overall strength and stamina. If it is well nourished and maintained and not unduly spent for sexual functions, then it supports the production of ojas, the life-giving essence of the body.

Factors That Cause Shukra Disturbance. Shukra is most easily disturbed by factors that deplete you of energy, immune strength, and nutrition, or that overtax your reproductive system, such as too much sexual activity or too frequent childbirth (babies less than two years apart). If shukra is disturbed, avoid unwholesome foods lacking in nutrients, mental or emotional stresses, carbonated beverages, baked goods made with baking soda or powder, and alcohol. Also avoid pesticides and other chemicals with carcinogenic, estrogenic, or DNA-damaging effects (such as Atrazine, DDT, DDE, dioxins, and PCBs), ionizing radiation (such as X-rays and radiation treatments), and drinking liquids or eating foods that have been stored in soft plastic containers, which can leach infertility-causing chemicals if kept in warm environments.

Lifestyle and Dietary Tips. To balance shukra, practice moderation in all your habits, including sexual activity. To resolve your shukra symptoms, get enough sleep (at least eight hours), go to bed by 10 P.M., and give yourself a daily oil massage (see Chapter 4). Eat nurturing foods (like the date milkshake and rice pudding described under majja), fresh asparagus two or three times a week, include walnuts, pecans, and blanched almonds in your daily diet, eat mangoes when they are in season, and eat one sweet, juicy pear or apple each day.

Purifying Your Wastes

Your three malas, or bodily wastes, are urine, stool, and sweat. Determine from the Chapter 5 quiz which ones are relevant to your symptoms and follow the dietary and lifestyle tips below to purify and rebalance your malas.

1. Urine

A generous intake of pure water every day, a diet rich in organic fruits and vegetables, and minimal or no toxins and junk foods are important for a healthy urinary system. To purify your urine, follow these recommendations.

• Avoid eating sour, acidic, or fermented foods or supplements (citrus, tomatoes, vitamin C, alcoholic beverages, and vinegar, including vinegar-containing condiments such as ketchup, mustard, and salad dressings), or very alkaline food, such as products made with baking soda and baking powder. All of these foods may irritate or inflame the bladder. They may also disturb the body's neutral pH (acid balance), causing the blood and urine to become too acidic or too alkaline, which can lead to bacterial growth and urinary tract infections.

• According to MAV, the following foods will help balance and neutralize your body's pH, improve urine flow, and reduce the tendency for infections. Every day, eat sweet juicy fruits (such as pears, apples, sweet plums, and sweet grapes), green, leafy vegetables at lunch and at dinner, squashes (winter and summer), a little cooked or grated daikon radish, and coriander and fresh cilantro in your cooking.

• Use the following blend of spices as your smart spice mixture instead of those described in the foundation program: 1 part turmeric powder, 2 parts cumin seeds, 3 parts coriander seeds, 4 parts fennel seeds, 1 part fenugreek seeds, and 1 part black peppercorns. Put all the ingredients in a dry pan without any oil and stir for a few minutes over medium heat until lightly browned. Remove from heat and allow to cool. Then blend and powder the ingredients together in a spice (or clean coffee) grinder. Place in a small airtight container and carry with you to sprinkle on food when eating out. Use a quarter to a half teaspoon per meal.

• Drink pure water. The purity of your drinking water is extremely important. Avoid drinking chlorinated water. If you have no choice, boil the water in a stainless steel or glass vessel for five minutes to allow the chlorine to evaporate out. If there are too many minerals in the water (as evidenced by a cloud of tiny white precipitates that appear as you boil it), let the water sit for twenty-four hours after boiling in a covered pan and then slowly pour the water off the top. The heavy mineral deposits will stay at the bottom. Don't use reverse osmosis (R-O) on a regular basis because it contains no

PURIFICATION

> ### For Yeast Infections (a Sign of Ama in the Genitourinary Tract)
>
> • Use turmeric and chopped fresh ginger root in your cooking. Eat plenty of cooked green, leafy vegetables. Avoid sugar, yeast breads, and other yeast products.
>
> • Put a tablespoon of fresh plain yogurt on a tampon, on a small piece of cotton gauze (approximately one-half by two inches), or in an applicator and insert into vagina. Leave it in place for thirty minutes. Do this once a day for at least a week.

minerals. Water should be naturally composed of both pure water and earth (mineral) elements. Fresh spring water containing a natural mineral balance from the earth is the best kind for your body.

• Do not delay visiting the bathroom when you feel the urge to urinate. Suppressing or delaying urination gives chemicals, toxins, and bacteria more contact time with your bladder, allowing them to interact with your urinary tissues. It also causes back pressure on the kidneys, which can be damaging, as well as downward pressure on the urinary sphincter, which can lead to urinary incontinence (leakage) over time. Finally, it can interfere with the functions of vata dosha in your lower abdomen, creating bloating, gas, or constipation.

2. Stool

Good digestion is critical for a healthy quality and quantity of stool. The following recommendations are aimed at correcting the imbalance in digestion that is at the root of problems with the bowels. There are two sets of recommendations, one for normal stool consistency or constipation and the second for loose stools or diarrhea. Note: Always check with your doctor if you have had a change in your bowel habits or have bleeding associated with a bowel movement.

For normal stools or constipation:
• Drink this culinary "lighter fluid" to fire up your digestive system before lunch and dinner. Bring a cup of pure water to a boil. Remove from heat. Add a quarter teaspoon of cumin seeds and let steep for ten minutes. Then add ten drops of lime juice. Drink before lunch and dinner whenever possible.

• Do not skip or delay meals, overeat at a meal, or eat between meals if you are not hungry.

• Go to the bathroom promptly when you feel the urge to eliminate. Do not suppress or delay eliminating once you feel the urge.

• Make a habit of drinking two cups of pure warm water in the morning on an empty stomach. If desired, add the juice of a quarter lime and 1 to 2 tsp. of raw honey for extra ama-busting power.

• Increase the amount of figs, prunes, and raisins in your diet. (All should be soaked in water overnight to soften and hydrate them.) Also increase the amount of cooked green, leafy vegetables you eat.

• Do not skip breakfast. Start your day each morning with a stewed apple or pear, cooked in water with one or two cloves added (even if you normally skip breakfast). If you usually have a bigger breakfast, eat your stewed apple or pear first and then continue with the rest of your meal. With your hot cereal of whole grains cooked with water (quinoa, whole-wheat couscous, amaranth, bulgur wheat, or cracked wheat) cook 1 or 2 tsp. of wheat bran.

• Avoid rice, cheese, red meat, and potatoes, *especially* after 2 P.M.

For loose stools or diarrhea:
The following recommendations are helpful in most cases. However, it is advisable to check with your doctor regarding further evaluation if your symptoms persist. Loose stools or diarrhea without an infectious cause (such as intestinal virus or dysentery) are referred to as *grahani*, meaning a disturbance in digestion and assimilation in the small intestine.

• Use 1 or 2 tsp. of pomegranate chutney with your meals instead of the smart spice mixture. Recipe: Separately grind up ¼ tsp. black peppercorns, 2 tsp. cumin seeds, and 1/8 tsp. cardamom seeds. Add one at a time, mixing well after each addition, to a mixture of 8 tsp. pomegranate seed powder (available in most Indian grocery stores as "anardana" powder) or freshly ground pomegranate seeds, 2 tsp. salt, and ½ cup organic whole cane sugar. After mixing all dry ingredients, add ¼ tsp. fresh lemon juice. Store in an airtight container for up to a month.

• Eat *kichari* (**kih**-cha-ree) at least once a day, either at mealtime or as a snack in between meals. It should be warm and fresh, not left over or refrigerated, and composed of 10 percent dahl and 90 percent rice. To make kichari, mix 1 Tbsp. split yellow mung dahl (available at Indian grocery stores and some health food stores) with a half cup white basmati rice. Rinse well in cold water. Add 1 ¼ cups of water and a pinch of salt. Bring to a boil, then simmer covered on low heat until soft, about 20 to 30 minutes. Then add ½ tsp. of your pomegranate chutney and enjoy this nourishing, easily digested dish.

• Drink up to four cups of *kanjee* (<u>kuhn</u>-gee), a special type of homemade rice "milk," with meals or between meals each day. Boil a half cup of organic basmati rice in eight cups of water for 20 minutes. Strain the rice out and pour the water into a thermos. Add ½ tsp. to a one-quart thermos or add a pinch of fresh cumin powder to each glass. Kanjee helps to rehydrate your body, slows down and firms up bowel movements, and provides electrolyte support.

• At lunchtime, drink one or two cups of fresh lassi made from nonfat yogurt. Add a pinch of baked, ground cumin powder to each glass.

3. Sweat

Purifying your sweat requires reducing "bad fats" and sugar in the diet and increasing exercise. Follow these lifestyle and dietary tips.

• Get more exercise.

• Avoid refined sugar and white flour entirely, reduce fat in your diet, consume more fiber, and eat organic foods as much as possible. Use only organic, unrefined olive oil or up to 2 tsp. of ghee per day; always sauté your olive oil/ghee in spices as described in the directions for smart spice mixture earlier in this chapter. Foods especially good for you include bran, whole cooked grains (especially barley and quinoa), green, leafy vegetables (chard, kale, spinach, and broccoli), legumes (lentils, dried beans, and peas), and dahl, so add them to your daily diet. (See the Resources for Web sites that provide recipes for these and other Ayurvedic healing foods.)

Ayurvedic/Indian Herbs and Spices

Effects of the some of the less common Ayurvedic herbs and spices used in this chapter are described below. The information has been derived from the classical texts of Ayurveda, including *Charaka Samhita*, *Bhavaprakash Samhita*, and *Sushruta Samhita*, as well as two reference books on Ayurvedic herbs, *Dhanvantari Nighunti* and *Nighunti Ratnakar*. Information on estrogenic effects is from recent scientific research.

Ajwan seed (Bishop's weed, *Carum copticum*) — This mildly heating spice is a powerful digestive aid, especially for vata-related problems of gas and bloating. It can also be helpful in relieving heart palpitations.

Bala root (Indian country mallow, *Sida cordifolia*) — This herb is revered in Ayurveda for its strength and immune promoting properties. It is recommended in conditions of low stamina, low immunity, or weakness, especially when due to vata imbalance. It is nurturing to the nervous system, good for the heart, promotes shukra and enhances ojas. It balances all three doshas and is cooling.

Cardamom (*Elettaria cardamomum*) — This spice aids digestion and fat metabolism without creating excess heat. It also helps move gas out of the intestines and eliminates mucus from the respiratory tract.

Coriander seeds (*Coriandrum sativum*) — This spice has a cooling effect and enhances urine flow and the removal of toxins from the blood, liver and kidneys. Overall it balances all three doshas, but especially pitta.

Cumin (*Cuminum cyminum*) —This spice is cooling overall, helps digestion, especially vata-related gas and bloating, and purifies the blood and uterus. Cumin also has a specific detoxifying effect on the whole body. It helps reduce any inflammation of the uterus and enhances the reproductive essence.

Fennel (*Foeniculum vulgaris*) — This spice is a premier digestive aid, and is especially helpful in moving gas downward and out of the intestines. It also helps to reduce spasms. Balances both vata and pitta. Also is mildly phytoestrogenic and balancing for the reproductive system of women.

Indian asparagus root (Shatavari, *Asparagus racemosus*) — Shatavari (literally "one hundred marriages") legendarily bestows the reproductive fortitude to handle a hundred husbands. It enhances libido through its nourishing effects on shukra dhatu, the reproductive essence. It pacifies both vata and pitta doshas. Is a tonic for the brain and nervous system, especially in women, and is good for the emotional and physical heart.

Indian hibiscus (Chinese or Egyptian hibiscus, *Rosa Sinensis*) — This flower is said to make women happy and is good for the emotional and physical heart. It has a balancing effect on hormones and helps to reduce heavy menstrual flow. It is very cooling and reduces heat in the body. (Note: do *not* substitute Western hibiscus, as it has opposite effects.)

Indian sarsaparilla (Sarsaparilla, *Hemidesmus indicus*) — Has powerful cooling effects and promotes purification of the blood and liver.

Manjistha (Indian madder, *Rubia cordifolia*) — An extremely beneficial herb for pitta-type skin conditions involving inflammation and redness, including rosacea and acne. Acts by gently purifying the blood and liver. Usually tolerated well by those who may otherwise have skin reactions to purifying herbs.

Marshmallow root (marshmallow, *Althea officinalis*) — Purifies the genitourinary tract, helps immunity against infections, lubricates the channels of the body, is cooling. Balances both vata and pitta. Has overall strengthening action similar to bala root — especially good for the immune system. Rose petals/buds (rose, *Rosa spp.*) — Available in a wide number of species, all rose is deeply cooling in nature and therefore can be helpful for hot flashes. Pacifies both vata and pitta. Specifically helps mood swings and irritability, promotes clarity of mind and enhances hormonal flow.

Part III

How to Overcome Specific Health Issues

7

Your Heart — Healthy and Happy, Naturally

To protect the heart and great vessels, above all take measures that are healthy for the heart and promote ojas, that cleanse the gaps and channels, and help create serenity of mind.
— *the* Charaka Samhita

Your beating heart is the quintessential indicator that you are alive. No other organ is more vital to sustaining your individual existence. It is therefore no wonder that coronary artery disease, the clogging of the arteries that causes heart attacks, is the most serious of all maladies. More than half of all the women alive now will die of heart disease.

As the number one killer of both men and women today, heart attacks and strokes account for more than twice as many deaths as all cancers put together. Yet, according to a recent Gallup poll, most women are largely unaware of their risk for heart disease. They tend to overrate the possibility of dying from breast cancer and underrate that of dying from heart disease. This misperception is probably due to the fact that before age fifty, twice as many men as women have heart disease, supporting the popular notion that heart disease is a man's disease. Also, until recently, most medical research was done on men, and the few studies that were done on women were not widely published.

In reality, however, heart disease claims more lives than the next sixteen causes of death combined, including breast cancer, lung cancer, and brain stroke. These statistics may sound shocking and indeed have been used to frighten women into taking hormone therapy for prevention. A better use for them is to motivate you to start exercising and eat a healthier diet, because the good news about heart disease is that nearly all of it is *preventable*, and much of it may be reversible.

The Good News About Lifestyle

Recent research shows that we have considerable control over the destiny of our heart health. Findings from a study of over 84,000 women participants in the Nurses' Health Study, as reported in the *New England Journal of Medicine*, reveal that by simply following a healthy lifestyle, you can lower your heart attack risk by as much as 82 percent!

This extremely low risk of heart disease applied to all women in the study who did not smoke, exercised at least one half hour per day, maintained a normal body weight, and ate a healthy diet. Even more startling is that this lowered risk applied to women with these habits regardless of their age, their menopausal status, their family history of heart disease, and whether or not they had been diagnosed with high cholesterol or high blood pressure.

These findings are especially relevant today, with millions of women looking for new ways to reduce their heart attack risk since HT's purported heart benefits were discredited by the Women's Health Initiative. While we now know that HT *increases*, not decreases heart attacks and strokes, the benefits of healthy lifestyle remain for the taking!

It is worth noting that the reason women taking HT in earlier observational studies had less heart disease than women who didn't was due to their thinner bodies and healthier lifestyle. Their healthy habits reduced their heart disease risk by half in spite of their taking HT, which has been found to *increase* heart disease by approximately 25 percent. If they had simply followed their healthy lifestyles and left the hormones in the medicine cabinet, they would have been even better off!

More good news from the Nurse's Health Study is that if you already have high blood pressure or high cholesterol, or you are overweight, *it is not too late* to get moving and improve your diet. With even these simple lifestyle changes, you can quickly begin to enjoy a *dramatic* reduction in your heart disease risk, and begin feeling really great to boot!

HT and Your Heart: The Latest (Astounding!) Research

In the early 1990s, medical scientists and physicians were confident in estrogen's ability to reduce cardiovascular disease. When the Heart and Estrogen/Progesterone Replacement Study (HERS) trial was planned in the mid-1990s to test estrogen's effectiveness in women who had already had a heart attack, the study was strongly opposed as a waste of time and effort, because the benefits of estrogen on heart health were considered already known.

The results, published in the *Journal of the American Medical Association* in 1998, were some of the most surprising medical findings of the century. Within the first year of the trial, early results showed such a disproportionate *increase* in the number of heart attacks in the women taking HT versus those who didn't, that the trial was nearly stopped prematurely to prevent further injury.

The HERS trial clearly indicated that giving estrogen to a woman who has already had a heart attack does *not* reduce the incidence of a second one, and, in fact, can lead to an *increase* in heart attacks in the first year. A HERS follow-up study seven years later confirms the lack of any benefit of HT at all for women who have had heart attacks.

The surprising results of the HERS study were eclipsed in July 2002 by the findings of the Women's Health Initiative, a randomized, placebo-controlled "gold standard" study on HT, involving 27,000 mainly healthy women between the ages of 50 and 79. The world medical community was shocked in July 2002 to find not only the absence of a protective effect against heart disease, but an actual *increase* in heart attacks, strokes, and blood clots in women taking HT versus a placebo.

Today, the American Heart Association (AHA) recommends against giving HT for the prevention of cardiovascular disease, a 180-degree turn-around from prior decades!

The Women's Health Initiative and the studies mentioned earlier make my point clearly: Much of what we hear initially (and sometimes for many years) about the benefits of the latest drug or hormonal approach may eventually prove to be just plain wrong. In the history of modern medicine, a host of drugs and therapies have been pulled off the market due to harmful and serious side-effects discovered after the fact.

Fortunately, these recent studies have proven what our common sense should tell us. Heart health doesn't come from a pill, whether it is a drug, a hormone, or a vitamin. A healthy heart doesn't need added hormones. What we *really* need to do is get moving and eat right!

TREATING HEART DISEASE NATURALLY

In contrast to the ineffective and harmful results of HT, research shows that certain non-drug treatments can actually reverse and prevent heart disease. One natural approach — using diet and lifestyle to reverse heart disease — has proven to be surprisingly effective and free of harmful side effects.

The Ornish Study: Diet and Lifestyle Changes Work

In the 1980s, Dean Ornish, M.D., led a landmark study addressing the question "Can lifestyle changes reverse coronary heart disease?" In 1990, the results of that study were published in a major medical journal, the *Lancet*. These results documented the first attempt to reverse established heart disease through a comprehensive lifestyle program of diet, stress reduction, exercise, smoking cessation, and group support.

The results were astonishingly positive. After one year, the lifestyle group had measurably *reversed* the degree of blockage in their arteries, while the group undergoing "usual medical care" experienced increased blockages despite cholesterol-lowering drugs. The lifestyle group also had markedly less chest pain, while in the other group angina had worsened. Follow-up at five years found that the lifestyle group continued to improve. Chest pains and heart attacks were about 50 percent less in the lifestyle group, while the usual medical care group experienced a 27.7 percent worsening of their blockages. Overall, the positive changes in the lifestyle group translated into not only better numbers but less disease and a higher quality of life.

The success of Dr. Ornish's program makes this choice clear: If you want to, you have the power to not only prevent heart disease but reverse it without drugs, HT, or surgery. The choice is yours. As you may remember, MAV identifies ages forty-five to fifty-five, the midlife transition years, as a critical decade for building the foundation of your future health. If you choose to follow a healthy lifestyle at this time, not only will you be easing your menopausal and midlife symptoms, but you will also be investing in good heart health for many decades.

Now let's examine the cause of heart disease from the perspective of Maharishi Ayurveda. What does this ancient, profound health science offer us today in the way of prevention and treatment for women?

ANCIENT VEDIC WISDOM FOR A HEALTHY HEART

Those who eat heavy, cold, and excessively oily foods in excessive quantity and do excessive mental work, suffer from disease of the vessels that nourish the heart.
— *the* Charaka Samhita

Thousands of years ago this classic Ayurvedic text identified the exact causes of heart disease as we know them today: eating too much fatty, rich food and suffering from chronic mental and emotional stress.

We are all too familiar with both of these factors in our modern Western lifestyles. Even our popular music testifies to our fast-food habits: "Eating dinner from a paper sack — a 99-cent heart attack." And it is no surprise to any of us that chronic mental and emotional stress can increase blood pressure and the risk of heart disease. Indeed, not "taking a break from it all" each year — skipping your annual vacation — can increase your risk of dying of a heart attack by as much as 32 percent, according to recent findings by University of Pittsburgh psychologist Karen Matthews and colleagues. More proof of the dangers of a lifestyle that is perpetually on the go!

In treating heart disease, MAV takes into consideration both diet and stress by recognizing that the human heart is actually two hearts: the physical heart muscle, which pumps our blood, and the emotional heart, which experiences love, joy, sadness, and every other human feeling. It says both of these hearts must be supported for health, the physical heart through diet and the emotional heart through stress reduction and enhancement of ojas, the bliss factor that keeps you immune to disease (see Chapter 5).

I will begin with the MAV treatments for the emotional heart, which emphasize reducing chronically stressful emotions, balancing your doshas, and enjoying the heart-healing effects of ojas-enhancing *rejuvenatives*. For healing your physical heart, I will present dietary and herbal approaches that help to clear toxic plaques (ama) from your arteries to give your heart full strength and stamina for its vital job of pumping blood through your body.

But first I want to introduce you to what MAV considers the most valuable approach for both emotional and physical heart health, the practice of the Transcendental Meditation technique.

Transcendental Meditation for Your Heart

Remember Dr. Ornish's program, the natural approach that worked so well to reverse heart disease? It is amazingly effective, but there's a catch: Ornish's program recommends that only 10 percent of total daily calories come from fat, whereas the average American eats a diet with *nearly four times* that much fat. While Ornish's diet may be ideal for reversing coronary heart disease, and is certainly doable for the most motivated patients, such a dramatic change in diet is very difficult for most people to achieve.

Maharishi Ayurveda provides a simpler approach for reducing heart attacks and strokes naturally without requiring a dramatic dietary change. Transcendental Meditation, introduced to the world in 1955 by the famous Vedic sage from India, Maharishi Mahesh Yogi, creates a state of "restful alertness" during two twenty-minute periods of meditation each day. Through the experience of this peaceful state of mind, Transcendental Meditation induces a beneficial mind-body chain reaction that leads ultimately to reduced atherosclerosis (arterial blockage), lower blood pressure, and lower risk of death from heart attack, stroke, and even cancer. See Chapters 9 and 10 for more about this technique.

TM and Reversal of Heart Disease

In April 2000, a remarkable result emerged from a National Institutes of Health (NIH)-funded study conducted by Robert Schneider, M. D., the director of the NIH-sponsored Center for Natural Medicine and Prevention at the Maharishi University of Management (MUM) in Fairfield, Iowa. Dr. Schneider looked at the effects of Transcendental Meditation in men and women with high blood pressure. He found that in less than nine months, the meditating individuals demonstrated a measurable reversal in the degree of blockage in their carotid arteries (the main arteries leading to the brain). A control group, who received health education but did not do Transcendental Meditation, showed an increase in arterial blockage.

These results caught the attention of media and experts alike because no stress-reduction technique alone had ever before been demonstrated to reverse arterial blockage. The success of Transcendental Meditation suggested the possibility of a "mind over matter" effect that was intriguing and, before this study, barely imaginable. To show that simply sitting comfortably with eyes closed for twenty minutes twice a day could lead to physical changes in the amount of plaque in the arteries was revolutionary for modern medicine. Further studies in larger numbers of people are now under way to investigate this healthful phenomenon further.

Transcendental Meditation and Your Blood Pressure

High blood pressure, or hypertension, is one of the leading risk factors for heart attacks. Some experts consider it an indication that blockage of the arteries is already present. Unfortunately, nearly half of all women over fifty-five have hypertension; by age sixty-five, that proportion rises to 60 percent. Controlling high blood pressure helps to lower risk of heart attack and stroke by about 30 percent, but to do this, most patients need to be on blood pressure medication for life.

There is some good news about hypertension, however, if you want to avoid or reduce your dependence on medication. Studies indicate that Transcendental Meditation effectively lowers blood pressure roughly as much as taking a blood pressure medication: by about ten points systolic and six points diastolic. A groundbreaking study published in the American Heart Association's journal *Hypertension* in 1995 found that Transcendental Meditation was *twice as effective* at lowering high blood pressure as other relaxation techniques.

Transcendental Meditation and Other Diseases

Transcendental Meditation is good not only for your heart but for disease prevention in general. In a study reported at the Society of Behavioral Medicine's annual meeting in 1999, the risks of heart attack and stroke were found to be reduced by almost 50 percent in Transcendental Meditation practitioners as compared to control subjects. Even more remarkably, the number of deaths due to cancer and all other causes was also reduced by nearly 50 percent in the Transcendental Meditation subjects, in the randomized trials completed thus far.

This fascinating result tells us that the beneficial heart effects of the Transcendental Meditation technique are not due merely to its lowering blood pressure or some other single factor. Rather, according to Maharishi Ayurveda, the practice of the Transcendental Meditation technique strengthens the body's inner intelligence in a holistic and integrated way, leading to healthier, *more balanced* functioning not only in the cardiovascular system but in the immune system, central nervous system, and probably other systems of the body as well.

Transcendental Meditation Compared to HT

Table 7.1 compares the dramatic spectrum of improvements in physical health Transcendental Meditation yields to the limited, and often harmful, effects of HT. The evidence clearly indicates that Transcendental Meditation is far more beneficial, as well as safer, than HT.

A Warning Note

I don't advise you to throw out your high blood pressure pills as you rush out to the nearest center teaching the Transcendental Meditation technique! Do learn the technique, but ask your doctor about the possibility of reducing your medication as you begin to accrue the benefits of your daily practice. (See the Resources for places where you can learn Transcendental Meditation.)

HEALING YOUR EMOTIONAL HEART WITH MAV

One who wants to protect the heart, the great vessels and the ojas, should avoid particularly the causes due to affliction of the mind.
— *the* Charaka Samhita

MAV long ago described the intimate connection between your emotional life and the health of your heart. According to MAV, your heart is not only a physical organ that circulates your blood but, like your brain, a seat of consciousness in the body.

Table 7-1: Comparing the Effectiveness of HT to Transcendental Meditation For Heart Health

Condition	HT	Transcendental Meditation
Hypertension (HBP)	0 % effective	Equivalent to taking a medication
Atherosclerosis	0 % percent effective	Reverses blockage
Heart Attack	Increases risk	50% reduced risk of death by heart attack
Stroke	Increases risk	50% reduced risk of death by stroke
Cancer risk	Increased breast and ovarian cancer risk	Cancer deaths reduced by 50%

Modern mind-body medicine, or psychoneuroimmunology (PNI), acknowledges that your brain and your heart speak the same language. Neurotransmitters, the chemicals your brain secretes in response to your ever-changing mental and emotional experiences, are simultaneously "understood" by your mind and "felt" in your heart. Candace Pert, Ph.D., a leading pioneer in PNI research, explains that it's as if both heart and brain were listening to the same conversation, with one organ reacting more intellectually and the other more emotionally.

These neurochemical conversations are seldom trivial. On the contrary, PNI research has shown that positive, uplifting thoughts and feelings can be good for your cardiovascular system by reducing *cortisol*, the stress hormone, thus lowering blood pressure, and increasing *serotonin*, the "well-being" brain chemical. On the other hand, "heart-hurtful" conversations can raise cortisol and trigger the fight-or-flight response, promoting heart disease via elevated blood pressure, elevated cholesterol, impaired immune function, and damage to the lining of the arteries.

OJAS AND YOUR HEART

Life known by sensory experience is located in the heart. It is also the seat of the essential ojas and reservoir of consciousness.
— *the* Charaka Samhita

In MAV, the heart is seen as the seat of ojas in your body. Ojas, you may recall from Chapter 5, is the finest, most subtle level of your physical body, so subtle that it is described as being as much consciousness as it is matter. Ojas is experienced as bliss: a pleasant, satisfying, soothing inner state of perfectly balanced mind, emotions, and physiology. Ojas is like a lamp in a doorway, lighting both inside and outside. In one stroke, ojas both infuses your mind with bliss and enlivens the healing intelligence of the physical body.

According to Ayurvedic wisdom, your life depends on the maintenance of a critical store of eight precious drops of ojas that reside in your heart. These eight drops are essential to life and to maintaining the connection between the soul and the body. They must be perfectly preserved in their wholeness since, according to the ancient texts, any diminution (even a tiny amount) results in the end of life.

Mental and emotional well-being plays an enormous role in preserving the eight essential drops of ojas in your heart. Positive inner experiences enhance ojas; negative emotions destroy ojas. Many a wife has implored her irate husband, "Calm down, honey, before you have a heart attack!" Such urgings are scientifically validated by studies that show a person is twice as likely to have a heart attack within two hours after an episode of sudden, intense anger as at other times.

For women with heart disease, another issue is stress in the marital relationship. How happy or unhappy you are in your marriage has been shown to affect recurrent heart problems. Increased marital stress contributes to more heart attacks, the need for further heart-related surgery, and heart-related deaths.

The *Charaka Samhita* says the positive qualities of the mind and emotions, such as inner calmness, positive thinking, happiness, and feelings of love and compassion, uphold ojas and lessen the risk of heart disease and all illnesses. It's beginning to appear that "Don't worry, be happy" is as important a prescription for heart health as exercising and eating a healthful diet!

Balancing Yourself to Enhance Ojas

You may recall from Chapter 3 that dosha imbalances are related to specific types of emotional symptoms. Each dosha can potentially damage your critical supply of ojas through the negative emotions it may cause. Worry, grief, and fear can dry up your naturally unctuous store of essential ojas through the effects of imbalanced vata. The searing flames of heated emotions such as anger and resentment can burn ojas through the action of imbalanced pitta. And deep, chronic sadness can create a heavy-heartedness that damages your ojas through the effects of sluggish, imbalanced kapha.

Each of these emotional conditions is rooted in an imbalance at a subsidiary level of dosha functioning, or subdosha. Three of these subdoshas, *prana vata, vyana vata,* and *sadhaka pitta,* all have dual residences in the heart and in the brain. In other words, action in the brain equals action in the heart, or biochemistry in the brain equals biochemistry in the heart. A passing thought, a fleeting emotion, a deep state of lasting grief are all felt in your heart as they are experienced in your mind and consciousness. Negative emotions like chronic anxiety, depression, anger, and hostility have all been repeatedly demonstrated to dramatically increase your risk of heart disease. Therefore, stressful emotions can create dosha imbalances and damage your heart, and vice versa.

Physical influences such as the wrong food, poor sleep, late nights, missed or delayed meals, heart surgery, and toxins like alcohol, drugs, and cigarettes can all cause imbalances in your emotional subdoshas. Indeed, depression is especially common after heart surgery and heart attacks and is commonplace in people suffering from addictions. Over time, all of these emotional imbalances can affect the health of your physical heart if they are not resolved. Keeping your doshas balanced and maintaining a healthy mental and emotional state are critical to nourishing your ojas and living a long, blissful, heart-healthy life. (See Chapter 10 for details on overcoming your emotional imbalances naturally.)

Using Rejuvenatives to Enhance Ojas

In Ayurvedic terms, ojas can be enhanced by *rasayanas* (ruh-<u>sah</u>-yuh-nuhz) or *rejuvenatives*, which refer to anything that causes ojas to be produced throughout the physiology. Rejuvenatives can be physical, in the form of herbal preparations, or behavioral, in the form of attitudes and behaviors. They operate at the deepest level of physiology, between intelligence and matter, consciousness and the body. There they nourish and uphold the fundamental health of the body by supporting and enhancing ojas, which unifies all aspects of the body into a seamless, harmonious whole.

Research over the past twenty years has revealed that many of the traditional MAV rasayana herbal formulations are especially rich in antioxidants, those important chemicals your body needs to fight off free radicals that cause damaging oxidation in your cells. In fact, several formulations are hundreds of times more powerful than the well-known antioxidants vitamin C and E. Like whole foods, these formulas contain a large variety of antioxidant components that counteract free radicals through many counterbalancing mechanisms (unlike high doses of one isolated vitamin or other substance, which could bring side effects) while at the same time supporting the body's own antioxidant defense system.

One of the most ancient and highly prized herbal rejuvenatives, formulated according to strict traditional guidelines, is produced today under the trade name Maharishi Amrit Kalash (MAK). Amrit Kalash (<u>Ahm</u>-rit Kuh-<u>lahsh</u>), or Amrit, literally means "immortality," and indeed its traditional purpose is the promotion of health and longevity.

Dozens of research studies have been performed on Amrit, showing a wide variety of benefits, including anti-inflammatory and anticancer effects, antioxidant effects that are a thousand times greater than those of vitamin C or E, cardiovascular

Problems with Antioxidant Supplements

Many of my patients are taking antioxidant vitamins and herbal extracts in hopes of avoiding heart disease in the future. It's true that people who eat diets rich in antioxidant vitamins have less heart disease, according to a number of studies. However, studies in which antioxidant supplements are given to people in randomized, placebo-controlled clinical trials (recall, that's the gold standard) have not yielded the same positive results. In fact, in some instances, such supplements have done more harm than good.

In two separate trials published in the *New England Journal of Medicine* in the mid 1990s, a group who took beta carotene actually had *more* deaths from both heart disease and lung cancer than a control group who took no supplements. Vitamin E also showed negative results in one of these trials, although other studies on vitamin E are mixed; a number of them show some benefit for reducing heart attacks and some show no difference. Unfortunately, for those who are looking for a shortcut to heart health that skips diet, exercise, and stress reduction, antioxidant supplements have not yet stood up to the test.

What *has* been especially effective at lowering heart disease risk is a healthy diet that is naturally rich in antioxidants. Recall the Iowa Women's Health Study, discussed in Chapter 1, which found that women with the highest vitamin E consumption from *food* had the lowest risk of death from heart disease. However, remarkably, this effect was stronger in those women who did not take vitamin supplements than in those who did.

These findings are completely in line with what we might expect given the principles of MAV. A wholesome diet rich in antioxidant foods and spices according to Nature's design naturally supports the inner balance that our bodies are striving to uphold. On the other hand, taking large amounts of single isolated nutrients is likely to throw off the body's intricate web of nutrient and biochemical interactions and generally should be avoided.

benefits, and protection against the side effects of chemotherapy treatments without reducing their efficacy.

In heart patients, Amrit has been shown to reduce chest pains and levels of oxidized low-density lipoprotein (LDL), an especially toxic, artery-damaging form of this "bad" cholesterol, indicating a possible reversal of the disease process. These early studies have been so promising that the National Institutes of Health is currently funding a placebo-controlled, double-blind trial of Amrit versus a vitamin C and E "cocktail" to see if it improves the health of individuals with heart disease.

Supporting Your Ojas through Behavioral Rejuvenatives

Not all Rejuvenatives are herbal preparations. Some prescriptions are simple daily activities. The Vedic tradition tells of a king who was interviewing a group of vaidyas for the position of royal physician. One of his test questions was: "What is the simplest rasayana available to the common man, of no material cost, that is both relaxing and invigorating and is available every day to everyone?" The correct answer was "A morning walk." Not only is an early morning walk in the fresh air invigorating, but it clears out any morning brain fog and creates a positive mood for the whole day — a side benefit for our emotional hearts!

> ### *Six Ojas-Enhancing, Heart-Healthy Tips*
>
> • Turn your attention to that which brings you bliss and upliftment. Do not dwell on thoughts or issues that evoke negative emotions like anger, resentment, worry, fear, sadness, or grief.
>
> • Eat a wholesome, fresh, and delicious diet that includes moderate amounts of pure, organic oils such as olive oil. Too little nourishment, a fat-free diet, and too much raw, rough, and dry food deplete ojas.
>
> • Avoid drugs, alcohol in excess (Ayurveda advises none on a regular basis), cigarettes, unnatural foods (such as genetically modified ones), and exposure to environmental toxins.
>
> • Learn the Transcendental Meditation technique and practice it regularly.
>
> • Get enough sleep and avoid staying up late into the night.
>
> • Stay active. Get at least thirty minutes of walking or other exercise each day. A morning walk in the rising sun is particularly ojas-enhancing.

HEALING YOUR PHYSICAL HEART WITH MAV

Enhancing ojas is the key to the health of your dual hearts, the emotional heart directly and the physical heart indirectly. However, the buildup of cholesterol and other artery-damaging substances in your blood and in your arteries may require some extra attention.

According to MAV, cholesterol buildup happens when you overwhelm your digestive tract with rich, fatty foods on a regular basis and cannot digest and metabolize them fully. The resulting accumulation of ama, as elevated cholesterol, triglycerides, and other artery-harming toxins, is the root physical cause of heart disease. Specifically, the Ayurvedic texts describe how ama builds up in the blood plasma (rasa dhatu) and from there damages the arteries carrying blood and oxygen (rasa vaha srotas) to the heart.

Modern medicine is recognizing that elevated cholesterol alone does not fully explain heart attacks. The role of internal toxins in heart disease is gaining recognition. Such toxins include free radicals; overactive immune cells creating inflammation, measured by "c-reactive protein"; homocysteine buildup due to a lack of folic acid and other vitamins; trans-fatty acids from impure oils in your diet; and environmental toxins, such as mercury from contaminated fish.

From the perspective of Ayurveda, these highly reactive toxins interact with ama, forming an especially vicious form of unstable, irritating ama called *ama visha*, which can directly damage the arteries. One example of this is LDL, which is not truly "bad" cholesterol until it is attacked by free radicals. Only then is it taken up by immune cells in the artery wall, beginning the process of plaque formation, which gradually blocks the passage of blood. The insidious process all too often culminates in inflammation, the body's response to irritating ama visha, increasing the likelihood of the plaque becoming unstable and rupturing, causing a heart attack. The rasayana MAK discussed earlier, as well as Maharishi Rejuvenation Treatment, have both been shown to lower levels of toxic oxidized fats in the blood, and may possibly lower the risk of heart disease.

After menopause, toxic ama buildup can lead to any number of heart health risks. Fortunately, most of my patients have responded well to dietary and lifestyle changes, often dropping their cholesterol by 50 points or more within a few weeks. The experience of my patient Margaret shows how improving digestion and metabolism can reverse cardiovascular ama buildup, lower cholesterol and lower heart attack risk.

Margaret's Story: Clearing Ama to Lower Cholesterol

Margaret, a fifty-three-year-old financial advisor, first came to see me after her annual checkup with her internist. She had learned at that her cholesterol was significantly elevated, and she was concerned about going on medication to lower it.

Margaret pulled out her lab report for my review. It showed her total cholesterol was 316, far above the desired level of 200 or less. Her good cholesterol (high-density lipoprotein, or HDL) was only mediocre, yet her bad cholesterol (LDL) was very elevated at 212 (normal is below 130).

Not surprisingly, Margaret's pulse showed a lot of ama. I assured her that if she was committed to making some lifestyle changes and would follow a careful dietary and herbal program for a few months, she could avoid what she feared would be a "downward spiral of more and more medication" as she got older.

Based on her evaluation, I advised Margaret to follow the diet prescribed for her particular dosha imbalance — a kapha-balancing diet — and the healing meal plan outlined in Chapter 4. I also asked her to completely avoid processed, refined, and restaurant foods, and to cook for herself with pure, wholesome, and fresh ingredients. I assured Margaret that her cravings for sugar, chocolate, and other unwholesome foods would resolve within a few days of sticking to the diet and she would soon find the program rewarding and satisfying.

Six weeks later Margaret returned with her latest report work in hand. Her total cholesterol had dropped nearly 50 points and was now 267, better than a 15 percent decrease in just a few weeks. Most of the decrease was in the bad cholesterol, now down to 174. This result was as good as might be expected with medication and translated into a 26 percent drop in her risk of heart disease.

Margaret continued her diet, along with a moderate exercise program, and after six months her cholesterol profile was nearly normal. On a follow-up visit, she told me: "I don't really mind not eating snacks any more, because I no longer have cravings like I used to. I've even lost a few pounds and am very happy with the way I feel — much lighter. And I have lots of energy again!"

Lower Your Cholesterol the Natural Way

If your cholesterol is as high as Margaret's was, you will obtain the best results by following the intensive program outlined below. However, if your cholesterol is only mildly elevated (between 200 and 240), you may not need to follow as strict of a program as Margaret's. Simpler dietary changes, such as reducing fat intake, can lower cholesterol effectively in most people. But remember, cholesterol is only one side of the coin. *Ama visha*, toxins and free radicals that join with cholesterol to narrow your artery walls, also increase the risk of a heart attack. A primarily vegetarian diet of fresh fruits and vegetables, whole grains and legumes, and nonfat organic dairy products will provide you with heart-protecting, cancer-preventing nutrition that delivers much more benefit than a simple low-fat diet can provide.

Making a few simple dietary changes can go a long way toward lowering your cholesterol. Increase your intake of fresh fruits and vegetables, whole cooked grains, legumes, and nuts and seeds. Eat less meat, cheese, and restaurant and packaged food. Limit your fat intake exclusively (or nearly) to small amounts of pure organic olive oil. And don't forget to exercise daily for at least thirty minutes — even a walk will do. Exercise also enhances your agni, your ability to digest your food well and metabolize ama out of your body.

If you have the time and desire for a total makeover of your diet, I encourage you to try a more intense, individually tailored program for quicker results. Study the guidelines that follow to design your own cholesterol-conquering program without drugs or hormones.

General Guidelines for Lowering Cholesterol

First of all, follow the "Eat Your Way to Balance: Kapha" diet and the "Healing Meal Plan for All Imbalances," both in Chapter 4. Avoid processed and packaged foods, fried foods, restaurant meals, and foods containing saturated, hydrogenated, or trans fats (especially margarine and the partially hydrogenated oils found in packaged foods and baked goods). All of these can elevate cholesterol and lead to the formation of free-radical cholesterol complexes, a particularly dangerous plaque-promoting type of cholesterol.

Dietary Tips for Lowering Your Cholesterol

The following recommendations will optimize digestion and help clear ama from your rasa dhatu and meda dhatu (plasma and fat tissues) for better metabolism — and lower levels of fats and cholesterol.

- Drink your herbal water daily as instructed in Chapter 6 and be sure to include the spices and herbs recommended for balancing meda, which governs your fat metabolism.

- Set a regular schedule of mealtimes and stick to it.

- Don't eat between meals except for fresh fruit or other healthful snacks, if you really feel genuine hunger.

- Eat until you are satisfied, not stuffed, and eat slowly. When you dine out, bring a bag of your favorite herbal tea to enjoy at the end of the meal instead of going back for seconds before what you've already eaten "hits bottom." This will help you avoid overeating.

- Drink a half cup of warm water before the meal and sip more warm water throughout the meal.

- Eat proportionately more vegetables and legumes (including soy) than other food types, such as breads, dairy, and meats.

- If you are not having hot flashes, you may include fresh garlic in your daily diet. (Garlic is "heating" according to MAV and could trigger more flashes.) Sauté one crushed garlic clove in a little olive oil. Mix into your vegetables, soup, or grains. (While studies have not shown garlic extracts or powders to be effective at lowering cholesterol, MAV describes many beneficial effects of fresh garlic on the heart and blood vessels and recommends it, especially for people with vata- and kapha-related problems.)

Emissaries of Heart Health: Three Special Ayurvedic Herbs

All MAV herbal preparations contain a balanced combination of herbs, spices, and other substances to avoid negative effects. Formulas for a particular purpose are designed around specific herbs that are known to be outstanding in their healing effects on that condition. *Arjuna myrabolans* and *ashwagandha* are two such gems in the Ayurvedic treasury of herbs for heart health. Their purposes and effects are described briefly here, along with those of another Ayurvedic superstar, *guggulu*, a tree resin with a remarkable ability to lower cholesterol. (For information on obtaining balanced MAV formulas containing these heart-healthy herbs, see the Resources.)

Arjuna myrabolans (*Terminalia arjuna*). Arjuna is the best herb overall for the heart, according to the Ayurvedic texts. It is named after Arjuna, the warrior hero of the classical Indian *Mahabharata*, who in the story of the *Bhagavad-Gita* was emotionally torn between his duty to fight for righteousness and his loyalty to family members whom he would have to kill in battle. Like Arjuna, you can get caught between two opposing desires, a situation that is deeply disturbing to sadhaka pitta, the subdosha governing your emotional heart. Such stress can evoke in your body a toxic biochemical state that raises the "heart-wrenching" hormones cortisol and adrenaline.

Arjuna myrabolans calms and soothes sadhaka pitta, easing emotional stress and reducing levels of heart-damaging hormones, according to scientific studies. It is useful for nearly any type of heart disease because it supports both the physical and emotional hearts.

Ashwagandha (*Withania somnifera*) This powerful rejuvenating herb for the heart and the whole body helps any condition of weakness, whether due to illness, stress, lack of sleep, overwork, or advanced age. It is included in many preparations for heart problems due to its ability to reduce stress hormones like cortisol and adrenaline, improve immune function, and promote good sleep, an important factor in heart health. (*Somniference* means sleep in Latin.)

Guggulu (*Commiphora mukul*). Guggulu is a gum resin and a relative of the Biblical botanical spice myrrh. Guggulu is combined with a variety of other herbs to make specific formulas for different health problems, including high cholesterol, arthritis, and other inflammatory conditions; uterine fibroids; and thyroid nodules. In one study, treatment with guggulu reduced total cholesterol by 22 percent while increasing good cholesterol by 35 percent. A word of caution, however: Do not take guggulu "straight." If not properly formulated in combination with cooling and balancing herbs, or if taken inappropriately, guggulu may cause heartburn and other pitta-related symptoms.

Dietary Tips that Nourish Your Heart

The following tips include specific foods and spices described in the Ayurvedic texts as *hridayam* (hrih dyuhm), meaning "directly nourishing and supporting heart health." (*Hridaya* is the Sanskrit word for heart.)

• Squeeze a wedge of fresh lemon or lime on your food just before serving.

• Add a few sprinkles of freshly ground black pepper to your meal.

- Use freshly ground cardamom (or the whole pod or seeds as you prefer) daily as desired in your cooked cereal, cooked vegetables, tea, and the like.

- Include fresh pineapple in your diet.

- Eat some unsalted blanched almonds or walnuts every day. (Recommended in Ayurveda for thousands of years, nut consumption has recently been found to be associated with a dramatic reduction in heart disease risk. It also provides a rich, vegetarian source of omega-3 fatty acids, which are very good for the heart.)

- Start your breakfast each day with a stewed apple or pear. This supports ojas, immunity, elimination, digestion, metabolism, and balanced emotions. (See the recipe for nourishing stewed apple in Chapter 4 under "The Pitta Cleanse.")

- If you are prone to high blood pressure, avoid herbal mixtures, foods, and teas that contain licorice root, unless it has been deglycyrrhizinated, a process that removes any blood-pressure-increasing components. Licorice root can increase sodium and fluid retention, especially in women.

Maharishi Rejuvenation Treatment: Deeper Cleansing for Deep-Rooted Problems

Both MAV and modern medicine agree that diet and exercise are essential for normalizing cholesterol and promoting heart health. However, if symptoms are stubborn or a problem is deep-rooted, MAV recommends an aggressive "roto-rooter" technique for clearing ama, provided by a series of purification treatments known as *panchakarma* in the classical prescriptions and as Maharishi Rejuvenation Treatment (MRT) in MAV (see Chapter 6).

Maharishi Rejuvenation Treatment is a series of gentle but deep cleansing procedures that systematically dissolve ama, mobilize it out of your tissues, and promote its removal through your digestive tract. If you have a stubborn case of high cholesterol that does not respond as quickly as you'd like to your lifestyle changes, or you would like to jump-start your metabolism as you work to establish better dietary and lifestyle habits, then a week of in-residence MRT may be just what you need. (See the Resources for MAV treatment centers.)

MRT has proven itself on the testing fields of modern medicine. A study performed by Hari Sharma, M.D., and colleagues of Ohio State University showed a sudden drop in total cholesterol during and immediately following the treatment. MRT also increased HDL cholesterol (which helps clear excess cholesterol from the body) by 7.5 percent within three months after subjects completed a three- to five-day treatment program. MRT also lowered lipid peroxide, a measure of toxic, oxidized fat in the body. Research by Fagan and Herron shows that levels of pesticide, another potent category of toxins that may increase heart disease as well as cancer, are reduced by half in as little as five days of MRT.

These findings are all compatible with the MAV prediction that Maharishi Rejuvenation Treatment brings about a mobilization of ama and toxic wastes out of the body. They suggest that MRT may be very helpful as part of a comprehensive program to lower your cholesterol and heart disease risks and improve your overall health naturally.

Adopting a Heart-Healthy Lifestyle

A wealth of information on heart health has been presented in this chapter. Nearly all of it relies on you to carry it out. In case you are not yet following any of the recommended lifestyle habits, I offer the following suggestions to help you adopt a heart-healthy lifestyle:

• Start by trying to establish *one* new heart-healthy habit. Pick the one that you have wanted to try for a long time but have never gotten around to, or one that sounded fun or inspired you in some way. For example, perhaps you have been meaning to exercise for a long time and an energizing morning walk sounds inviting. Give it a try!

• Once a new habit is second nature to you, add another heart-healthy habit of your choosing. Perhaps this time it will be eating a lighter evening meal, with lots of vegetables and a cholesterol-lowering lentil soup, complete with the heart-healthy, antioxidant spices turmeric and fresh garlic. Continue gradually adding the recommended habits until you are reaping the benefits

• At any time, learn Transcendental Meditation to reduce your mental stress and directly lower your risk of heart disease. It's effortless to practice and so easy that anyone who can think a thought can do Transcendental Meditation.

• If you find it difficult to change your habits on your own, or you feel you are a tough case with lots of ama, or you just want to get a jump-start to better health, take a week of in-residence Maharishi Rejuvenation Treatment. You will make a quantum leap toward better health, inner calm, and new lifestyle habits for making vibrant health your reality.

* 8 *

YOUR BONES: STRONG WITHOUT DRUGS OR HT

Aggravated vata affecting the bones and bone marrow leads to porous bones.
— *the* Charaka Samhita

Since the advent of widespread bone density testing in the past decade, women and their doctors have become much more concerned about bone density and the prevention of osteoporosis. Indeed, the health of our bones should be a concern. Women of Asian and Caucasian heritage have nearly a 50 percent chance of breaking a bone due to low bone density after age fifty, and major fractures can seriously alter your life. Yet, while the concern about osteoporosis is justified, both the popular notion that osteoporosis is a disease caused by lack of estrogen after menopause and the usual treatments for low bone density, have been recently called into question.

ESTROGEN AND YOUR BONES

Prior to July 2002, when the Women's Health Initiative discovered that HT's risks outweigh its benefits, women often inquired about taking HT to prevent osteoporosis. Usually, their concern was voiced in an all-too-frequently asked question: "Without taking estrogen, won't I get osteoporosis?" Their concern reflected the still common misconception that osteoporosis is caused by declining or insufficient levels of estrogen after menopause. What follows, of course, is the assumption that estrogen therapy must be the key to prevention and treatment.

While such conclusions played handily into drug companies' marketing plans, it is just not that simple. Osteoporosis is not the inevitable result of declining estrogen levels, and declining estrogen is *not* the cause of osteoporosis. In actuality, scientists estimate that only about 15 percent of the bone mass we lose after age 30 is due to estrogen-related factors. An equal amount, roughly another 15 percent, is lost due to other factors, such as poor diet and lack of exercise. While lack of estrogen *contributes* to the development of osteoporosis in vulnerable women, it must share the stage equally with diet, exercise, and other factors.

Aging Not Solely Responsible

What role does aging play? Figures are often cited stating that women begin to lose 1 percent of their bone mass each year starting around age thirty, accelerating to 2 percent loss per year for the five years around menopause. This rate slows again, until a similar surge in loss occurs again after age 65 or 70. These statistics have lead many women and their doctors to conclude that bone loss and deterioration of the female frame is an inevitable part of the aging process.

But is it? More careful, longitudinal studies have since shown that such an inevitable decline is *not* normal for every woman. In fact, rates of loss vary considerably from woman to woman. Some lose very little bone over time and others lose a lot. Only about one-third of women were found to experience a rapid rate of loss around the time of menopause.

An interesting study on the bones of women of 19th century England found *no* bone loss at all before menopause and a rate of loss after menopause that was much slower than that documented in women today. The authors attributed the healthier bones of the 19th century women to a more wholesome diet and a more physically active lifestyle.

These studies substantiate the view that rapid bone loss is not inevitable with menopause, but varies with lifestyle habits and probably with genetics. And although losses of 1 percent or more per year after age thirty may be considered "normal" for our population today, they do not represent healthy aging. They reflect something that is *wrong* with our aging process. Getting older does not have to mean getting weaker, in our bones or otherwise.

Osteoporosis is *Preventable*

While most medical doctors and menopausal women have yet to get the message, leading experts in the field are now proclaiming that osteoporosis is not inevitable, is not a normal consequence of aging, and is preventable in almost everyone if its root causes are addressed and bone-weakening habits eliminated.

A recent National Institutes of Health Consensus Panel on Osteoporosis Prevention, Diagnosis, and Therapy declared: "Once thought to be a natural part of aging among women, osteoporosis is no longer considered age- or sex-dependent. It is largely preventable..." The report goes on to state that prevention of osteoporosis depends on optimizing our bone health from birth onward and that this process must occur *throughout* our lives, as an essential aspect of our lifestyle.

Peak Bone Mass Is an Important Factor

The NIH Panel report also emphasized that the amount of bone lost as we grow older is not the only factor that leads to osteoporosis. The amount of bone we start out with in early adulthood, our *peak bone mass*, is as important as later bone loss in the development of osteoporosis and largely determines whether later loss is significant enough to increase the risk of fractures.

Simply put, if you have very strong, dense bones to begin with (having achieved a good peak bone mass as a young adult) then losing 30 percent or more due to reduced estrogen, poor lifestyle habits, and "aging" over several decades probably won't weaken your bones enough to cause fractures. But if you start with low bone mass and a delicate skeleton, losing 30 percent could lead to vulnerable bones and a high risk of fractures in the future.

Table 8.1 will alert you to the factors you can and cannot change to reduce your risk of osteoporosis.

WHAT EXACTLY *IS* OSTEOPOROSIS?

Osteoporosis is a condition of the bones characterized by *decreased bone strength*. When bone strength decreases, you are more likely to have abnormal breakage or fractures. Your bone strength relies on two factors: *bone density*, the solidity of your bones, which depends on calcium, collagen and other substances, and *bone architecture*, the underlying structure and design of your bones.

Low bone density, caused by decreased calcium content in the bone structure, is the factor best known to cause bone weakness. There is so much attention on the

Table 8.1 Medically Known Risk Factors For Osteoporosis

Factors You Can Change	Factors You Cannot Change
Diet deficient in calcium	Family history
Diet deficient in vitamin D	Caucasian and Asian ethnicity
Lack of exercise	Advanced age
Cigarette smoking	Small frame
Excessive alcohol intake	Female gender
Underweight	History of major depression
Abnormal loss of menstrual periods	
Anorexia nervosa or bulimia	
Over-exercising associated with loss of menstruation	
Iron deficiency anemia	
Excessive ingestion of acidic foods and phosphate-containing soft drinks	
Excessive vitamin A intake (from supplements)	
Medications, such as certain anticonvulsants and steroids (including inhaled steroids)	
Some injectable contraceptives	
Hormone-suppressing treatment (such as for endometriosis)	
Hyperthyroidism (including excessive or inappropriate use of thyroid hormone therapy)	
Hyperparathyroidism	

density of bones today that it is easy to think of osteoporosis as simply very low bone density. But the density of your bones, which accounts for about 70 percent of your bone strength, is only one of several factors that may weaken your bones and lead to fractures. It just happens to be emphasized because it is currently the only factor that we can directly measure.

Another important factor determining how strong your bones are is *bone architecture*. Bone architecture, just like house architecture, refers to how well-designed and well-built your bones are, and is a bone attribute that also tends to deteriorate with age.

When looked at under a microscope, your bones appear like the steel skeleton of a skyscraper under construction. If the construction quality of the many supporting "girders" is poor, the bone will be brittle, even though there is plenty of calcium present to cause good density. Imagine the skyscraper is built of the densest, hardest steel, but the girders are poorly aligned to handle the weight of so many stories. The floors may collapse, even though the raw material itself was strong.

Table 8.2 summarizes the myths and facts about the modern medical understanding and approach to osteoporosis.

Age and Your Bone Strength

Our risk of bone fracture tends to increase as we get older because bone density, bone architecture, and bone strength all tend to decline over time. But as you may recall, lack of estrogen and aging are not enough to cause osteoporosis in most women. It takes lack of calcium, inadequate exercise, and other preventable factors over a lifetime to make bones vulnerable to breaking. Nature did not intend for us to fall apart as we age!

And despite your doctor's concern over low bone density results, such reports don't necessarily mean you have brittle bones. Your bone strength depends partially on your age. Even if a woman has low bone density at age fifty, she is much less likely to break your hip than a woman with the same bone density who is in her seventies or eighties. This is generally attributed to better quality of bone architecture in younger women. Younger bones are better able to withstand the stress of a fall or sudden impact without breaking. What this means is that you can be diagnosed as having "osteoporosis" simply from a low reading on a bone density test, when in actuality, your bones may still be quite strong.

Recent research has uncovered further "good news" regarding bone strength and the body's incredible ability to compensate for hormonal and other shifts as we age. As estrogen level drops, the bones may lose density, but they also tend to gain actual *thickness* as measured by the diameter of the bone. This means that if your bones were shaped like a hollow pen, the outside of the pen is getting bigger around, as if more plastic is being added to the outer surface. This adaptation helps to strengthen the bone and compensate for loss of bone density on the inner surfaces of the bone as we age.

Finally, regardless of our age, our bone cells remains extremely sensitive to increases in weight-bearing (i.e., exercise), and respond by laying down more and stronger bone. The result of more exercise is stronger bones, whether we are eight or eighty!

The most important action you can take if you are diagnosed with low bone density or osteoporosis is to *stay active*. Curtailing your exercise and activities out of fear of breaking a bone will only make you *more* likely to fracture over time. Get moving, keep moving, and enjoy the feeling of agility, self-sufficiency, and energy that you gain as you build your bone and muscle strength through a regular exercise program. Treating this condition *can* be fun and empowering!

Bone Changes at Menopause

At menopause, your bone's architecture undergoes changes that directly affect the strength of your bones. Two processes of bone growth are involved: bone remodeling and bone turnover rate.

Your bones are not static. They are constantly undergoing a process of *remodeling*, or rebuilding. Just as a jet plane must be inspected regularly for tiny cracks in its steel structure, your bones are continually monitored for weak areas and then repaired by this remodeling process. To accomplish this, *osteoclasts*, or bone-eating cells, continually chew holes in your bones to get rid of weaker, older bone, and *osteoblasts*, or bone-making cells, fill in these holes with new, stronger bone.

The speed at which remodeling of your bone occurs is your *bone turnover rate*, and it depends on the coordination between removing old bone and making new bone. If bone is chewed up faster than the resultant gaps can be filled, your bones may develop thin, weak spots where breaks can easily occur. And this is exactly what tends to occur in some women at menopause: Tiny cracks and empty "potholes" accumulate faster than they can be filled in, making the bone weaker and more prone to fracture.

Modern medicine doesn't know why this increased rate of bone breakdown occurs at midlife, but it does have treatments that have been shown to slow the process. In women with osteoporosis, these treatments have been shown to reduce fractures, at least in the first few years of taking them. However, for women with *osteopenia*, a milder degree of bone loss than osteoporosis (the category in which most midlife women with low bone density fall) none of these treatments have been proven to prevent fractures or to be without side effects.

Let's look at the benefits and pitfalls of some of the treatments for osteoporosis available today, both medical and nonmedical. Then I will show you how Maharishi Ayurveda can be used to improve your bone health and prevent osteoporosis without drugs and without hormones, in a truly natural approach.

HORMONAL AND DRUG TREATMENT FOR OSTEOPOROSIS

Let's review the most common drug and hormonal approaches for preventing osteoporosis used by women today, which include hormone therapy (HT), bisphosphonate therapy (such as Fosamax and Actonel), and "natural progesterone" creams and pills.

Hormone Therapy (HT)

It is well-established that HT improves bone density — 6 percent within the first few years of use — in the hip and spine. And results from the Women's Health Initiative, the first large-scale trial to test HT's effect on fractures — the *bottom-line* issue in osteoporosis treatment — confirmed that fracture risk of the hip and spine was reduced by about 33 percent compared to women on placebo. However, the HT regimen used in the Women's Health Initiative resulted in so many excess heart attacks, strokes, blood clots, and breast cancers that use of HT solely for the prevention of osteoporosis is no longer recommended.

Researchers are now testing the effects of "ultra-low" HT regimens on bone density using bioidentical estrogen at one-quarter the usual dose, in an effort to reduce negative side effects. This regimen resulted in increases in bone density over three years with no evidence of the side effects usually associated with HT. However, longer term follow-up is needed to assess whether this increase in bone density results in actual reduction of fractures and to be sure that increased breast cancer risk and other negative effects do not occur with long-term use.

Ultra-low-dose estrogen may someday prove effective at reducing fractures, especially in women with very low endogenous (naturally-present) estrogen levels after menopause who are at increased risk of fractures. For now, however, it is probably wise to avoid taking HT simply for the prevention of osteoporosis.

Bisphosphonate Therapy (Fosamax and Actonel)

Women who don't want the risks of HT, but are at risk for osteoporosis, are often encouraged to take Fosamax, a drug belonging to the class called *bisphosphonates*. These drugs dramatically reduce the rate of bone turnover (your bone's repair cycle) and within the first year of use can reduce the risk of fractures by as much as 65 percent. At first glance, such statistics make these drugs seem too good to pass up for a woman with low bone density concerned about fractures. Yet, their long-term safety and efficacy has been brought into question by some experts.

The results of one of the most important studies on osteoporosis treatment to date, the Fracture Intervention Trial (FIT) at the University of California, San Francisco, showed that in the first year of bisphosphonate treatment, bone density increased by about 6 percent and fractures were reduced a dramatic 50 to 60 percent. Extra bone density *plus* reduced fractures sounds either too good to be passed up or too good to be true. But in medicine, as in life, there is no free lunch. If we manipulate the body powerfully, without the guidance of the body's own inner intelligence, there is likely to be some fallout somewhere.

Remember the process of *bone remodeling*, the process in which your bones are in a constant state of breaking down and building up? Bisphosphonates work by slowing down the speed of your bone's chewing cells (osteoclasts), so that the repair crews (osteoblasts) can catch up and fill in bone, shoring up critical weak points in the bones where fractures are more likely to occur. But in later years, slowed bone turnover rates may mean that tiny stress fractures are not removed and replaced in a timely manner, resulting eventually in *weaker* bones that are *more* prone to fracture. It is altogether possible that women who take these drugs for ten years or more may end up with weaker bones than they started with.

Indeed, research is showing that the benefit of these drugs at reducing fracture *is less* with each successive year of use. A follow-up study to FIT found that after seven years, bone density was greater in the women on Fosamax, but fracture risk was *the same* as those who were not taking it, supporting the concern that the benefit of these drugs may be short-lived.

Currently Fosamax is being recommended if you have already had a fracture due to osteoporosis, test in the severely osteoporotic range, or are over age seventy and at high risk of fracture. The assumption is that you might benefit from the quick, short-term reduction in your risk of breaking a bone. However, if you are younger, you may be trading off early protection that you don't really need for further problems down the line. A thorough discussion with your doctor is in order if you are advised to take one of these drugs.

"Natural Progesterone"

In the widely read book *What Your Mother May Not Tell You About Menopause: The Breakthrough Book on Natural Progesterone*, Dr. John Lee popularized the notion that "natural progesterone" cream, more accurately called *bioidentical progesterone*, is a dramatically effective way to increase your bone density. His research involved observations and data on about sixty-five women in his practice who took bioidentical progesterone cream for three years. All of them were reportedly following his recommendations for exercise, diet, and vitamin and mineral supplementation, and 40 percent of them were also taking estrogen. He reported as much as a 23 percent increase in bone density in the lumbar spine over a three-year period in those patients.

However, there are several problems with this study. Besides the fact that there is no control group, the use of estrogen along with progesterone in almost half the subjects, as well as the effects of exercise and vitamin/mineral supplements on all the subjects, confound the picture. A follow-up study by other researchers — a randomized, controlled trial with 102 postmenopausal women — compared the effects of bioidentical progesterone cream with a placebo on bone density at the spine and hip. After one year, there was no difference in bone density between the women taking progesterone and those on the placebo.

Another larger trial, the Postmenopausal Estrogen/Progestogen Intervention Trial (PEPI), also failed to show that bioidentical progesterone, when taken orally, increases bone density beyond that of estrogen alone. Add to this the recently discovered breast cancer-increasing effects of progestins and it is clear that taking *any* kind of progesterone, whether synthetic or "natural," to increase bone density is not advisable based on the best evidence available today.

Osteoporosis: Myth vs. Fact

Below is summary of the myths and facts about the modern medical understanding and approach to osteoporosis.

NATURAL APPROACHES TO BONE HEALTH

None of the modern medical approaches available, notably HT and Fosamax, are FDA approved or recommended if a woman is premenopausal or perimenopausal and in her thirties or forties; appropriately so, given that they have not been proven helpful. Yet, many women in that age range are being tested and told they have *osteopenia*, bone density that is lower than normal but not yet osteoporosis. In fact, a recent study found that approximately 28 to 45 percent of midlife women currently have osteopenia, depending on what measuring device is used for diagnosis. This includes many women in their fifties, who are increasingly being prescribed drugs to increase their bone density. A Merck study estimates that about one-third of women diagnosed with osteopenia are currently taking a drug for it.

Yet, due to lack of convincing data and the potential for long-term side effects, the best experts in the field are recommending *against* drugs or HT for these midlife women. Given the age limitations recognized by the FDA, and researcher's doubt about long-term use of these drugs, what should you do if you are one of these women with osteopenia?

First of all, don't panic. Keep in mind that your condition of low bone density can in many cases be improved as effectively through changing your diet and exercise habits as by taking drug or hormone therapy. You are not at immediate risk of

Table 8.2 Osteoporosis: Myth vs. Fact

MYTH	FACT.
#1. Osteoporosis is a disease of postmenopausal women that originates in childhood.	Osteoporosis is a disease of women and men.
#2. Osteoporosis is a disease caused by lack of estrogen.	Osteoporosis is a degenerative and nutritional disease, due to lack of proper diet and exercise over a lifetime.
#3 Your bone density determines your risk of fracture.	Bone density is only one factor affecting fracture risk. Bone quality, calcium and vitamin D intake, age and your level of muscle strength and fitness also affect it.
#4. If you have osteopenia (low bone density) but not osteoporosis, Fosamax will increase it so that you won't get fractures.	Fosamax has *not* been shown to be effective at reducing fractures in women with osteopenia if they have not yet had a fracture, even though it increases their bone density.
#5 "Natural progesterone" is an effective treatment or prevention for osteoporosis.	Bioidentical progesterone cream was not shown to have any effect on bone density in the only controlled clinical trial conducted so far. The oral capsule form has not increased bone density or reduced fracture risk beyond the effects of estrogen given concurrently in clinical trials thus far.

fracture, and you have plenty of time to accrue the benefits of new bone-health habits for stronger, healthy bones later in life — if you get started now.

Besides, just because your doctor gives you a drug or hormone tablet does not mean you are suddenly immune to getting a fracture later in life. Estrogen therapy does not prevent two-thirds of fractures, and Fosamax may not prevent any in later life. Rushing off to your doctor for a pill to cure your low bone density or "osteopenia" as diagnosed by a test in midlife is not justified by the research thus far, and is discouraged by the best experts in the field.

Experts, such as Dr. Bruce Ettinger, senior researcher at the Kaiser Permanente Medical Program in northern California, are advising women in their forties and fifties with osteopenia to stick to natural, nondrug, and nonhormonal interventions He has stated: "Drugs for osteoporosis should be reserved for those at highest risk and should not be used for healthy women in their fifties who have osteopenia… Alendronate (the generic term for the leading drug in this class, Fosamax,) is accumulating in bone and staying there, possible forever. Will this eventually be a good or a bad thing? We don't know. Recent five- to seven-year data on alendronate give us reason to be concerned… Stay with nondrug interventions for younger women at risk."

Regardless of your age, natural therapies like soy products in your diet, enough calcium and vitamin D, and regular exercise offer a preventive treatment approach for improving your bone density years *before* osteoporosis fractures are likely to occur. An added plus is that these approaches can be continued indefinitely without side effects.

Soy Products

There is some scientific evidence that soy protein and soy *isoflavones*, the phytoestrogenic ingredient in soy products as well as whole soy food, may increase bone density in the spine. So far, research has not demonstrated any increase in bone density in the hip and more research in needed to assess soy's effect on fractures. However, concentrated isoflavone pills, in addition to being less effective than whole soy, are quite estrogenic and may turn out to have side effects similar to estrogen itself. Whole soy protein and foods such as tofu, soy milk, and tempeh, may be safer. They tend to be rich in calcium and exert a gentler estrogen-like effect on bone. Stay tuned for more research and more dependable findings on soy for your bones in the coming years.

Calcium Supplementation

An adequate supply of calcium is essential for healthy bones and should be a gained from your food rather than supplements if possible. If you already have enough calcium in your diet, taking calcium supplements will not improve your bone density.

An adequate supply of calcium in your body requires a balance between what you consume and what you excrete. A diet high in protein, especially animal protein, can cause you to excrete more calcium through your kidneys. A recent study by Dr. Sellmeyer and colleagues at University of California, San Francisco, found that women over the age of sixty-five with diets high in vegetable protein and low in animal protein (as in a vegetarian diet) lost bone at a slower rate and had a lower risk of hip fractures than those consuming higher amounts of animal protein. Caffeine in coffee and black tea, phosphorus in commercial soft drinks, and sodium (either from table salt or hidden in prepared and packaged foods), all leach calcium and threaten bone density. Reducing your intake of these bone-leaching foods and drinks, and eating a more vegetarian diet are positive steps you can take to protect your bones naturally.

How Much Calcium Is Enough?

The recommended daily allowance for calcium intake in postmenopausal women is currently 1,500 milligrams per day. This means the total calcium present in your food plus any supplements you may take. Women often think this means they need to take 1,500 milligrams of calcium supplement in addition to diet. That is not the case. In fact, it could be dangerous.

If you are digesting and assimilating well, you may not even need 1,500 milligrams of calcium per day after menopause to prevent bone loss. Studies have shown that rural Chinese women and native Argentineans, in whom osteoporosis is rare, typically consume as little as 400 milligrams of calcium per day, mostly from vegetable sources. Their active lifestyle and the good metabolism that follows from that, and possibly the soy in the Chinese diet, all contribute to their healthy bones.

The danger of overdosing on calcium supplements was brought home to me by the experience of one of my patients, who followed the advice of her doctor to take 1,500 milligrams of calcium citrate supplement each day. Within three months, she noticed a strange metallic taste in her mouth and started feeling tired and nauseated. She returned to her internist for evaluation. A blood test revealed a serum calcium level above 15 (normal is less than 11). She was in serious danger of cardiac arrhythmia and her kidneys had begun to fail, which was the cause of her symptoms. Fortunately, a treatment of aggressive hydration to flush out the calcium quickly returned her serum calcium and kidney function to normal. Of course she stopped taking the supplements, and no serious ill effects persisted.

This was an unusual incident, to be sure. However, it was a valuable lesson that calcium supplements in excess can be too much of a good thing. This incident further points out that overloading your body with large doses of single nutrients (the magic bullet effect again) is not natural. It is always better to get what you need from your food. If you are not getting enough calcium from your diet, supplement the *difference* according to your need and be cautious not to go beyond it. (Refer to the sidebar to help calculate your daily intake and guide you in including more calcium-rich foods in your diet.)

Vitamin D: The Sunshine Vitamin

Another important ingredient for normal bone metabolism is vitamin D. You can get your daily dose from your diet or from supplements. Or you can expose a

Common Dietary Calcium Sources	
Dairy	**Nondairy**
Milk: 1 cup, 275 mg Yogurt: 1 cup, 296 mg Cheese: 1 1/2 oz., 306 mg	Tofu: ½ cup, 204 mg Sesame seeds: 1 Tbsp, 87 mg Almonds: 1 oz. (about 24 almonds), 70 mg Cooked spinach: 1/2 cup, 122 mg Cooked broccoli: 1 cup, 62 mg Chickpeas (garbanzo beans): 1 cup, 80 mg Boiled fresh collard greens: 1/2 cup, 133 mg

sunscreen-free area of your skin, equivalent to the face and arms, to sunlight for about twenty minutes per day, year round. Because vitamin D is fat soluble, your body can store enough of it to last several months at a time, so lots of sun on the body in the warmer months may be adequate enough to get you through the winter.

If you don't want to expose your skin without a sunscreen for protection, you need to know that sunscreen reduces vitamin D synthesis in the skin. A reasonable solution is to take a supplement of 400 to 800 International Units (IUs) of vitamin D per day. Also, walking outdoors before 9 or 10 A.M., when the sun is less direct, works well for many women.

Exercise

Starting an exercise program, especially if you have been previously inactive, can increase your bone density by as much as 6 percent in a year, a rate that is similar to that seen in women taking HT or biphosphonate therapy (Fosamax). And it's never too late to start. One study found that women in their eighties could increase the bone density in their hips simply by holding on to a chair and stomping their feet for several minutes each day! However, as with HT, bone density starts to go down again if you stop exercising. That's good motivation to start exercising and stick with your program — it's the most effective method of improving your bone density naturally.

Like most natural approaches, exercise gives benefits in more ways than one. Exercise reduces the risk of falls, another major cause of fractures, by 25 percent, according to randomized clinical trials reported by the recent NIH Panel on Osteoporosis Prevention, Diagnosis and Therapy. As we get older, we have a tendency to fall more easily due to problems with balance, vision, reaction time, and reduced muscle power. However, most of this deterioration is not due to inevitable effects of aging, but due to lack of "practice" as we get more sedentary in later life.

Regular exercise and balance training through Tai Chi, yoga, sports, Pilates and other coordination-enhancing exercises can help keep reactions youthful and should be included in every lifelong exercise program.

Combining exercise with adequate calcium and vitamin D intake can reduce your risk of fractures by over 30 percent, about the same amount seen in osteoporosis patients treated with Fosamax for three years — a little known fact the drug companies do not care to publicize! Given these very real benefits of exercise, you'd be wise to start your exercise program today if you haven't already, no matter what your age.

Studies have found that in general, the stronger your muscles are, the stronger your bones are. Any activity that builds your muscle strength will help to build your bone strength at the same time, although exercises that use your largest muscles against gravity — *weight bearing* — are most effective. Good news for swimmers: Recent studies have found that swimming can increase bone density in your back, contrary to prior belief that it was not weight bearing and therefore not effective at building bone. Another example of how strengthening adjacent muscles can strengthen your bones.

What is the ideal exercise regimen for your bones? One study found that women could increase their bone density by 6 percent in only six months with a regimen of aerobics for 1 ½ hours and weights for ½ hour three times a week. If this sounds too rigorous for you, schedule some regular walking, jogging, dancing, bicycling, or aerobics — even 20-30 minutes a day will do it. Just get started with *something* and the well-being you begin to feel will keep you coming back for more!

Healthy Bones through MAV

In MAV, osteoporosis is known literally as "porous bones" and is believed to result from physiological imbalances, not from aging. Osteoporosis is described as a disorder of vata dosha, which most commonly occurs in the vata time of life (or the latter third). This is the time after menopause when degenerative, vata-related disorders are most common.

The medical establishment commonly cites figures indicating women lose 1 percent of their bone mass each year after age thirty and 2 percent or more each year during perimenopause and into postmenopause. But, as we have seen, as many as two-thirds of women do not fit this profile. Indeed, I have seen this midlife bone loss completely obliterated and women *gain* bone at this time of life, simply by applying MAV therapies to balance vata and supporting bone health naturally, from the inside out. What it takes is proper attention to diet and exercise, as well as some specific vata-balancing approaches to enhance calcium absorption and utilization by your bone tissue.

The following story of Jennifer's treatment with MAV demonstrates the very real results possible for bone health through this nondrug, truly holistic approach.

Jennifer's Story: Gaining Bone in Midlife, Naturally

Jennifer, an interior designer, came to see me at age forty-two, when she noticed that her periods had become irregular. A blood test revealed that Jennifer's FSH level was elevated, indicating the onset of menopause, a bit on the early side of the normal 45-55 age range. Within a year, Jennifer's periods had stopped altogether.

"I've had very few hot flashes, more like a few warm flushes, and only if I'm under stress or not getting enough rest," Jennifer reported. "But I *am* concerned about my bones. My twin sister had a bone density test, and it was low. She's starting on HT. But our mother died of breast cancer and I don't want to risk taking hormones."

A bone density test of her hip and spine revealed a moderate degree of low bone density, or osteopenia, at the hip, although the spine was normal.

I explained to Jennifer that since her bones were still basically strong and fractures due to low bone density wouldn't be a concern for many years, it was completely safe to try some natural approaches to improving her bone density. I assured her we would monitor the result, and change our treatment approach if what we were doing wasn't working.

Jennifer decided to pursue a completely natural approach, focusing on balancing vata dosha through diet and lifestyle, continuing her regular exercise, and getting adequate dietary calcium. I also advised Jennifer to undergo the purifying process of panchakarma, or Maharishi Rejuvenation Therapy (MRT), once a year for the profound balancing effect it has on vata dosha, as well its ability to rid ama from the body. Classical texts of Ayurvedic medicine recommend panchakarma as the best treatment for osteoporosis.

Finally, I recommended a traditional herbal supplement from MAV that contains organic sources of calcium (derived from pearls and conch shell) plus herbs to help their absorption. (See the Resources for information on where to obtain this and other products.)

Four years later, Jennifer had another bone density test. Instead of losing 8 percent or more, as is commonly predicted for the average woman during the first four years after menopause, Jennifer had *gained* 4.5 percent.

Not only did Jennifer's gain in bone density bode well for the future health of her bones, but her achievement confirms that bone loss is *not* inevitable at menopause. Loss of bone is due to an imbalance that can be corrected, not an inevitable result of menopause *per se*, or of "aging."

Several other women in my practice over the past 10 years have had comparable or even greater improvements in their bone density, without hormones or drugs. These women, either perimenopausal or early postmenopausal, and ranging in age from forty-two to fifty-five have experienced similar gains in their bone density at a time when they technically are expected to be undergoing accelerated rates of bone loss.

Most of these women followed a combined approach of improved diet and calcium intake, increased exercise, daily oil massage, and MAV supplements for better assimilation and utilization of dietary calcium. One fifty-four-year young patient, Maria, achieved a gain of 15 percent in her hip bone density after only one year of MAV herbal calcium alone, without even increasing her exercise. While I wouldn't expect every woman to have this dramatic a result, and certainly recommend exercising for increasing bone density *as well as* so many other reasons, it was an impressive indication of the potential power of the MAV calcium supplements to support bone health.

Balance Vata to Build Bone

Balancing vata dosha is critically important to improving your bone density and treating osteoporosis. Anything that disturbs vata dosha — whether from diet or lifestyle choices — can reduce assimilation and affect your bones and other tissues. Such factors as irregular meals, late nights, mental stress, inadequate nutrition, overwork, and lack of exercise can all throw your vata dosha out of balance and thus contribute to weakened bones.

You may recall how vata dosha governs all movement and flow in the body. This includes assimilation of nutrients, such as the flow of calcium across the intestinal lining and delivery of nutrients directly to the bones through your circulatory system. As the governing intelligence of all bodily activity, vata is also responsible for keeping the rate of your bone turnover balanced.

I have described how your bones are in a constant state of renewal and repair through the process of remodeling. For most of your life span, the remodeling proceeds at a steady pace in healthy bones. Around the time of menopause, however, the pace of remodeling, and thus bone turnover, tends to speed up (a decidedly vata-like turn of events, since vata is associated with quickness and dominates at the time of menopause).

However, excess vata also tends to create a *kshaya*, or wasting effect on your tissues. In other words, excess vata tends to make you lose mass from your tissues, including your muscles and bones. This is exactly what can happen at menopause, when old bone is eliminated faster than new bone is formed. Translated into modern medical terms, this means your osteoclasts begin to chew up your bone up faster than your osteoblasts can fill in the gaps, resulting in a net loss of bone density. MAV provides a way to treat the root of this speedup by restoring overall balance to the body, rather than by slowing down the process with a drug like Fosamax.

How to Balance Vata

Here are some specific recommendations you can incorporate into your life to ensure a more balanced vata dosha for bone health. Also see Chapter 4 for more information on balancing vata dosha.

- Give yourself abhyanga (self-massage with oil) every day. Oil is the most vata-pacifying physical substance there is. Applying oil to your body daily is a powerful way to balance your vata, calm your nerves, increase assimilation, and ultimately strengthen your bones. Choose your massage oil according to the guidelines given in Chapter 4. For added effect on your bone tissue, add eight drops of pure essential oil of peppermint to one-eighth cup of your oil for application on your legs, hips, and spine area.

- Eat your meals on time and do not skip any meals, especially lunch.

- Go to bed early, preferably by 10 P.M.

- Walk for twenty to thirty minutes each day in the early morning sun.

- Take measures to reduce mental stress and worry.

Strengthen Your Digestive Fire to Build Strong Bones

MAV states that good digestion and metabolism are both fundamental to bone health and gives you practical ways to maximize these critical functions of your body.

We have seen how the imbalance of a dosha cannot by itself cause disease — it is when the tissues of your body themselves become disrupted that disease develops. This happens through a weakening of your agni, or the digestive fire that breaks down your food before it can be delivered to your cells and tissues for their nourishment. Weak digestion can cause lack of assimilation of calcium and other bone nutrients, as well as ama build up that further blocks the delivery of nourishment to your tissues, leaving them starved, weak, and vulnerable to disease.

At menopause, buildup of wastes and impurities can disrupt the remodeling that is necessary for your bones to remain strong. The influence of vata at this time throws off the coordination of bone chewing and bone repair. According to MAV theory, this ama build-up creates more trouble by choking off the maze of tiny channels called *canaliculi* that carry nutrients into the bone, and wastes out. Estrogen, calcitonin, parathyroid, and other important bone hormones course through the bone along canaliculi, guiding and adjusting the process of remodeling in a way that keeps your bone metabolism balanced. When they are blocked, your bones can become weak and porous, making them increasingly vulnerable to osteoporotic fractures.

How to Banish Bone-Breaking Wastes

Keeping your digestion and assimilation strong and your bones ama-free are important factors in bone health. Follow these recommendations to improve your digestive fire for good bone-building metabolism.

• Drink your herbalized water daily for three to six months. Refer to Chapter 6 for your personalized recipe and be sure to add the herbs and spices listed specifically for your bone tissue, as well as for meda, your fat tissue, which "cooks" for your bones. Your herbal water helps clear wastes from your tissues and its various herbs and spices give phytoestrogen support.

• Eat regular meals of wholesome, fresh ingredients.

• Eat your main meal at noon and have any nonvegetarian foods, which are harder to digest, at lunchtime only.

• Eat a lighter meal in the evening, preferably vegetarian without cheese, yogurt, or other curdled products, which can cause channel-blocking ama when eaten late in the day.

• Eat plenty of green, leafy vegetables, cooked until tender for better assimilation.

• Include sesame seeds in your daily diet. They are high in calcium and especially nourishing to the bones, according to MAV. Try adding them to stir-fry vegetables or your morning cooked cereal. Grinding them first in a spice grinder will aid assimilation. Or eat tahini (ground sesame butter) with a little jam or jelly, or try hummus made with tahini and chickpeas, both of which are good sources of calcium.

• Eat eight to ten blanched almonds several times per week. Soak in water overnight and remove the skins before eating for greater digestibility and for pitta-balancing effect. Almonds are high in calcium and especially nourishing to bones.

• Include dairy in your diet, but do not drink milk with a full meal or with fresh fruits or anything salty. Milk is best as a snack with grains, unsalted nuts, or dried sweet fruits such as dates or raisins. Boiling it with a pinch of cardamom and ginger and drinking it at bedtime is a good habit for most women, if your evening meal was light. Boiling your milk enhances digestibility and reduces its kapha- or mucus-increasing effect.

• Include some power grains (see Chapter 6) in your diet each day. They are rich in minerals and provide phytoestrogen support.

Are You Concerned About Low Bone Density?

If you are age forty to fifty-five and have osteopenia (low bone density, not yet osteoporosis) and have not had a fracture related to it, these guidelines provide a balanced approach to your bone density problem:

If your last bone density scan was more than a year ago, get a baseline DEXA scan of your hip and spine, or alternatively a peripheral bone density measurement (which has been shown to be as effective at predicting fracture risk). Make sure that your doctor checks for other contributing factors such as thyroid disease, parathyroid problems, or medications you may be taking, and get those addressed. Then proceed with the following all-natural treatment program for at *least* one year and at most *two* years. After that time, repeat your bone density test, ideally on the same machine. Discuss the results with your physician and, if needed, re-evaluate your approach with his or her input.

If you already have osteoporosis, or had a fracture due to low bone density, discuss treatment options with your physician and make a collaborative decision that you are comfortable with regarding HT or drug therapy. Make sure your doctor monitors your progress at least once a year with a bone density test. Meanwhile, be sure to follow the guidelines below to ensure that you are doing everything possible to strengthen your bones.

- Exercise for at least 30 minutes every day on average, including weight-bearing and aerobic forms.
- Include calcium rich foods in your daily diet, totaling 1,500 mg/day, with supplements if needed.
- Be sure to get adequate sunshine. If you can't, take 800 IU of vitamin D daily.
- Give yourself an abhyanga — oil massage — daily to help balance your vata and nourish your bones.
- Reduce meat intake and include a variety of organic, non-GMO soy products in your diet.
- Give your bones phytoestrogen and metabolic support by drinking your wise water and using your smart spice mixture daily (see Chapter 6).
- Follow the other tips given in this chapter for balancing vata and improving your bone strength and metabolism.

• Exercise daily for at least thirty minutes at about 50 percent of your capacity. Include light weights or other resistance exercise to build muscle and bone strength, as well as brisk walking or other aerobic activity to improve circulation, digestion, and metabolism.

• If you are not getting enough calcium in your diet, you may supplement with over-the-counter calcium. However, MAV holds that nutrients in your food are assimilated better and less likely to imbalance your system in any way. You may also wish to take the MAV herbal calcium supplement that I mentioned earlier. (See the Resources for product information.)

• To enhance absorption, use your digestive spice mixture from Chapter 6 in cooking and when eating out. This will help you digest and assimilate the calcium in your diet.

Your Elimination and Your Bones

Another factor involved in bone health, according to MAV, is the health of your colon, that part of your large intestine that extends to the rectum. Vata dosha is said to have its main seat or "home" in the colon, underscoring again the pivotal role of vata in bone health.

The colon is lined with a thin mucous membrane (*purisha dhara kala*), which absorbs water and electrolytes back into your body before elimination. This membrane is described in the Vedic medical texts as intimately associated with the membrane surrounding the bones (*asthi dhara kala*, or "periosteum" in Latin) and is key to both healthy bones and a healthy colon. Any disorders of the colon, such as chronic constipation or chronic diarrhea, can affect the colon's mucous membrane and thus bone health, so any treatment program for osteoporosis should consider them. (See my recommendations for correcting these elimination disorders at the end of Chapter 6.)

Maharishi Rejuvenation Therapy (Panchakarma): The Ultimate Bone-Building Treatment

Diseases due to the vitiation of bone tissue should be treated by panchakarma (five elimination therapies)
— *the* Charaka Samhita

You recall that vata dosha is key to bone health, that oil massage balances vata, that toxic ama buildup can weaken the bones, and that the colon is the home of vata in the physiology. So it is no wonder that MRT, which uses oils, a mild herbal enema, and heat application to balance vata and eliminate ama, is the ultimate, most intensely balancing treatment for osteoporosis in MAV.

As in Jennifer's case, I have observed that MRT can be very helpful in restoring strength to the bone tissue and normalizing bone metabolism. While it takes months or even years to reverse low bone density, imbalance in vata dosha and the accumulated layers of ama in the tissues that are causing further loss can be greatly reduced in just a week of treatment. And while medically effective, MRT is also one very nurturing, deeply rejuvenating, and relaxing week of pampering and luxury. As well it should be, for to balance vata dosha, your mind, emotions, and nervous system must also be deeply soothed.

Unfortunately, not everyone has the time or resources to take advantage of MRT. However, everyone can make the time to do a mini-MRT at home, every day, by giving herself an abhyanga (oil massage). And following the three-step foundation program described in Chapter 6, along with the dietary points in Chapter 4 for optimizing your diet and assimilation and eliminating ama, will allow you to gain some of the cleansing benefits of MRT on your own.

Healthy Bones Are within Your Reach

I hope these approaches from MAV, along with other natural approaches like exercise and increased calcium intake from food, will give you tools that quell your apprehension about osteoporosis at a time when low bone density is being diagnosed for so many midlife women. You are not helpless and you do have options other than drugs and hormones — regardless of what your health care practitioner may be telling you. Put some or all of these bone-saving therapies into effect right now and enjoy living the rest of your life with strong, healthy bones to carry you forth.

9

Your Mind — Out of the Fog, Into the Light

Complete transcending is the best among the sources of health.
— *the* Charaka Samhita

If you are over forty years old, you may have begun to notice that your memory or mental reflexes are sometimes slow or off. At first, it may be merely annoying to find you have forgotten the name of a family friend, an important client, or a fact you need at work. As this age-related "brain fog" becomes more frequent, however, it can become concerning. Our worst fear is that at the peak of our lives some sort of irreversible decline is setting in, leading gradually to dementia in old age.

But there is no need to panic. Walking into another room only to wonder what you were going to get, losing your train of thought in mid-sentence, or losing your keys are all normal midlife memory lapses. For the overwhelming majority of women over forty, such lapses are *not* a harbinger of Alzheimer's disease, the disease of the brain that afflicts the elderly and robs them of memory, identity, and even the ability to recognize their loved ones. Such "senior moments" occur from midlife on in both men and women, as any woman with male peers or a spouse can attest, and are a normal part of the midlife shift.

Estrogen Replacement and Your Brain

Mild memory loss is a normal midlife phenomenon for both men and women. However, significant memory impairment is present in as many as one third of older adults in America, and by eighty-five years of age, fully one-half of our population suffers from Alzheimer's disease, and two out of three are women. With such a female predominance, one must address the questions of "What role does estrogen play in this disease?" and "Can replacing hormones after menopause help prevent cognitive breakdown later in life?"

HT and Your Brain: What the Studies Show

Women who naturally have higher levels of their own estrogen (*endogenous* estrogen) after menopause do perform better on memory tests than women of the same age who have lower levels, according to some studies. But we must ask: Is their improved memory a direct result of having more endogenous estrogen, or are both better memory and higher estrogen levels secondary to other lifestyle factors, such as better nutrition and exercise, or to metabolic factors? If it really was the higher estrogen, then women who had early menstruation and late menopause would be likely to have less Alzheimer's disease and cognitive decline due to longer exposure to their own natural hormones. However, studies show they do not.

In fact, some experts suggest that *taking* estrogen as a therapy may not create the same beneficial effects as the estrogen produced by your body. Continuous exposure to HT, taken at the same dose day after day, can lead to a desensitization of the "target" cells. In other words, your cells "close their doors" to more estrogen entering by decreasing the number of estrogen receptors available, a natural adjustment called *down-regulation*. We can understand this as the body's inner intelligence telling it that this amount of hormone is unnatural and unhealthy, and the cells adjust accordingly.

Indeed, taking HT for the first time after the age of sixty-five, as in the Women's Health Initiative, was not associated with any benefit. In fact, women in the WHI who took HT after the age of sixty-five had *more* dementia and more cognitive decline than women taking placebo. Clearly, studies now indicate that it is not beneficial to take HT for prevention of dementia or to improve memory and cognition after sixty-five and may, in fact, be harmful.

When given around the time of menopause, HT *has* proven helpful in improving memory, but only for women who had menopausal symptoms, such as hot flashes and sleep problems. The authors of one of these studies, Dr. Erin LeBlanc and colleagues, suggest that HT improved memory in flashing, sleep-deprived women because it reduced their hot flashes and night sweats and improved their sleep. Good sleep is essential for optimal memory and cognitive function. Given the lack of cognitive improvement from HT in women who were already sleeping well and not having hot flashes, this seems to be the logical explanation.

In regard to HT as a treatment for Alzheimer's disease, unfortunately, estrogen does *not* seem to improve the symptoms of Alzheimer's disease, once the disease has progressed. Two trials thus far involving women with mild-to-moderate Alzheimer's disease showed no difference in cognitive performance after four and twelve months on estrogen.

A Better Brain without Drugs or Hormones

With modern medicine unable to provide magic bullet for midlife forgetfulness and brain drain, more and more doctors are advising what has become the midlife mantra of natural, non-drug, non-hormone approaches: *diet and exercise.* Just as with heart disease and osteoporosis, there is no substitute for feeding your body properly and keeping it physically active. A healthy diet and proper exercise are the indispensable foundations of preventing mental decline and most other diseases.

Research on exercise shows that more is better when it comes to optimizing brain function. In a recent study of six thousand women age sixty-five and older reported at a meeting of the American Academy of Neurology in 2001, women who walked regularly and engaged in moderate exercise were found to be less likely to experience memory loss or other declines in mental function that can accompany aging. Activities measured included walking, climbing up stairs and other normal daily activity. A little bit of exercise was good, but more exercise daily was even better. Obviously, use common sense and moderation in your exercise habits. You don't have to run marathons to reap the benefits of exercise.

"People who think there's a pill that is going to keep the mind in top form are mistaken," says Robert N. Butler, M.D., president of the International Longevity Center USA and former director of the National Institute on Aging. Dr. Butler makes the point that not only is physical activity important for brain health, but so is varied mental activity, such as reading, learning a new language or skill, playing music, doing math, or otherwise engaging your mind in stimulating pursuits, especially ones that are novel or not part of your "mental routine." It seems that the saying *use it or lose* it is just as true for your brain "muscle" as it is for your quadriceps.

Dr. Butler's advice is further validated by a study on leisure activities and the risk of dementia performed by researchers at the Albert Einstein College of Medicine. Men and women over the age of seventy-five who participated in reading, board games, card games, crossword puzzles, playing a musical instrument and dancing were found to have reduced risk of dementia, by as much as 75 percent. The amount of reduction in risk was directly related to how many times a week the person participated in these activities — the more, the better.

In regard to a diet for a healthy brain, modern research is in its infancy when compared to our understanding of diet for a healthy heart. Initial studies point to a promising role of antioxidant vitamin E intake from food in preventing Alzheimer's disease. No effect was found from supplements for prevention, although a possible slowing of progression may occur from vitamin E supplements in patients who already have Alzheimer's disease. Results from randomized trials will be the most dependable, but for now, eating your walnuts, wheat germ and avocados can't hurt!

In general, we do know that your brain needs good fats, adequate protein, the requisite vitamins and minerals, and healthy carbohydrates for optimal functioning. Later in this chapter, I will cover sources of vital brain foods, including a wealth of Ayurvedic wisdom on how to nourish your brain for a healthy and intellectually agile old age, *without* the risks of hormone therapy.

The MAV Understanding of Mind and Memory

In my practice, many women in their perimenopausal years complain of lack of mental clarity — "brain fog" or "fuzzy thinking" — and report more memory gaps than usual. The good news is that this is often a passing stage rather than the beginning of a downhill spiral. One sexagenarian patient of mine remarked that she finds her memory sharper in her sixties than when she was in her forties.

Maharishi Ayurveda understands temporary memory lapses and brain fog in terms of your doshas and how they govern key functions of your brain. You use your brain to learn, process, and retain new information, and finally to recall it. In MAV, these three intimately connected functions are referred to respectively as *dhi* (dhee), *dhriti* (dhrih tee), and *smriti* (smrih tee). Just as with every other function in your body, the orderly interaction of all three doshas is involved in memory. Each dosha, however, plays a predominant role in just one aspect of the remembering process.

Dhi (learning and immediate memory) is governed by vata dosha. For you to have good focus of mind to learn and acquire new knowledge, your vata dosha must be balanced. Otherwise, your attention will be easily distracted by outside stimuli like a radio playing, your co-worker speaking on the phone next to you, or your own inner thoughts or emotions. You may recall that vata dosha relates to air and space. It may be no coincidence that a distractible, forgetful person with a vata imbalance is often referred to as an "airhead" or "space cadet"!

Your ability to retain what you learn, dhriti, involves chemical and electrical processing in the brain and is therefore governed by pitta, which is responsible for all metabolism. When pitta gets out of balance, the laying down and retention of memory is impaired.

Finally, smriti, the holding and storing of memory deep within your brain and then retrieving it, is governed by kapha dosha. When kapha is out of balance, slowness and obstruction come to the forefront. If you are having slow recall, find yourself at a loss to remember something you *know* that you know, or frequently say, "I'm blocking," then your kapha dosha is in need of some help.

Your doshas work together to coordinate these three key functions of your mind, keeping it clear and sharp. Imbalance in any one of them can cause problems with memory, concentration, or mental clarity. Fortunately, to improve your mind and memory at midlife and later it is not necessary to analyze which aspect of dhi, dhriti, and smriti is responsible for your "brain fog." Rather, MAV addresses all three simultaneously in its herbal prescriptions for the brain, as well as specific foods, spices, and behaviors (such as sleep, exercise, and stress reduction for enhancing brain function), all of which will be addressed later in this chapter.

Midlife Brain Fog and Vata Dosha

According to Ayurveda, temporary fuzziness, forgetfulness, or lack of mental sharpness at the time of hormonal fluxes is natural, and is understood in terms of vata dosha. At menopause, these symptoms are due to the transient aggravation of vata dosha that occurs with the change from a pitta to a vata-dominated time of life (see Chapter 3).

You may recall that vata dosha, which governs the brain and nervous system, tends to become aggravated by change. At menopause there is plenty of change going on, including an overall decline in your hormone levels across the menopausal transition, as well as frequent and wildly erratic hormonal shifts on an hourly, daily, and monthly basis. As a result of these changes, vata dosha and your nervous system are thrown off kilter temporarily, just as they are during premenstrual, postpartum, and pubertal hormonal fluctuations earlier in your life.

However, as the hormonal fluxes of the perimenopause smooth out and sleep and temperature control become more stable again, so does your brain function. You naturally regain your mental clarity *without* hormone therapy. I have found that natural vata-balancing approaches, with special attention to *prana vata*, a subdivision of vata which governs all mental activity, are usually enough to bring back clarity and memory, even in the midst of menopausal transition.

The story of one of my patients who suffered from memory loss due to prana vata imbalance serves to illustrate MAV approach to treating memory loss due to aging.

Graciela's Story: Balancing Prana Vata

Graciela, a forty-seven-year-old marketing representative and single mother of a teenage son, came to see me for help with heavy menstrual bleeding that lasted for several weeks at a time. Her gynecologist had prescribed progesterone, but Graciela had to stop it after a week due to intolerable side-effects, including weight gain, bloating, and fluid retention. Fortunately, an herbal and behavioral program from MAV was able to normalize her flow within a few weeks.

"Now that my periods are under control, I need some help with my memory," Graciela confided in me. "I'm concerned my boss is going to notice I'm not performing as well, and I've already embarrassed myself by forgetting important details about my clients and their projects."

I explained to Graciela that the same hormonal fluctuations and imbalances that were affecting her menstrual flow were also affecting her brain during this perimenopausal time. However, certain factors in her life could be making her memory worse, and if modified, could improve her memory and mental clarity. I asked her if she was experiencing much stress in her life currently.

"Oh, yes," Graciela confirmed, nodding vigorously. "I have a thirteen-year-old son who needs lots of attention, and I commute in heavy traffic on the beltway for over two hours every day. Business is going well, but I have many clients and a lot to keep track of." Further discussion revealed that on top of her hectic schedule during the day, Graciela frequently stayed up late to finish household chores and never got quite enough sleep.

Upon checking Graciela's pulse, I found that she had an imbalance of *prana* (prah nuh) vata, the subdivision of vata that governs the mind and all mental activity, including memory. Her daily commutes in heavy traffic, late nights, hectic business schedule, and single parent duties, all on top of a shifting hormonal status, added up to an overload on her brain and nervous system — in short, a prana vata aggravation. In order to correct her memory problem, we needed to balance her prana vata.

I advised Graciela of the three key points for balancing vata — a daily oil massage, regular and early bedtime, and a vata-balancing diet (see Chapter 4). I also recommended several lifestyle and dietary tips specific for balancing prana vata, which are described later in this chapter, and an MAV supplement containing a number of special brain-nourishing herbs that help to balance prana vata (see the Resources for product information).

At her follow-up a couple months later, Graciela enthusiastically reported that her memory problems had disappeared. "The recommendations really worked. I am so relieved. My memory is back to normal again."

Vata and the Fast Pace of Modern Life

You may recall from Chapter 3 that vata is the only dosha that can move and is therefore the leading or dominant dosha. In that role, vata controls and guides the function of both pitta and kapha doshas. Within vata dosha, prana is like the head — it governs the actions of all the other subdivisions of vata. In other words, as goes your brain — your *thinking* — so goes the health of your whole body.

It makes sense then that if prana vata is disturbed, the first clues may be mental fuzziness or "brain fog," sleep problems and trouble remembering things. Since prana vata is fundamental to the balance of all three doshas and to the entire body, prolonged imbalance in prana vata can lead to disturbance in the basic functions of the body, such as digestion, elimination, and immunity.

In today's fast-paced, high-stress lifestyle, a balanced prana vata is hard to maintain for most women. Activity of any kind, especially the hurried, stressed kind, tends to increase or aggravate vata, particularly when it is not compensated for by an adequate amount of rest. We rush to finish daily "to-do" lists that have a week's worth of tasks. We race to and from each day in airports and shopping malls and along busy city streets and highways. Moving, rushing, and stressing with the convenient, yet overstimulating, style of modern life all put a strain on the nervous system and pressure on your mind. Stay up late to get it all done, night after night, and you have a sure formula for serious prana vata imbalance.

Check Your Brain's Vata Balance

How do you know if your brain's prana vata is out of balance? Take the mini-quiz below to rate your own balance of prana vata:

- Do you often feel spacey or scattered?

- Do you find that you are forgetting things frequently?

- Do you find it difficult to concentrate on your work?

- Are you frequently having tension headaches?

- Are you having trouble falling asleep at night?

- Do you frequently feel irritated or overwhelmed by with extra pressures or workload that you might be handed?

- Are you often feeling worried or anxious?

If you answered yes to at least three of these, your brain's vata is most likely out of balance. Follow the tips below to help get your prana vata back into balance and resolve your symptoms naturally.

Calming Your Overactive Brain

Here are some tips to ensure that your prana vata is balanced for a clearer, more rested mind:

- Follow a regular routine of bedtime and mealtimes. Go to bed early, before 10 PM.

- Do one activity at a time, not two or three. When you are driving, don't talk on your cell phone and listen to talk radio shows. After a week, or even a single morning drive to work without cell phone or talk radio, you'll find you are more relaxed and mentally clearer when you get to work.

• Breathe in and out slowly and deeply through your nose whenever you feel tense during the day. (Prana also means "life breath," and prana vata governs your respiratory tract and breathing along with your central nervous system.) This will help to relax your mind, as well as energizing it with oxygen pumped deeply into the lungs. Slow, deep breathing from the abdomen has also been shown to be useful in reducing hot flashes, according to studies performed by Dr. Robert Freedman at Wayne State University, perhaps by balancing the hypothalamus as described for pranayama below.

• Practice *pranayama* (prah-nuh-yah-muh) for 10 minutes anytime during the day. Pranayama is a Sanskrit term referring to a breathing technique from the traditional Vedic discipline of yoga that helps to create balance in the mind, body, and nervous system. According to Ayurvedic medicine, this simple technique enables oxygen to penetrate deeply into the cells of the body, including the brain, to create balance in prana vata and the nervous system. It this way, it may also help to regulate your *hypothalamus*, the part of your brain which controls temperature, as well as the constriction and expansion of blood vessels in your skin, both of which are also involved in hot flashes.

To practice pranayama, sit comfortably with your eyes closed, preferably in a room with plenty of fresh air. To begin, place your thumb on your right nostril and close it. Breathe in through your left nostril. Then close off your left nostril with your third finger and release your thumb from your right nostril. Breathe out slowly through your right nostril then in through your right nostril. Now close your right nostril off and breathe out through your left nostril. Begin this cycle again by breathing in through your left nostril and then repeat the same steps as already described. Keep going for about five to ten minutes.

• Eat several fresh, organic fruits and vegetables each day. Juice them fresh for a powerful energy boost to your mind and body. Remember that prana means "life breath." The more freshness and purity in your food, the more prana it has. Try to find tree-ripened fruits, which pack the most "prana punch," having absorbed and utilized the life-giving energy of the sun more fully.

• A cup of warm milk boiled with a pinch of cardamom, taken before bedtime, can help calm your prana vata and promote good sleep.

The next section gives tips for restoring your mind and memory by banishing your sleep deprivation, feeding your brain wisely, and reducing your stress to transcend the fast pace of modern-day life.

A Maharishi Ayurveda Prescription for Brain Health

The Ayurvedic texts state that your health rests on a foundation supported by three pillars: sleep, diet, and balance of life. In Ayurvedic terms, a balanced life means moderation on every level and in all activities, and specifically implies that pursuit of material success is balanced by a lifelong dedication to spiritual development.

If any one of your three key lifestyle pillars is weak, your entire health is threatened. Let's look at how each of your health pillars can be strengthened for improving your memory and mind as you pass through and beyond menopause.

Overcoming Sleep Disturbance

Proper sleep, like proper diet, is essential for the maintenance of the body. Untimely, excessive and insufficient sleep (excessive vigil) take away happiness and long life. — *the* Charaka Samhita

During midlife, the Ayurvedic recommendation for sleep couldn't be more relevant, since hot flashes and night sweats awaken as many as 36 percent of menopausal women, as shown in a recent poll of the National Sleep Foundation. Sleep disturbance alone can lead to a significant decline in memory and cognitive function during the day.

Among the many menopausal patients I've encountered, sleep deprivation is the number one reason why women eventually opt for HT, at least for the short-term. Daytime fatigue, decreased alertness and mental clarity, and frequent mood swings are the common effects women experience when sleep is interrupted, and many women just can't bear the resulting decline in their quality of life.

In addition to menopausal sleep issues, sleep in both men and women tends to be lighter, more interrupted and generally less in quantity as we grow older. According to Ayurveda, this is a result of accumulated vata imbalance more than an inevitable effect of aging. That's good news, because imbalance is potentially reversible!

In my experience, sleep can usually be improved, along with mental clarity and mood during the day, through natural approaches. The main aim is to balance vata, especially prana vata, which governs all mental and brain activity and the hypothalamus, the structure in your brain responsible for regulating your body temperature through the night.

How to Improve Sleep

In general, improving your sleep as you transit menopause is a matter of getting your hot flashes and night sweats under control through dosha balancing and clearing your gaps and channels from toxic wastes or ama. For guidelines on how to do this, please refer back to Chapters 4 and 6. You can also break the cycle of sleepless nights and brain-fogged days at any stage of life by following these recommendations.

- Reduce stimulating activities in the evening, especially after 9 P.M. Rather than watch TV or work on your computer, take a walk, read your kids a bedtime story, fold laundry, relax with an uplifting or spiritual book, or make a "to-do" list for tomorrow to set your mind at ease.

- Eat a light, easy-to-digest meal for dinner. Avoid eating meat, cheese, potatoes, or salad in the evening. Meat and cheese are heavy and hard to digest and potatoes and raw vegetables aggravate vata in the digestive tract. All can disturb your sleep with overactive digestion.

- Eat your dinner by 7 P.M. Eating early improves sleep and also helps prevent joint pains and sinus congestion caused by ama formed when the food is not digested properly.

- Avoid alcohol in the evening. While alcohol can help some women feel sleepy, it interferes with sleeping through the night and can trigger more hot flashes.

- Avoid caffeine, which can both trigger hot flashes and make it harder to get to sleep. The caffeine habit also increases fatigue and mind and memory problems over time. By preventing the breakdown of the energy molecule adenosine triphosphate (ATP), caffeine chemically holds your cells in an energy-expending, "on" mode when they might otherwise rest and recuperate. This gives you an energy boost and mental focus that lasts a few hours. But afterward, your brain and body cells are *more* tired than they would have been without caffeine, and you're tempted to have another fix. Better to get off the caffeine merry-go-round and get back in touch with your body. You'll find that the end result is increased energy, more stable moods, and more mental clarity on a daily basis.

- At bedtime, apply a little coconut oil to your scalp and the bottoms of your feet. Rub the coconut oil on the palms of your hands to melt it, then slip the flats of your hands underneath your hair to apply directly to the scalp. Oil is the most vata-balancing physical substance, and coconut oil also chills out your pitta. Since your head is the seat of prana vata in the body and your feet are representative of the body as a whole, massaging oil into these two areas at bedtime can be extremely relaxing.

- Ayurveda recommends sleeping with your head pointing toward the east or south, and never toward the north. Studies on both humans and animals have shown that sleeping with the head toward the north increases restlessness, confusion, and irritability, accompanied by increases in stress hormones (cortisol, epinephrine, and dopamine). This simple change has improved sleep dramatically in several of my patients.

Feeding Your Brain: Supply and Delivery

To function optimally as you age, your brain needs nutritional support in two ways. First, it needs proper delivery of nourishment, and second, it must be able to assimilate and use that nourishment. The right nutrients must be supplied through diet, but also the channels within your brain must be open and free of ama so that those nutrients can penetrate into your brain cells.

Supplying Your Brain with Nourishment

Your brain needs four basic types of nourishment: oxygen, glucose (blood sugar), fat, and protein. Let's look at how each of these affects the health and functioning of your brain and how you can make sure your brain is getting what it needs.

Oxygen. Your brain is exquisitely sensitive to oxygen deprivation. It can survive only four minutes without oxygen, and then often with irreparable damage. Proper oxygen delivery, of course, relies on good circulation. Primarily, arteries must be free of atherosclerosis to deliver oxygen-rich blood to the brain. Healthy lungs and red blood cells are also key elements for delivering adequate oxygen to the brain. (We women must be particularly alert to the latter. Iron deficiency, with or without anemia, can lead to reduced brain oxygen, less productivity, and poorer mental performance.)

Exercise (especially in unpolluted outdoor settings), pranayama, more deep breaths during the day, small amounts of black pepper (which clears the channels in the brain) in your food, and "prana-filled" fresh fruits and vegetables can all enhance oxygenation of the brain and thereby mental function.

Glucose. The brain's preferred food is *glucose*, or blood sugar, although it can also adjust to burning *ketones*, a type of fat metabolite, for its primary fuel. Refined sugar, however, is not good for the brain, as any women who has had tiredness, moodiness, or other types of mental backlash after overdosing on chocolate chip cookies knows.

Instead of refined, sugary foods, keep your brain fueled with slower-release carbohydrates like whole grains, fruits, and vegetables. Sweet juicy fruits, such as pears or a rich medjool date, are especially good. Eating these foods instead of a candy bar or cookie when your energy dips in the late afternoon will give you *tripti* (<u>trip</u>-tee), a feeling of being truly nourished and satisfied. Also include the following special "brain foods" in your diet: almonds, walnuts, warm boiled milk, panir, stewed apples, sweet mangoes, couscous, coconut meat in small amounts, and sweet, juicy pears.

Fat. Your brain is an astonishing 60 percent fat. Every one of your neurons (brain cells) is insulated by a layer of fat. So it is no wonder that your brain needs fat for nourishment. However, the *quality* of the fat you give it determines the quality of the brain constituents your body will make from your diet. It is important to eat healthy, pure oils, like organic olive oil. Stay away from nonorganic, mechanically processed (overheated), hydrogenated, or otherwise altered fats. Avoid trans-fatty acids, such as margarine and other foods containing partially hydrogenated fats. And stay away from fatty cuts of meat.

Recent research has elucidated the importance of the essential fatty acids (EFAs) for normal mood and brain function. For example, omega-3 fatty acids, found in wheat germ, walnuts, dark, leafy greens (like spinach and kale), some fish, and flaxseed, are especially important in regulating mental functions and mood. Walnuts in particular are considered brain food in Ayurvedic medicine, and the fact that they *look* like the brain itself is considered no coincidence!

Ayurvedic medicine extols the virtues of dairy products for ojas, overall health, and more brain power. It especially recommends consumption of a specific dairy-derived fat — ghee. Despite the fact that ghee is nearly 70 percent saturated fat (a fact that would raise the eyebrows of any cardiologist), it is revered in MAV as an oil that *in small amounts* is extremely beneficial to brain function, helps protect the brain from degenerative diseases, and promotes overall health. Indeed, ghee is a source of omega-3 fatty acids, and contains monounsaturated fats as well as saturated ones. It is also highly resistant to oxidation. Unlike other dairy and meat fats, the saturated fats in ghee are composed of *short*-chain fatty acids that are readily used for energy and tend to be metabolized quickly rather than building up in your system.

There is an Ayurvedic saying that speaks to the importance of moderation in ghee consumption: "Ghee should be sipped, not drunk." One or two teaspoons per day, is considered a rasayana, or rejuvenative, for the brain. But rather than adding your ghee to foods after cooking or slathering on bread, sauté it with spices like turmeric (antioxidant and detoxifying) and a pinch of black pepper and add to your vegetables and grains. This will help the ghee cross the blood-brain barrier to fortify your brain, not your waistline.

Protein. Your brain also needs protein, especially certain *amino acids* (building blocks of protein), such as tyrosine, tryptophan and cysteine. The first two are essential for manufacturing key neurotransmitters (brain messenger chemicals) like dopamine and serotonin, which support your mood, while cysteine detoxifies the brain and body of certain chemicals and heavy metals.

If you are a vegetarian, you may find yourself relying on soy products as your main source of protein. This may be a concern. A study conducted at the University of Hawaii on Japanese-Americans raised questions about the long-term effects of midlife tofu consumption. Subjects who consumed tofu at least twice a week had a substantially higher risk of dementia and brain atrophy later in life than those who ate tofu less than twice a week. Researchers suggest that the high levels of certain enzyme inhibitors in tofu, or its high levels of isoflavones, may be responsible.

Until we have more research on the connection between tofu and dementia, I recommend that you broaden your selection of protein-rich vegetarian foods and consume tofu no more than once or twice a week. Soy products that are fermented, such as tempeh, do not have such high levels of enzyme inhibitors and may provide a suitable alternative. However, a wide variety of whole grains (especially high-protein grains like quinoa and amaranth), legumes, dairy, nuts, and seeds is always wise, since each food comes with its own inherent complement of vitamins, minerals, and other micronutrients, helping to ensure that you are getting all the nutrition you need.

The brain also needs vitamins and minerals, specifically B_{12}, which can get too low in vegetarians who do not take vitamin supplements. Deficiency in vitamin B_{12}, which is reliably found only in dairy or meat products, prevents the proper synthesis of myelin, the insulating sheaths that coat the nerves. This can result in memory loss, numbness and tingling in the arms and legs, depression, poor mental performance, and a host of other psychoneurological symptoms. Taking a B_{12} supplement can often reverse the symptoms and is a good precaution for vegans and vegetarians who do not consume two to three servings of dairy on a daily basis. Another risk of B_{12} deficiency is buildup of the toxic amino acid homocysteine, a metabolic by-product of protein metabolism. If you are low in B_{12}, folic acid or B_6, homocysteine can build up in your blood and in your brain. Better known in the past as a risk factor for cardiovascular disease, recent research indicates that homocysteine is an even more potent brain toxin. Even a mild elevation can double your risk of dementia and of stroke. If you are concerned about your brain health, and prefer not to take B vitamins regularly, it is probably a good idea to have your doctor check your homocysteine level, especially if you are vegetarian.

Clearing the Channels to Your Brain

According to Ayurvedic wisdom, any toxin or waste (ama) that lodges in the brain tissue will obstruct the brain's microcirculatory channels and interfere with the mind's smooth functioning. The modern medical version of this principle is Alzheimer's disease.

One of the most extensively researched toxins implicated in Alzheimer's disease is the amyloid-beta-peptide, or *abeta*, a type of protein waste (think "ama"-loid) that builds up in the brains of Alzheimer's patients and interferes with normal brain function. Japanese and American scientists studying mice found that activity of the enzymes that break down amyloid, such as the "cleaner-upper" enzyme *neprilysin*, tends to decline with age and is especially weak in the mice with Alzheimer's. They suggest that keeping neprilysin in top form may help prevent both Alzheimer's and age-related declines in cognitive ability.

From the Ayurvedic perspective, these latest insights into keeping the brain healthy are not new. MAV states that balanced metabolism (agni), which includes the activity of all enzymes in our bodies, is key to good health and longevity. Neprilysin is just one of those key enzymes.

Tips for Improving Your Brain's Metabolism. To clear ama, amyloid, and other wastes more effectively, follow these few simple dietary tips:

• Cook with a little freshly ground black pepper. MAV says black pepper is the greatest enhancer of brain metabolism, and modern research suggests that it also enhances the uptake and utilization of oxygen by your brain cells. (Go easy on this if you are suffering from frequent hot flashes, as any heating spice, such as pepper, can trigger them.) Add after cooking and grind fresh for maximum effect.

• Cooking with a little fresh ginger root, which Ayurveda describes as the best enhancer of overall metabolism of all the spices, helps you digest your food well without forming ama, can help you assimilate your food better, and clears all the channels throughout the body and brain. Add at the start of sautéing vegetables or midway through cooking a lentil soup. Boil a slice in milk to create a warm spiced beverage that is easy to digest and delivers good nutrition to the brain. Both ginger and milk contain tryptophan, an essential amino acid used by the brain to make serotonin and other neurotransmitters that are important for good sleep and a good mood.

• Avoid eating foods high in refined, "bad" sugar, which can damage your brain's enzymes, including neprilysin, thereby promoting the buildup of amyloid, ama, and other undesirable substances.

• Avoid exposure to heavy metals (like lead, mercury, and aluminum), which reduce cognitive ability. Aluminum in particular has been implicated in Alzheimer's disease, although any causative role it may play is still controversial. Some researchers and health professionals recommend avoiding aluminum-containing deodorants and cookware. I advise avoiding *all* potential sources of brain-busting heavy metals, including mercury amalgam fillings; ocean and Great Lakes fish that are high in mercury (including swordfish, whitefish, sea bass, tilefish, shark, king mackerel, and even tuna); lead-containing calcium supplements (check with the manufacturer for a no-lead guarantee); and the many potential sources of environmental lead (including paint, old water pipes, and lead crystal glassware and pottery).

- Avoid alcohol and other "recreational" chemicals. If you feel you must drink, do so in moderation and not every day. Recent research indicates that women's brains are more sensitive to the brain-damaging effects of alcohol than are men's brains; female alcoholics show greater brain atrophy than male alcoholics.

Three Brain-Boosting Herbs for a Clear Mind and Memory

An elite class of Ayurvedic herbs has earned the distinction of *medhya* (<u>may</u> dhyuh), meaning best for enhancing the functions of the mind and memory. Each herb acts in a unique way to bring about improved clarity of mind. They are most effective when combined with other herbs that balance your physiology as a whole. Here are three of the premier brain-boosting medhya herbs from the Ayurvedic herbal treasury. (See the Resources for product information.)

Shankapushpi (Aloeweed, *Convolvulus pluricaulis*) is considered the very best herb overall for supporting the brain and mind. It is described as *somanasya janana*, or giver of great mental power and bliss. It enhances memory and thinking, calms the mind, and improves tolerance to mental stress.

Brahmi (Bacopa, *Bacopa monniera*) is *mastishka shamaka*, or balancing to the mind overall. It also has specific hormonal-balancing effects in women. Scientific studies show that it can enhance learning and memory, reduce the negative effects of drugs (like the antiseizure drug Phenytoin) on mental ability, and provide antioxidant support for the brain.

Gotu kola (Indian pennywort, *Centella asiatic*) is described as *smritida*, or best at enhancing memory. It also protects the heart, supports women's hormonal systems, enhances collagen formation in the skin, promotes good complexion and healing of the skin, and slows the aging process. Gotu kola also contains asiatic acid, a potent inhibitor of the amyloid formation seen in Alzheimer's disease.

Herbal Combinations. As I mentioned earlier, it is important to take herbs in combination formulas prepared according to strict traditional principles, both to enhance the effects of the primary herbs in the formula and to prevent negative side effects. For example, it is not in accord with Ayurvedic principles to take gotu kola as an isolated herb.

Research has shown the excellent results possible when classical guidelines of formulation are followed strictly. Study Power, for example, a traditionally prepared MAV formula for the mind, was shown in a randomized, double-blind trial to increase students' intelligence without creating side effects. In another double-blind, placebo-controlled study, Maharishi Amrit Kalash improved age-related attention problems, alertness, and visual discrimination. Laboratory studies demonstrate that both formulas protect the brain from free radicals and the effects of aging.

A Mind in Balance: Reducing Stress

We have seen how mental stress, over-stimulation, and over-activity are all brain busters that throw off vata dosha (which is already in transition at midlife), eroding your memory and mental clarity. You are left with a life out of balance, one in which your outer activity is not balanced with the inner state of rest. In today's terms, you are stressed out.

Medical science describes that the negative effects of mental and emotional stress are caused by the stress hormone cortisol, which is secreted by your adrenal glands. Cortisol increases alertness and provides quick energy to the muscles for the "fight or flight" response needed in extreme and dangerous situations. But when chronically secreted in response to the endless daily stressors of modern life, cortisol can damage the *hippocampus*, a structure in the brain involved with memory, resulting in a decline in memory and other mental functions.

In general, chronic cortisol secretion is at the root of the burnout and mental fog that many women *and men* experience at midlife. Add to that the effects of fluctuating hormones on the female brain during perimenopause, and the need for truly effective stress-relievers becomes self-evident. Two of the best techniques are Transcendental Meditation and Maharishi Rejuvenation Treatment (MRT).

The Transcendental Meditation Technique

Fortunately, everything you do to balance vata will help to lower your stress level and turn down your production of cortisol. But to boost your ability to reduce stress, I recommend the Maharishi Transcendental Meditation program, which I introduced in Chapter 7. Transcendental Meditation has been shown to directly lower cortisol levels in just the *first four months* of practice. As might be expected, Transcendental Meditation practice has been shown to improve short-term memory, as well as creativity and intelligence.

Transcendental Meditation is a simple, natural mental technique that is practiced quietly twice a day for about twenty minutes. Transcendental Meditation allows the mind to spontaneously settle down to its most silent and peaceful state — a state of "restful alertness," the quiet inner source of our thinking. This most silent level of the mind is called *Atma* in the Vedic tradition, or the inner "Being" of each of us.

Even beginning to experience our Atma or inner Being for a few minutes twice a day through the practice of Transcendental Meditation turns out to be very beneficial to health. More than 600 published scientific studies from 216 universities and research institutes in 30 countries, published in over 100 different scientific journals, have verified the beneficial effects of Transcendental Meditation for the mind, body, behavior, and environment.

I have used Transcendental Meditation in my practice with thousands of patients and in my own personal life for over twenty-five years, and as a result, am

YOUR MIND

very confident that it delivers the many benefits that research has shown. The Transcendental Meditation technique is taught only by qualified teachers according to traditional and authentic Vedic procedures passed on from teacher to student over many generations. The procedure is completely standardized and its results and benefits are reliable and verified by scientific research.

Why Transcendental Meditation Is More Effective. All techniques of meditation are not the same and do not give equal results. Comparison studies show that different techniques yield different and varying degrees of benefit. Specific benefits of the Transcendental Meditation program include lowering blood pressure, enhancing longevity, reducing anxiety, reversing atherosclerosis, reducing mortality from heart attacks, strokes and cancer, enhancing creativity and self-actualization, and reducing aging. They are unparalleled by any other technique of meditation or stress reduction to date.

At a recent medical conference where I gave a talk on the benefits of Transcendental Meditation, a doctor in the audience asked me why I thought the Transcendental Meditation program was more effective than other stress reduction techniques. I thought for a moment and responded that I suspected the reason lay in the effortlessness and simplicity of the technique and its teaching. The Transcendental Meditation program instruction has been refined over thousands of years by devoted yogis meditating for many years of their lives, resulting in a very precise mental technology that is capable of yielding maximum benefits from meditation with the least amount of effort.

But perhaps even more important, the Transcendental Meditation program is a technique for *transcending*, which means literally "going beyond." To go beyond thinking, to experience one's own Atma (or state of silent pure awareness) is, according to the Charaka Samhita, "the greatest of the sources of health." So a technique that results in the maximum degree of transcendence should give the maximum health benefits. Transcendental Meditation, more than any other technique of stress reduction, helps you to effortlessly transcend the active thinking level of your mind, and may explain why it yields superior benefits.

In summary, to get out of the memory-eroding fight-or-flight habit and increase your mind and memory power, you need to reduce your stress and give your brain some deep rest and rejuvenation. To accomplish this, follow the tips given earlier for balancing your prana vata. And for maximum benefits, learn the Transcendental Meditation program.

Maharishi Rejuvenation Treatment (MRT)

For those of you who can go for an intensive in-residence stress-reducing experience, consider a five- to seven-day treatment of Maharishi Rejuvenation Treatment (MRT). While every treatment — from *abhyanga* (gentle massage and oil application) to *basti* (mild herbal enema) — helps to rebalance vata, none is so powerful for the mind as *shirodhara* (shih-roh-<u>dhah</u>-ruh), an ancient technique regarded in Vedic medicine as the treatment of choice for all stress-related or mental disorders.

In shirodhara, a warm, gentle stream of herbalized sesame oil is poured on the forehead in a prescribed pattern that induces a profound state of relaxation in the mind and brain. Three or more consecutive days of shirodhara treatment at an in-residence program is recommended for chronic insomnia, stress-related conditions, worry, anxiety, memory loss, and other disorders of the mind and emotions. (See Resources for information on locations of centers.)

Melodies for Memory: Mozart and *More*

Various types of music can profoundly affect our mind and emotions. Several studies have showed that listening to Mozart's music, in fact, improves short-term memory, a phenomenon referred to as the Mozart effect.

One investigator recently put Mozart to the test, comparing the effects on short-term memory of listening to Mozart's music versus listening to *Gandharva Veda* music, the classical Vedic music. After listening to Mozart, subjects showed a 16 percent improvement in short-term memory and learning ability. After listening to Gandharva Veda music, they showed a *36 percent* improvement. Although the study has not yet been published, it earned its talented young investigator, Deborah Swartz, first prize in her division at the Eastern Iowa Science and Engineering Fair in 2001.

Gandharva Veda music is described in MAV as "that melody from which all melodies have sprung" and is said to "create balance in nature, eliminate stress in the atmosphere, and produce a healthy influence for the individual and peace in the world family." So if your memory leaves something to be desired, maybe what you really need are a few more melodies in your life!

ET, GO HOME!

I hope this discussion has helped you to move beyond thinking about your brain health solely in terms of your estrogen levels. Estrogen therapy (ET) is not *the* key factor in staying mentally agile as we age. Remember that complete transcending (experience of your Atma), quality sleep, physical exercise, mental "calisthenics" and varied experiences, proper foods, spices, and herbs can all help nourish and flex your brain cells on a daily basis, keeping them in shape for a mentally alert and fulfilling life. With the help of these interventions, your senior moments will be flashes of deeper insight and creativity, growing inner wisdom, and an enhanced enjoyment and love of life.

* 10 *

Your Emotions — Transforming Blues to Bliss

When the emotional heart is balanced, one gains pure knowledge, the desires of the mind are always righteous, and one experiences unbounded bliss.
— *the* Sushruta Samhita

Shifting hormones can mean shifting emotions for women at midlife. Certainly, most women have become used to the emotional sensitivity that for so many years has accompanied our menstrual cycles, ranging from irritability and quick temper to sadness and hurt feelings, the blues or other upsets. Around menopause, we can expect to experience similar emotions as hormones fluctuate and begin to fall off.

While fluctuating hormones and moods are a normal part of a woman's life, they can trigger more serious mood disorders. During our reproductive years, women are two to three times more likely to experience an episode of serious depression or anxiety than men of the same age. The exact cause of this gender gap in emotional and mental health is not known. While extremely stressful events can trigger depression in men and women alike, studies have shown that women are not more prone to depression because of a greater sensitivity to stress and are not more often exposed to stressful events, as popular belief might hold. Rather, major depression and anxiety often coincide with times of maximal hormonal shifting — as do premenstrual dysphoric disorder (PMDD), a severe kind of PMS, and depression after childbirth. These disorders are most likely linked to those shifts.

Does Menopause Cause Depression?

Given the link between hormones and mood, it makes sense that the dramatic biological shifts that occur around menopause would contribute to increased emotional instability for women at this time. Fortunately, shifting moods during the perimenopause are not usually serious or debilitating. Studies like the Massachusetts Women's Health Study, which looked at large numbers of women at midlife, have found that serious conditions like major depression are *not* more common at menopause.

There are a few exceptions. Women who undergo an abrupt withdrawal of their hormones at menopause from a hysterectomy, or from taking chemotherapy or Tamoxifen, do have an increased risk of depression, as do women who are particularly prone to emotional upheavals associated with their menstrual cycle or other hormonal shifts. But the good news is that most women are not more depressed as menopause approaches than at other times in their lives.

And there is more good news about emotional health after menopause. According to the most recent research, the general trend is that mood disorders become less common as women advance beyond menopause. Age, it seems, actually grants us some protection against mood disorders. We might conclude that as far as emotional health goes, the popular axiom is true: You aren't getting older — you're getting better.

HT Is Not the Solution

Can taking hormone replacement therapy help with your emotional ups and downs? Since the loss of estrogen at menopause does not appear to cause serious depression, we wouldn't expect HT to be of particular help. And indeed, an analysis by Pearce, et al., of over one hundred studies showed that taking HT did not clearly lead to improvement in women's depression symptoms.

For women who had undergone surgical menopause for benign gynecological conditions, however, HT did help. This may be because surgical menopause involves a sudden, severe hormonal withdrawal, causing a truly estrogen-related depression in a way that a more gradual, natural menopause does not.

Recently, a small randomized trial of fifty perimenopausal women with mild to major depressive symptoms found that giving bioidentical estrogen in patch form *did* significantly relieve depressive symptoms as compared to placebo. This is only one small study that goes against the grain of previous findings, and more research needs to be done in this area. In my clinical experience, I have found that a minority of women with depression that has persisted despite intensive nonhormonal therapies *do* improve dramatically when started on HT.

I have also seen many women who report feeling *worse* on HT, emotionally and otherwise. In my experience, 80 to 90 percent of women can recover their emotional balance naturally, without medication or hormone therapy. Regardless of future research conclusions, as always with any drug or hormone which carries risk, it is best to try to balance yourself naturally first, and resort to drugs or HT only if really necessary. But if it is necessary, don't feel bad about it. Use your newfound energy and positivity to make the necessary life changes to take your health and well-being to a higher level of fulfillment.

I hope you are encouraged to know that perimenopause is not associated with an increase in serious mood disorders, that hormonal shifts do not spell emotional disaster for most women at this time, and finally, that HT is not required to keep you sane and emotionally stable. However, you may be suffering from a variety of milder emotional symptoms that are known to coincide with the time of perimenopause and are troublesome enough to demand treatment of some type. If it's not simply hormones, then what other factors might explain why you feel the way you do?

Other Causes of Your Midlife Moods

There are many theories that attempt to explain the emotional ups and downs that perimenopausal women experience so often. These include psychological and stress-related factors, as well as the "domino theory" that hot flashes and sleep disturbance result in mood swings.

Psychological adjustment to the fact that childbearing is no longer an option is also emotionally challenging for some women, especially those who are childless and *not* according to plan. Other women tell me they miss the cyclical rhythm of menstruation and the feeling they get of being cleansed and more vibrant after their period is over.

Coinciding life stressors may also contribute to fatigue, sadness, irritability, or an overwhelmed feeling. Multiple stressors are common at midlife and may include teenage children with behavioral issues, children leaving home (empty-nest syndrome), older children returning home, working outside the home for the first time or other career changes, caring for sick or dying parents, and marital, financial, or other stressors.

Stress has a biochemical reality that does not depend on your reproductive hormones. As we have seen, chronic stress increases cortisol, the hormone released to help the body cope with challenging circumstances, and can lead to a wide variety of health disorders and rapid aging. Chronic stress can also cause imbalances in your brain chemicals that can trigger mood disorders, including major depression.

Stress can also cause anxiety. Fear naturally arises when you perceive something as a threat. Anxiety is how you feel when your nervous system activates its fight-or-flight mode to cope with the stressful situation. A heightened state of activity and alertness in the sympathetic nervous system sets your heart pounding, your pupils dilating, and blood surging to your muscles so you can make a quick escape to avoid danger or even death.

While this response may have been helpful to our cave-dwelling ancestors fleeing a saber-toothed tiger, it is not necessary and is clearly unhealthy when we have the same response day in and day out as we are driving on a crowded freeway, worrying about our children, or rushing to a meeting. A state of chronic anxiety does not help us cope with these stresses.

The domino theory of perimenopausal mood disorders suggests that when hot flashes and night sweats interrupt normal sleep patterns, women are more vulnerable to fatigue, anxiety, irritability, easy crying, and other disturbances during the day. This is the most common scenario I see in my practice. Mood swings usually resolve after healthy sleep patterns are restored.

Your Sexuality and Menopause

Many women worry that declining hormones mean an inevitable decrease in their sexual desire. But this is not necessarily so. According to an American Association of Retired Persons (AARP) survey, 57 percent of women reported that they considered a satisfying sexual relationship to be one of the most important quality-of-life issues. Only 37 percent of women in the study agreed with the statement "sex is less important as people age." When Gelfand surveyed the frequency of sexual activity in women over 39, it was women 65 and older who reported being the most active sexually.

There are many factors involved in your sexual mood during and after menopause, some biological and others psychological. According to a recent analysis of several studies, vaginal dryness is the only biological condition that is clearly linked to a decrease in a woman's desire for sex. Without sufficient lubrication, intercourse can fail to arouse and even be a painful, discouraging activity. Other psychological and emotional factors affecting your sexual desire include how you feel about your partner, your need for intimacy, and your overall health and well-being. According to some studies, sexual motivation in women is often guided by desire for emotional intimacy rather than by a need for sex, in which case the dynamics of your relationship will have more to do with your sexual interest than your hormones do.

Recent studies on sexual function in women during the perimenopausal transition verify that interpersonal, psychological, sociocultural and biological elements all play an important role in sexual functioning. Sexual dysfunction is rarely completely psychological, nor is it likely to be based solely on hormonal changes.

The most troublesome physical problem affecting sexual function in women as they get older is vaginal dryness and atrophy. It affects from 34 percent to over 80 percent of postmenopausal women, and accounts for at least 7 percent of sexual dysfunction in postmenopausal women. Lack of lubrication, pain with intercourse, spasms and tension of the vaginal muscles, and difficulty reaching orgasm are common difficulties. Lack of estrogen is cited as the primary cause, whether from natural menopause or following radiation, chemotherapy, and a variety of estrogen-blocking drugs. We know from discussion in earlier chapters that vata imbalance (recall that vata is dry) and accumulated wastes and toxins can also block the effect of estrogen on the vagina and other tissues, promoting dryness and atrophy. Indeed, research bears this out, with a number of common everyday factors contributing to dryness (vata imbalance) in women after menopause. For example, a variety of prescription medications, use of chemically-treated sanitary products, chemical sensitivity to deodorants, soaps, douches and perfumes, as well as tight-fitting or synthetic underwear, have all been implicated in vaginal dryness.

The modern medical approach uses topical estrogens intravaginally, which can usually reverse the symptoms within a few weeks. They are available in a variety of forms including creams, tablets, and a vaginal ring. It is not clear yet whether topical use of estrogen, without also taking a progestin, increases uterine cancer. More research is also being called for to study the effects of topical estrogen on the body as a whole. While the amount absorbed is less than taking estrogen orally, some of it does get absorbed into the general circulation and may cause side effects similar to those of oral estrogen.

Natural Approaches to Improving Sexual Function

Research on natural approaches for improving vaginal lubrication and reversing atrophy is in its early infancy. One study by Wilcox in Great Britain found that supplementation for six weeks with phytoestrogens from soy (isoflavones) and linseed (lignins) resulted in maturation and increased lubrication of the vaginal lining. Two case reports suggest an estrogenic effect on the vagina from the use of ginseng. One woman reported improvement in vaginal dryness (confirmed by microscopic examination) after prolonged use of ginseng, and similar effects have been reported with use of a topical ginseng cream. Vitamin E suppositories and a variety of over-the-counter nonprescription and herbal lubricants can be effective for mild cases.

An Ayurvedic homemade lubricant that is soothing as well as moisturizing is a mixture of equal parts aloe vera gel and coconut oil, used nightly for long-term nourishment of the vaginal tissues. If you are experiencing vaginal dryness, also be sure to add marshmallow root, a natural lubricant and moisturizer, to your wise water as described in Chapter 6. If your libido is flagging in an unwelcome way, also add shatavari to your wise water. Shatavari means "one hundred husbands"!

One of my patients, Jean, found herself in a frustrating cycle of dryness and pain with intercourse that ultimately resulted in complete avoidance of sex with her husband. She developed extreme anxiety about the entire sexual experience, and her husband likewise became anxious that he would cause her pain. The effect on their intimate relationship was devastating with both partners avoiding sexual activity entirely. Due to the severity of Jean's condition, treatment required use of a topical estrogen cream initially to help restore thickness and strength to her overly sensitive vaginal lining. Gradual reintroduction of sexual contact without intercourse helped Jean and her husband to break the cycle of pain and anxiety and eventually regain a normal sex life. Over time, Jean was able to substitute natural lubricants for the estrogen cream, reducing her dependence on estrogen, and her risk of long-term side effects.

Paradoxically, stopping sexual relations when initial symptoms begin can accelerate the atrophy of the vaginal tissues. Regular sex is actually a means to keep the vagina youthful, since stimulation and stretching of the tissues helps to increase blood flow and lubrication naturally.

Diminishing Desire is Also Natural

On the other hand, a decline in sexual desire can also be a natural and welcome consequence of passing beyond your reproductive years. One of my postmenopausal patients told me that she experienced a decline in sexual interest that paralleled a maturing sense of security and trust she felt in her marriage. "I feel so bonded to my husband, so secure and fulfilled after 20 years of marriage," she told me. "I don't experience a strong need for the emotional intimacy that comes with intercourse. While it's an enjoyable exchange at times, we are so deeply nurtured by each other in so many other ways, sex almost seems unnecessary."

Other women have told me that with a gradual decline in their interest in sex they experience new energy for other pursuits in life. Many find this a time to focus on their spiritual development, an opportunity to grow in wisdom, and welcome the availability of energy that had previously been focused on achieving sexual fulfillment. Whatever your particular sexual mood is at this time, my advice is to look at it not only in terms of hormones but in terms of what else is going on in your life and your relationship. Perhaps your emotional life is affecting your sexual behavior, and is the area where you should look for answers.

THE MAV APPROACH TO MANAGING EMOTIONS IN MIDLIFE

While our modern medicine doesn't have safe and natural solutions to the emotional swings you may be experiencing at midlife, the ancient wisdom of MAV does. When we look at what's happening with your doshas at this time, we can see the bigger picture of mind and body involvement in menopausal moods. We have greater access to a wealth of approaches that can bring about stabilization, even bliss, during the midlife transition.

According to MAV, menopause marks the transition from the pitta phase of life (ages twenty to fifty) to the vata phase (after fifty). Since pitta and vata are the two doshas most involved in this midlife transition, any emotional symptoms you may experience can be understood and treated in terms of these two doshas.

Once you know the doshic root of your emotional symptoms — anxiety, mood swings, irritability, and even depression — they can usually be resolved using natural dosha-balancing approaches without drugs or hormones. I encourage you to start by revisiting Chapter 3 to determine your dosha imbalances and then Chapter 4 for remedies and prescriptions to bring your doshas back into balance. Throughout this chapter I will be giving you additional recommendations for your specific mood and emotion imbalances.

The case study of my patient Martha, who recovered from perimenopausal stress-related anxiety and mood swings using MAV therapies, illustrates a natural and effective approach to treating your mood disturbances.

Martha's Story: Back from the Brink

Martha is a forty-five-year-old single mother of a teenage son and the owner of a management consulting business whose work takes her on frequent trips around the country. In hearing her story of perimenopause-related symptoms and how they were affecting her life, I was struck by the contrast between her highly organized, successful professional life and the utter lack of control she was experiencing in her personal life, particularly with her emotions.

"I'm having difficulty holding myself together during presentations to my clients," Martha told me, "and that is extremely unlike me. I've never been so anxious before. Also, I'm easily irritated and constantly struggling to keep my temper over little things."

Martha related that she had noticed some changes in her menstrual cycle over the previous six months. Her periods were now coming every twenty-three days instead of her usual twenty-eight. The flow had become heavier, accompanied by her usual severe cramps. Her sleeping pattern had deteriorated into long nights of waking episodes, with hot flashes and sweats occurring every hour and a half.

"Between the anxiety and the insomnia," she complained, "I find I've been drinking more and more wine every day to try to calm myself. And I'm beginning to worry about that."

Martha had been to her family doctor, who offered her anxiety medication, but she declined it because she felt it would only suppress her symptoms. "Whatever you recommend, I am willing to try it," she told me, obviously desperate for some relief. "If I don't do something, I'm going to go off the deep end."

After completing a history and taking her pulse, I explained to Martha that a generalized increase in vata and an imbalance in *sadhaka* (sah-dhuh-kuh) pitta were at the root of her anxiety, temper, and insomnia. Her frequent traveling, public speaking, and irregular lifestyle were aggravating her vata dosha, promoting more severe perimenopausal hormone fluctuations and therefore more severe symptoms. Her drinking was complicating the matter by directly aggravating her pitta dosha. Alcohol is the most pitta-aggravating substance there is, and it contributes directly to sleep problems and irritability.

To get to the root of Martha's symptoms, I suggested a number of recommendations from MAV, including a diet and herbal program to balance her vata and pitta doshas (see Chapter 4), a regular, early bedtime, and a nightcap of warm milk and nutmeg rather than wine. Most importantly, I urged her to learn the Transcendental Meditation technique to help manage her stress, reduce the anxiety, and eliminate her need for alcohol. I explained that Transcendental Meditation is about twice as effective for anxiety as other stress-reducing techniques, including the relaxation response, progressive muscle relaxation, biofeedback, and several other types of meditation. There is a substantial body of research indicating that Transcendental Meditation may be helpful in reducing addictions. (See Chapters 7 and 9 for more information about the healing effects of Transcendental Meditation.)

At her next visit two months later, Martha was doing much better. She had started to meditate using Transcendental Meditation and found it extremely helpful. After only one month of regular practice, twice each day for twenty minutes, Martha was feeling much less anxious throughout the day, and her sleep had started to improve. By the second month of practicing Transcendental Meditation and following a full MAV program of diet, herbs, and routine, her severe menstrual cramps had disappeared and her nighttime hot flashes had ceased.

About her new meditation practice, Martha told me: "It has been so effortless and simple that I almost didn't notice anything had changed until I stepped back and remembered how I used to feel just two months ago. I was flying off the handle at nothing. Now I don't feel so upset or tense even about important things. And it's only been two months!" She concluded: "I feel like I'm taking control of my life, instead of taking a drug or hormone for my symptoms. I feel better than I have in a long time."

Martha's experience is not uncommon for highly motivated career women who enter perimenopause with their plate already full, having pushed emotions and body to the limit on a daily basis for a long time. Martha's doshas were barely in balance before menopause, and with the onset of hormonal shifts her vata and pitta doshas quickly went awry.

Remember that menopause is a shift from the pitta-dominated stage of life to the vata-dominated stage of life, and both pitta and vata dosha are very active during this transition. If care isn't taken to keep their functioning smooth, both doshas can easily get out of balance and wreak havoc for you physically and emotionally. Irritability, mood swings, anxiety, and depression — the predominant emotions women experience during perimenopause — are due primarily to imbalances in vata and pitta doshas and can be corrected by careful attention to diet, lifestyle, and behavioral habits.

Symptoms of Vata Imbalance: Worry and Anxiety

Excessive worry and anxiety at midlife are often due to an imbalance in vata dosha, according to MAV. Vata is the moving dosha, associated with the element of air, and it governs your central nervous system. When vata gets disturbed as a result of too much activity (such as frequent travel, excessive exercise, or overwork) or other factors, such as lack of sleep, irregular eating, and excessive caffeine, you can become vulnerable to vata symptoms in mind and body, including the emotions of worry and anxiety and even panic attacks.

Stress and Your Vata

Specifically, midlife anxiety stems from imbalance in your prana vata, the same subdosha involved in brain fog and memory problems that we encountered in Chapter 9. Prana vata governs the flow and speed of your thinking and memory as well as the "tone" of your nervous system.

Your nervous system responds to stimuli much as a rubber band responds when stretched. The tighter you pull the rubber band, the tenser it becomes. Your nerves, too, can feel tense and be stretched beyond the breaking point when you are under pressure. This is exactly what happens when prana vata is aggravated. When your nerves are tightly strung, any little thing can start you worrying, and even minor upsets can create panic.

Anxiety is as physical as it is mental and emotional. The good news is that it doesn't always require years of psychotherapy or introspection to get your anxiety under control. The following story illustrates how anxiety can be the result of stress, especially as it accumulates over a lifetime, and how simple MAV treatments can alleviate it.

Josephine's Story: A Case of Nerves Unknotted

During our consultation, Josephine, a fifty-four-year-old museum curator and mother of three grown children, confided to me that she was puzzled by anxiety attacks that had begun a year after she went through menopause. Her children were now living their own lives and doing well, she loved her work, and she and her devoted husband were financially secure.

"I've had my share of stress and hardships over the years, but I never had this kind of anxiety," she related. "These years are the best in my life so far, and I just don't have a clue why I should have so much anxiety *now.*"

I explained to Josephine that in our culture, we usually understand our emotions as immediate reflections of our current life circumstances. While awareness is growing that most physical health problems arise from years of unhealthy living, that understanding has yet to extend to our emotions. Yet this is exactly what happens. It may seem odd to think of it this way, but a backlog of stress from the past can be just as toxic to your body, mind, and emotions as a buildup of chemicals, pesticides, free radicals, or other forms of toxic ama in your body.

To explain how stress affects the nervous system, let's return to the rubber band analogy. Each incident of stress becomes a knot in the band, tightening and stretching it to the breaking point. While one knot may not be a problem, ten or twenty knots can be, causing the band to lose all flexibility and eventually snap when stretched. Unless you take steps to relax on a regular basis, you become less and less able to respond as a result of accumulated stress, until *you* snap.

Exercise, yoga *asanas* (poses), artistic expression, time spent with nature, getting enough sleep, and good eating habits are all effective ways to prevent the buildup of stress over a lifetime. In addition, the Transcendental Meditation technique reduces chronic anxiety and gives the nervous system a deep rest, allowing it to rejuvenate, heal, and dissolve inner tensions in a spontaneous manner.

For Josephine, learning Transcendental Meditation was instrumental in her recovery by helping her to clear the backlog. Regularizing her diet and bedtime also helped.

"I'd never guessed that stress could be cumulative," Josephine remarked at her next visit. "I'm feeling more relaxed day by day. During my meditation, I can sometimes actually feel the tension releasing from my muscles. It's great to know I am getting freer of stress each day. I only wish I had learned this thirty years ago!"

Vata and Your Deeper Nature

The wisdom of Maharishi Ayurveda tells us that anxiety is fundamentally rooted in a lack of connection with the deepest, innermost nature of your mind. There lies the experience of pure silence and infinite calm. It is not a state of sleep but a state in which you are fully awake to your deepest essence, which is *bliss*. Opening your awareness to this state of blissful, restful alertness every day is the key to enjoying perfect health.

But in our modern, stressful lives, we spend too little time in deep restfulness and even less in bliss. We are overexposed to constantly changing events and experiences outside ourselves, resulting in anxiety and stress, the opposite of our true inner nature. When we don't complement outer activity with the balancing effects of inner silence through meditation, relaxation, recreation, and proper sleep, our vata dosha (specifically prana vata) is thrown out of balance. Fight or flight, supported by chronic cortisol release, becomes a habit of our nervous system we can't turn off when we want to relax, go to sleep, or simply stop to smell the roses. The "on" button has become stuck and we have no real peace.

Fortunately, unsticking your "on" button can be as easy as closing your eyes, if you know what to do. To calm prana vata and restore your deep sense of peace, follow the recommendations for balancing the mind given in Chapter 9, including the pranayama breathing technique. You'll find that just adding these simple techniques to your daily routine will put you more in touch with your deeper, inner nature, and anxiety will have no place to lodge. In addition, get your vata dosha under control by adhering to the guidelines below.

Balance Vata to Banish Anxiety

By now you are probably getting familiar with the mainstay of any vata-balancing routine: a regular schedule for sleeping and eating; a daily oil massage; and a vata-pacifying diet, which favors warm, cooked foods over raw, dry, cold, or crunchy ones. Let's look at these recommendations in more detail.

• Establish regular times for sleeping and eating. Eating at about the same time and sleeping at the same hours automatically helps to regulate your nervous system, which has an inner rhythm naturally attuned to the cycles of day and night. It helps your nervous system to function more smoothly and with less internal stress. An early bedtime improves the quality of rejuvenation you can get from your sleep, leaving you fresher and more resistant to stress the next day.

• Give yourself a massage with oil daily. There are over 1,300 nerve endings in every square inch of your skin, making it your most densely innervated organ aside from your brain. Since oil is the most vata-balancing physical substance, gently applying warm oil and massaging it into the skin is a very effective and direct way to soothe and calm your nerves. I find the oil massage second only to Transcendental Meditation for quelling anxiety and the physical symptoms of shakiness, oversensitivity, gas and bloating, constipation, dryness, and muscle tension that often accompany anxiety.

• Eat a vata-balancing diet. If you are in the habit of quick meals on the run, with lots of salad, cold foods and drinks, and caffeinated beverages, you are setting the stage for anxiety simply by aggravating the vata functions of your physical body. Slow down, eat while sitting down, and favor warm drinks and warm, cooked foods over cold and raw ones. Notice how you feel after eating a warm, balanced meal, topped off with your favorite herbal tea, rather than a salad and a soft drink. I suspect even one such meal will leave you feeling calmer.

Herbs for Calming Anxiety

Several Ayurvedic herbs can calm anxiety, most safely and effectively when combined in specific formulations. According to Ayurveda, Indian valerian root

(*Valeriana, spp.*) and muskroot (*N. jatamamsi*) are both prosedative, meaning they can calm you down and also help to you to relax into sleep. But as discussed previously, it is important not to take such herbs in isolation to avoid addiction, oversedating, or other side effects. With the synergistic action of a variety of herbs, formulated according to strict Ayurvedic principles, no groggy feeling or morning tiredness should occur (in contrast to many modern drugs and some single-ingredient natural remedies).

The potential danger of long-term use of single-ingredient herbal formulations was underscored in late 2001 in Germany, when one very popular anti-anxiety herb, *Kava kava* (*Piper methysticum*) was taken off the market by its manufacturers due to strong evidence linking it to 24 cases of liver damage. Diagnoses indicated liver failure, hepatitis, and cirrhosis, and resulted in one fatality and three people requiring liver transplants. While the German government did not ban Kava kava entirely, pending further scientific investigation, this case underscores the need for caution in the use of single, isolated herbs, and the wisdom of limiting their use to short periods of time.

Ayurvedic herbal combinations are in principle safe, and have been found to be effective against anxiety disorders. A recent study at the University of California at San Diego by Dr. Paul Mills showed that the MAV formulation Worry Free herbal supplement, a balanced formula containing both Indian valerian and muskroot, is effective in reducing day-to-day anxiety as well as reducing anxiety associated with public speaking. The study also showed that Worry Free reduces cortisol, the wear-and-tear-promoting hormone that's released when you're under stress.

Herbs like brahmi (*Bacopa monieri*) and ashwagandha (*Withania somnifera*) alleviate chronic anxiety by restoring the body's own inner intelligence to improve sleep and mental functioning. Again, these herbs should be taken only when combined with other herbs for a balanced effect. (See the Resources for more information on traditionally-formulated MAV herbal products.)

PITTA IMBALANCE: MOOD SWINGS OF IRRITABILITY, ANGER, AND THE BLUES

Although worry and anxiety result from a vata imbalance, mood swings of irritability, anger, sadness, and crying — the blues — all involve pitta dosha, specifically sadhaka pitta, your emotional heart.

In my clinical experience, irritability and angry outbursts are the most common emotional symptoms women report during perimenopause. The classical Ayurvedic text *Harita Samhita* agrees when it says that a midlife woman "becomes sharp in speech and manner" at this time. Prolonged sadness, crying, and grief are also signs that your sadhaka pitta is imbalanced and are often accompanied by feelings of apprehension and anxiety.

Pitta and Your Emotional Heart

You may recall that pitta dosha is involved in metabolism, the digestion and absorption of food for energy to run your body. Sadhaka pitta is concerned more with *emotional* metabolism, specifically how we interpret, process, and react emotionally to the various experiences of life.

Sadhaka pitta has dual residence in your heart and brain, where it governs and coordinates both thinking and feeling. If you have a feeling that is not supported by your mind, such as a longing for an experience or person that you know isn't good for you, your emotional heart is affected. Sadhaka literally means "to achieve or fulfill" and therefore is intimately connected with your ability to fulfill your innermost desires. If you are thwarted in your desires and you do not experience fulfillment in your life's pursuits, you may feel frustrated, disappointed, and resentful. Such feelings often underlie the erratic mood swings of midlife and are reflected in sadhaka pitta aggravation.

When your emotional heart is aggravated, you are vulnerable to impatience when things don't go your way, leaving you with an overall sense of irritability and discontent. You may find yourself blaming your spouse or significant other with little cause, wondering if he really loves you, or suspecting him of cheating on you when you have no real evidence. More severe emotional problems can result from sadhaka pitta imbalance, including depression or even psychosis.

A potentially frightening sign that your emotional heart is out of balance is the occurrence of sensations in the area of your heart, such as palpitations, burning feelings, or even chest pains, that may be a direct result of your emotional distress. Or you may wake up in the middle of the night, often with an accelerated heartbeat, and be unable to return to restful sleep. While vata imbalance tends to cause difficulty falling asleep, pitta imbalance is often the cause of sleep interruption that keeps you awake for hours reading or watching TV in order to try to get back to sleep.

My patient Laura had all of these symptoms, including anxiety.

Laura's Story: The Cure of Fulfillment

I met Laura, a petite forty-six-year-old, when she approached me after a lecture I gave on menopause at a local health conference. She appeared tense and anxiously asked me numerous questions, including whether her problems could be solved without drugs or hormones.

When I inquired further, Laura told me that she had been suffering from crying spells and occasional panic attacks as well as frightening heart palpitations that woke her up in the middle of the night. She had been to see several doctors, but all of them had wanted her to take antidepressants and tranquilizers. She had declined. "I didn't want to feel like a zombie all day," she told me.

I explained to Laura that psychological symptoms in midlife are often unmasked as symptoms due to hormonal changes and usually don't require medication. In fact, for many women, treating emotional problems with antidepressants prevents ever getting at their root causes and restoring balance for full functioning in later years.

Laura came for a consultation the very next day. Her pulse indicated a strongly imbalanced sadhaka pitta, which governs the emotions in both heart and mind, telling me that unfulfilled desires and other frustrations were likely the source of her emotional distress.

"Have you been feeling less content or less fulfilled in your life in the past year of so?" I probed, hoping to begin to draw Laura's attention to the call for help that was going on in her emotional heart.

"As a matter of fact, I have," Laura reflected. "I'm a computer programmer, but I don't really like my work. I'm more of an artistic type. I always wanted to pursue painting as a career."

I encouraged Laura to listen more to her inner desires and begin to fulfill them little by little, even if it meant simply taking an art class and drawing in her spare time. Meanwhile, I gave her a concentrated program of diet and daily routine recommendations to get her symptoms under control quickly. I also recommended a Worry Free tea and tablet, a daily oil massage with pitta-pacifying coconut oil, and rose-petal jam in warm milk before bed. Last but not least, I emphasized the importance of getting to bed early so she could slip off to sleep before her hot, overenergized pitta dosha kicked in at 10 P.M.

Fortunately, results came quickly. Within two weeks, Laura called to tell me she was feeling happier and less anxious and that her sleep had improved. "What I'm most excited about is that I have signed up for a painting and drawing class. I realize that I'm happiest when I'm painting, because art is an important part of who I am. I realize now that I need to make time for that."

Quiz: How Balanced Is Your Emotional Heart?

If your sadhaka pitta is out of balance, you may already have diagnosed yourself by the preceding descriptions. However, if you are in doubt, or wish to gauge the balance of your emotional heart, ask yourself the questions on the following page.

Your Score. If you answered yes to none or only one question, your emotional heart is basically balanced. Follow measures for overall pitta balance listed below for prevention. If you answered yes to two or three questions, your emotional heart is mildly out of balance. Follow the basic steps for pitta balance given in Chapter 4 and here. If you answered yes to four or more questions, your emotional heart is *very* out of balance. Follow the recommendations for pitta balance and sadhaka pitta balance that follow. If you continue to have difficulties, consult a health-care

Quiz: How Balanced Is Your Emotional Heart?

___ Do you tend to feel insecure, doubt yourself, or feel chronically anxious about whether you are doing a good enough job in your various roles as professional, wife, mother, friend?

___ Do you feel that you lack tolerance in the face of emotional stress?

___ Do small things get you upset?

___ Are you easily irritated, or do you have frequent angry outbursts?

___ Do you find yourself doubting your spouse's fidelity without any particular reason, or whether he loves you?

___ Do you wake up frequently throughout the night, or wake up and find you're unable to get back to sleep?

___ Does your mouth often feel dry or as if no amount of water is able to satisfy your thirst?

___ Do you have trouble making decisions and wind up unsatisfied with either option?

professional or a therapist/counselor in addition to following your overall pitta-balancing program.

Balance Pitta to Eliminate Mood Swings

Balancing your pitta dosha can frequently soothe and eliminate your rough, disturbed emotions. As discussed in Chapter 4, the following key steps are important for balancing pitta at menopause: Go to bed before 10 P.M. as a habit and get enough sleep. (This alone can cure 90 percent of irritability and the blues.) Never skip or delay your meals, avoid hot spicy foods and alcohol, and remove impurities with the pitta cleanse.

In addition, there are some very specific foods, drinks, and herbs that directly soothe sadhaka pitta and, at the same time nourish life-giving ojas (your bliss factor). Follow these recommendations if your quiz answers revealed an imbalance in your emotional heart.

• *Sweeten your heart with a rose bouquet.* Rose has a very special role in the treatment of emotional disorders in MAV, due to its unique and direct action on sadhaka pitta and the heart. The scent, taste, sight, and touch of rose all directly squelch the flames of emotional imbalance, enhance positive feelings, and intensify the experience of happiness and bliss. It is no wonder that in cultures around the world, roses are given to say "I love you" to someone special. Rose oil has been prized throughout the ages as a way to calm the emotions, soothe stress, and cultivate love and other nourishing feelings.

If your emotional heart imbalance rated four or higher, make a point of treating yourself to roses in some form every day. Rose is available for medicinal purposes as aromatherapy (use essential oil of rose), as rose water (for use in drinks or in cooking), as a tea (made of rose petals in boiling water), or as a food. Yes, certain roses are actually edible as food-grade dried rose petals or in a convenient Rose Petal Preserve.

In MAV, *rosa centifolia* (literally "a hundred petals") is chosen out of hundreds of varieties of wild and cultivated roses for food and medicinal uses. Be sure that any rose petals or products you use are pesticide free and made from the highest-quality food-grade roses available.

Here are some suggestions to get the benefits of rose in your diet and routine. (See the Resources Appendix for more information on products using roses.)

• Add a dash of rose water to rice pudding or other milk desserts for a pitta-cooling snack.

• Add one or two teaspoons of crushed dried rose petals to boiling water. Steep for ten minutes and strain. Add organic sugar to taste if desired. Drink once or twice a day for emotional calming effects.

• Use eight to ten drops of essential oil of rose in a potpourri pot or four to five drops on a handkerchief next to your pillow to chill your emotions and balance your pitta while you sleep at night.

• At bedtime, drink a cup of milk boiled with a pinch of cardamom powder. Add a teaspoon of rosewater after it cools down a bit.

• Drink a sweetened lassi with lunch whenever your pitta is on edge, and all summer long if you live in a hot climate.

• Keep a jar of rose-petal preserve in your desk drawer at work or in your purse for "pitta emergencies." Eat a teaspoon straight off the spoon, or on bread or a cracker, when you are feeling especially irritable.

• *Eat a pear* or other sweet, juicy fruit when you feel cranky, irritable, or upset. Pear is the number one fruit to nourish ojas immediately. The combination of natural sugars and complex carbohydrates gives the ideal nourishing fluid directly to ojas in your heart and brain. If a pear is not available, any sweet, juicy fruit will do. Grapes, plums, mangoes, watermelon, cantaloupe, papaya, and berries are all good pitta pacifiers. The main criterion is that the fruit tastes sweet, not sour. Citrus fruit in general is not effective for pacifying pitta.

- *Avoid environmental factors that trigger excess pitta.* Don't go out in the hot sun or heat when you are hungry or thirsty. Be sure to drink water or have a sweet, juicy fruit beforehand.

- *Be "pitta-wise" in your relationships.* Never discuss sensitive or potentially anger-provoking issues on an empty stomach or with someone who is hungry. Avoid the time right before lunch, when pitta is most active. Feed your spouse or friend a delicious meal before discussing touchy or difficult topics. Also, avoid angry, negative people as much as possible. You may need to set limits with friends, relatives, or acquaintances who constantly drain you emotionally by their focus on problems and bad news.

When you feel rough emotionally, the Vedic prescription is to be on your best behavior in your relationships with others. Take responsibility to balance your pitta with the above recommendations and try to be as pleasant as you can. This will aid in damage control when things go awry in your relationships and will also protect your own emotional heart.

Herbs to Soothe Your Mood

Since our physical and emotional hearts are so intimately connected, it is no surprise that the all-around best herb for heart health, Arjuna myrabolans (*Terminalia arjuna*) powerfully nourishes and supports "both" our hearts. Arjuna is the main ingredient in a carefully balanced MAV formula that is very effective for balancing the emotions. In my practice, it has "cured" many a case of perimenopausal blues, relationship heartbreak, and out-of-control irritability.

Likewise, our minds and our hearts jointly govern our emotional responses. Therefore, herbs for balancing the mind and calming the nerves are often blended with herbs for the heart, such as Arjuna, for maximum emotional support. Brahmi and Shankapushpi are two such herbs used in MAV preparations for emotional well-being. (Refer to Chapters 7 and 9 for more details on these herbs and to the Resources for product information.)

Cultivate Ojas to Eliminate Mood Swings

The heart is home not only to sadhaka pitta but also to ojas, the life-giving essence that so intimately nourishes your immunity and brings you happiness and bliss. If your emotional heart gets out of balance and anger and irritability become the norm, Vedic wisdom states that the critical repository of ojas in the heart can become scorched or burnt. It is believed that such damage to *even one drop* of essential ojas in the heart can lead to death.

This explains why chronic anger, depression, and anxiety all set you up for cardiovascular disease and can directly cause a heart attack (see Chapter 7). The quality of your thoughts and emotions can actually damage your physical heart, as well as impair immunity and cut short your life span, by creating biochemical changes that harm or destroy precious, life-giving ojas.

Dealing with Your Anger

You may recall that ojas is enhanced by the practice of specific behaviors known as rasayanas or rejuvenatives. According to the Vedic text, a person who practices rasayana and behaves in a way that protects ojas "does not entertain negativity." The wording is very precise here. It does not advise you to suppress negative emotions when they arise or avoid dealing with situations that might bring out your anger. "Stuffing" your feelings is never a good idea and only drives the emotional stress deeper into your body-mind to manifest later as chronic physical or mental illness. Rather, not entertaining negativity refers to not dwelling on or stewing over wrongs and injustices that may have come your way. Deal with them as best you can and move on. Otherwise, it is your own health that suffers.

The practice of rasayana also does not include venting your anger at a person or situation you perceive has done you wrong. This can lead to even more damage (including actual damage to your physical heart) than holding that anger inside (as research in mind-body medicine has verified). Instead, try to identify the exact source of your frustration and deal with it as rationally and calmly as possible later, after giving time for your pitta to cool down.

For instance, if your husband has overspent your budget for the third month in a row, sending you into a mini "pitta fit" of rage as you review the latest bank statement, curtail your desire to call him on the phone and let him have it at that very moment. Instead, have a sweet, juicy fruit or a cool drink or take a walk to chill out. Then choose a time when you can sit down together and discuss the issue in a more relaxed and open environment. And be sure to hold the discussion after a delicious meal so *his* pitta is also less likely to rear its sometimes ugly head!

Programs that train you to be more assertive or deal with chronic anger can be helpful, especially if sadhaka pitta imbalance is your lifelong tendency. But fortunately, as several of the patient stories in this chapter have illustrated, anger, irritability, and mood swings at perimenopause are usually transient, due more to physiological causes than psychological ones, and can generally be relieved without extensive psychotherapy or medication. The key is to reestablish balance of your mind-body system, especially in your emotional heart, and take measures to enhance ojas.

To enhance ojas, MAV provides a very pragmatic approach called "the principle of the second element." This means that whenever you experience darkness, instead of dwelling in it or spending your time figuring out who turned out the lights and why, simply turn them on again! In other words, a heart filled with love, bliss, and wholeness leaves no room for negativity. Practice the Transcendental Meditation technique to dissolve your stress, read your favorite spiritual or religious books, engage in some healthful activity that makes you happy. Fill yourself with balance, fulfillment, and bliss. This doesn't suppress, stuff, or explode your negative reactions. Rather, it dissolves and eliminates them from within.

When the Blues Have a Hold on You

Mild depression — gloominess and the blues — is common at midlife and does not usually require antidepressant medication to be reversed. Instead, try the simple but powerful Ayurvedic recommendations below.

Walking in nature, especially in cool environments like the woods, mountains, and lakes, and walking into the rising sun, can knock out a depression that nothing else seems to shake. According to MAV, the rising sun and fresh morning air filled with prana have a revitalizing effect on the emotions (as opposed to the setting sun, which tends to cause tiredness). If you can awaken early enough, take a walk into the rising sun, letting its light fall on your face, chest, and abdomen. These bodily regions benefit most from the sun's melting effect because they are areas where negative emotions can become blocked and accumulate. The sun in the Vedic system represents your deepest self, Nature's intelligence within you, whose life-giving light dispels all gloom and negativity.

Arranging your sleeping environment so your head is pointing east or south can also lift a gloomy mood. We know this from the *Sthapatya Veda,* an aspect of the Veda concerned with how you place things in relation to the natural environment around you (*vastu vidya*). (In fact, the Vedic tradition includes a whole science of building and furnishing designed to support dosha balance and clarity of thinking, with everything in its special place, similar to the Chinese *feng shui* but with some important differences.) Modern science validates this theory in studies showing that when people sleep with their heads to the north, they report significantly more irritation and confusion in thinking and show elevated levels of serum cholinesterase — a marker of increased stress — the next day. For a better sleep tonight and a better mood tomorrow, remember: "Sleep east, *never* north."

Cleansing Ama to Lift Your Mood

A diet of pure food, along with good digestion and metabolism, can also keep gloomy moods and depression at bay during menopause. The catch is that when hormones shift, you may be tempted to eat more sweets and junk food to relieve emotional stress. For example, during the holidays, painful memories or family conflict can stimulate you to overeat, resulting in imbalanced sadhaka pitta. While eating junk and overeating may be comforting emotionally, it can actually create more digestive impurities (ama), intensifying depression and trapping you in a vicious cycle of mood swings and weight gain.

To clear the hormone-blocking, mentally depressing wastes from your body, drink an herbalized water daily, eat phytoestrogenic grains like quinoa, couscous, and amaranth, and use smart spices in your cooking (the foundation approach I recommend in Chapter 6). Once your channels and tissues are cleared, the inner intelligence of your body can work more effectively. Your hormonal balance will improve and along with it your mood.

Dealing with More than the Blues

Occasionally feeling down and crying easily can be normal at midlife, but if your mood doesn't seem to lift over time, you may be suffering from serious clinical depression. As mentioned earlier, major depression is no more common during perimenopause and is less common after menopause than it is earlier in a woman's life.

Still, if you are *persistently* experiencing the symptoms listed below (meaning that several of them are present daily for at least two weeks), or you are having suicidal thoughts, then you are experiencing more serious depression and should see a health professional immediately.

Here are the most common symptoms of major depression.

• Persistent negative thoughts with overriding feelings of guilt, self-blame, hopelessness, and worthlessness

• A feeling that life is not worth living or suicidal thoughts

• Difficulty getting to sleep, waking up too early with trouble getting back to sleep, chronically oversleeping, or finding it impossible to get up in the morning

• Loss of appetite with significant weight loss, or overeating and significant weight gain

• Severe, persistent aches and pains for no apparent reason

• Trouble concentrating to the point that it interferes with your work or family duties.

If you have any of these symptoms, don't try to treat yourself with natural, at-home remedies from this book or any other source. Instead, consult your health professional without delay for a further evaluation of your symptoms. Certainly you can also follow all the recommendations for emotional well-being you find in this chapter, but do consult your health professional before taking any herbs (other than foods, spices, and herbs you use in cooking) to make sure they are compatible with the treatment program he or she prescribes for you.

MAV's Big Guns to Fight Mood Disorders and Chronic Conditions: Transcendental Meditation, MVVT, and MRT

In my seventeen years of clinical, I have found three approaches of MAV to have the most all-encompassing power in healing. I have already described two of them and cited numerous cases that illustrate their healing power, but I include them again in case you are having anxiety, worry, and other mood swings. First is the Transcendental Meditation technique for stress reduction (*and* unfolding your mental and spiritual potential). Second is Maharishi Rejuvenation Treatment, which consists of authentic, medically supervised panchakarma cleansing treatments done at a spa or treatment center. The third is a fascinating ancient Vedic healing technique, known as Maharishi Vedic Vibration Technology, which uses very subtle Vedic sounds to re-create balance in the mind and body.

All three of these health approaches require you to take advantage of MAV services beyond the at-home approaches in this book and involve significant expenditure, but I believe you will find them well worth it. The Resources lists centers and locations that offer these services.

The Transcendental Meditation Technique

For treating the emotions and mood, a technique that increases calmness, inner stability, and positivity *and* decreases stress and negative emotions would be ideal. Such a technique should develop the mind's capacity for inner silence, bliss, and refinement of the emotions and at the same time clear accumulated stress, fatigue, and strain from the nervous system.

This is an accurate description of the dual effects of Transcendental Meditation. The mind experiences deeper levels of its own silent, blissful nature, and the nervous system purifies itself of stress. Since the nervous system is the instrument through which your mind and emotions are created and expressed, the purity and strength of that instrument determines how sweet and harmonious your emotions will be.

In short, research on Transcendental Meditation and my years of clinical experience seeing the benefits in well over a thousand of my patients have convinced me that nearly everyone's mental, emotional, and spiritual health can profit from it.

Maharishi Vedic Vibration Technology

Maharishi Vedic Vibration Technology (MVVT) is a unique and elegant non-medical approach to chronic health conditions that works by realigning your physiology with Nature's healing intelligence through the subtle use of Vedic sounds. According to modern physics, the deepest level of the body consists of wavelike fluctuations or vibrations of the unified field that underlies all material creation. According to Vedic science, these vibrations can be understood as very subtle sounds, which are unique for each area of the mind and body. Directing these specific Vedic sounds to the area of the physiology that is imbalanced, by traditional Vedic experts trained in this approach, can rebalance that area of the body, much as a tuning fork can be used to tune an instrument.

Unusual as this may sound, research on the use of this healing technology attests to its effectiveness. A recently published, double-blind, placebo-controlled experiment found MVVT to be very effective at reducing pain from arthritis and other chronic pain conditions. Mental health research on over two hundred individuals has shown its usefulness for anxiety, depression, grief, anger, and emotional instability, documenting an average reported improvement of 55 to 75 percent for these conditions. The improvement was relatively stable at follow-up an average of seven months later.

I mention this extraordinary nonmedical treatment here because, in the two years since this technology has been available, I have seen dozens of my patients gain quick relief with MVVT from longstanding, chronic conditions of grief, anxiety, depression, fear, chronic pain, and even hot flashes As a physician, it is gratifying to see patients, many of whom have "tried everything" and are on medication for their conditions, improve dramatically and gain quick relief from long-term suffering. Remarkably, all that's involved are three one-hour-long, totally effortless sessions of MVVT, with no required change in lifestyle. While no health approach works for everybody, two out of three participants experience significant improvement in disorders that have been present for fourteen years on average. For most, it is a shortcut to attain balance quickly, effortlessly, and for many, blissfully.

Writes one participant with chronic anxiety, "Dr. Lonsdorf suggested that the program might address the fear and anxiety I reported during my physical exam. The

MVVT consultation gave me a burst of confidence that I could *do anything*. Right afterward, I was exhilarated and excited. Now everything in my life is much more enjoyable, easy, fun, and loving."

Maharishi Rejuvenation Treatment

The other major Ayurvedic healing technology that I have found to be extremely powerful and to create miracles, both big and small, is Maharishi Rejuvenation Treatment, traditionally referred to as panchakarma. MRT consists of a variety of gentle purification techniques, including relaxing herbalized oil applications and massage (imagine getting your abhyanga performed *for* you by two angelic women technicians working in synchrony on either side of your body), bliss-inducing warm oil treatments, and mild cleansing treatments. These treatments together act in a systematic way to stimulate your digestion and metabolism, loosen and remove deep deposits of toxic ama, and enliven the silent wholeness of Nature's healing intelligence within you.

Conducted in a clinical spa setting staffed by professionals trained in MAV, this therapy almost always improves chronic health problems. In treatments lasting just a week, I have repeatedly witnessed dramatic improvements in stubborn menopausal symptoms, multiple sclerosis, fibromyalgia, chronic pain, digestive problems, chronic fatigue, and a host of other chronic disorders. MRT also improves mental and emotional well-being by the same dual mechanism as Transcendental Meditation, by deeply settling the mind while ridding the nervous system of stress.

Be alert, however, that not all panchakarmas are alike. Many spas today offer isolated treatments or "tastes" of panchakarma, such as the relaxing abhyanga (oil application and massage) or shirodhara (oil poured on the forehead). But very few offer authentic Ayurvedic panchakarma treatment, prescribed and supervised by Ayurvedic and Western-trained physicians, that is capable of improving your chronic health conditions in any real or lasting way. While doing a full week of the real thing is not inexpensive, the genuine and profound benefits you will receive are well worth it.

One patient, a fifty-seven-year-old career woman in the federal government, describes how MRT improved her menopause-related mood swings.

"For a six-year period following menopause, I experienced depression for the first time in my life. Antidepressants and HT gave me side effects, and I had to stop all of them eventually. I couldn't sleep well at night. I felt depressed and miserable every day, had terrible mood swings, and gained twenty pounds that I just couldn't take off.

"When I began my first week-long MRT treatment, I was at the end of my rope. Yet, I found the whole experience very enjoyable. The treatments of massage, warm oil treatments, and mild cleansing therapies were gentle and health-giving.

Every day I felt better and better. I started to sleep better at night, weight started to drop off effortlessly, the depression lifted for the first time in six years, and even my sense of smell returned.

"During the education sessions, I discovered that the food I had been eating, though nutritious, was not good for me in other ways. I learned many dietary, cooking, and other behavioral approaches that I have followed at home with continued good results.

"It's even easy to follow the new lifestyle I've adopted because I want to keep this wonderful feeling of energy and vitality that's been restored through my MRT treatment. It's now over a year since my treatment and I still feel great.

"It absolutely changed my life."

Turning Midlife Blues into Midlife Bliss

Now that you have an arsenal of remedies and techniques under your belt for doing battle with your midlife mood swings — and, I hope, preventing them from striking in the first place — there is no more need to be cranky, ornery, weepy, or mad! Instead, you can tap into your emotional reserves and start experiencing the menopausal zest that is your natural state. Expand your idea of what it means to be menopausal by freeing yourself emotionally, enhancing your ojas, and spending this time of your life getting to know bliss.

* 11 *

Your Skin — A Program for Ageless Beauty

Inner and outer beauty are the foundation of lasting beauty — beauty that does not fade with age.
— Maharishi Ayurveda

Beauty is an essential aspect of our being. As women, we invest a tremendous amount of time, energy, and money in how we look and feel. Yet, we are often frustrated and disappointed with the outcome, because we measure beauty by standards set by the fashion and cosmetic industry — the "perfect" faces and bodies seen on every magazine rack. We are left feeling flawed and inferior by comparison and long for an ideal of beauty that has the power to unlock what is magnificent and unique in each of us.

After menopause, these challenges only increase. The pharmaceutical and medical industries, take advantage of our vulnerability, and offer us Botox, facelifts, prescription exfoliants, and the HT "solution," promising through drugs and surgery what we can have naturally when our physiology is in balance — youthful beauty that lasts.

Feminine Forever — The Myth Of HT

Published in the 1960s, the best-selling book *Feminine Forever*, by Dr. Robert Wilson, promised a cure that offered youth and beauty through drugs, specifically Premarin, made from the urine of pregnant horses. According to the *New York Times*,

Wilson's son stated in 2002 that the drug company Wyeth-Ayerst (the makers of Premarin) had paid for writing the book and had financed Dr. Wilson's lectures to women's groups on the benefits of hormone replacement. In those youth-obsessed times, when Marilyn Monroe was the ideal, women quickly bought into the idea that a single pill, HT, could keep them wrinkle-free, with lustrous hair and sensuous bodies, well after their ovaries had ceased to produce eggs.

Although the myth of HT hangs on, scientific studies do not support the idea that loss of estrogen causes the wrinkling and sagging of skin, which often marks beauty's decline at midlife. *Aging* does that, and aging effects can be largely prevented with the natural, holistic approaches already presented in this book. Even if taking estrogen *were* helpful to your aging skin, the risks revealed in the Women's Health Initiative make the cost too high. We now know better than to trust a single drug or hormone therapy to keep us youthful.

Scientifically, there are very few studies on estrogen's ability to prevent wrinkles and sagging skin. Estrogen has been known to bolster *collagen* — the protein that provides firmness to connective tissue — for a smooth skin, but a Spanish study showed that estrogen didn't prevent the expected loss of collagen that occurs with age. Another study assessed collagen content of the skin of women taking HT and found that these women had slightly more collagen than those who weren't on HT. However, this study isn't very significant since most women who chose to take HT were healthier in the first place.

Many women tell me they stopped taking HT, or were unhappy with it because of the effect it had on their skin. The package insert for Premarin clearly states that it does not help your skin, and even lists as one of the side effects "a spotty darkening of the skin, particularly on the face." Ayurvedically, pitta dosha is responsible for the metabolism, coloration and glow of the skin, and HT throws it out of balance, causing such effects. Some women have further pitta disturbances from HT, such as acne in their fifties or red, itchy patches (usually after sixty).

Still, many women cling to the hope that by taking HT they will achieve eternal, wrinkle-free youth and sensuality. This belief persists, even though there is no scientific evidence to support it. When HT is no longer seen as a viable option, we are faced with a sobering dilemma: Without drugs or hormones, how do we maintain a youthful appearance at menopause and beyond? Ayurvedically speaking, we must first ask a more profound question: What do we mean by *beauty*?

A NEW PARADIGM OF BEAUTY

The ancient science of MAV presents a "new" paradigm of beauty for modern women that cannot be mass marketed, but rather allows you to become the most radiant and peaceful expression of your own unique self. In the MAV ideal, beauty is not about conforming to a specific facial structure, eye color, or body size — it is about the entire vision of beauty that shines outward from within. Your outer appearance reveals the depth of your wholeness as a person, including your intelligence, personality, emotions, and your relationship to those around you.

In Western cultures, youthful appearance is worshipped, while we rarely appreciate beauty in older women. Growing older is dreaded as a passage in which we lose our outer, or surface, beauty, and have no other paradigm to fall back on. But in the more traditional culture of India, older women are the gurus, or teachers, of the young. Aging is associated with wisdom, authority, and prestige, and women wear the glow of inner knowing that brings confidence, self-respect, and self-worth. They seem to grow more beautiful with age, not less.

Subhanga Karanam — The MAV Definition of Beauty

Maharishi Ayurveda offers a precise term for beauty — *subhanga karanam* — based on three root words from Sanskrit: *subha*, which means "auspicious"; *anga*, which means "body part"; and *karanam*, which means "transformation." True beauty is present when all parts of your body are transformed to the most auspicious, or promising level. To paraphrase this ancient description, we might say that beauty is the promise of your unique being radiantly transformed and shining through your physical body.

Have you ever met a woman who looked especially radiant and unforgettable, attractive beyond beautiful? This is the inner power of subhanga karanam shining through to the surface. You can read a woman's sense of self-worth on her face, and when it is there, it makes her beautiful. The better we feel about ourselves, the more attractive we look to others.

The Three Pillars of Beauty

Maharishi Ayurveda believes true beauty as supported by three pillars. *Roopam*, or outer beauty; *gunam*, or inner beauty; and *vayastyag* or lasting beauty. Together, these three pillars give a balanced approach to beauty that guides us in specific care and treatment regimens to bring about the transformation to true beauty.

Roopam (Outer Beauty)

The outer signs of beauty — your skin, hair, and nails — are direct reflections of your overall health. The physiological functions that are responsible for health must be in balance if you want to maintain outer aspects of your appearance. This depends more on the strength of your metabolism, the quality of your diet, and the purity of your blood and plasma than on external creams or your hairstylist's skill.

Keeping your tissues clear of ama, and supporting your digestion as well as eating a pure diet, make all the difference. Follow the Healing Meal Plan (Chapter 4) and drink your personalized wise water, (Chapters 6), to see quick results in your skin. This regimen has yielded rewarding results for many of my patients, especially those with adult acne and rosacea, conditions that may easily worsen with less gentle approaches.

Also, follow the more specific recommendations in Chapter 6 for clearing your dhatus, especially *rasa* (for wrinkles and lack of luster), *rakta* (for inflammation and redness), *mamsa* (for acne and boils), and *meda* (for excessive oil or inflamed sweat glands). This will eliminate ama and toxins that may be irritating or dulling your skin. It will also improve your digestion (agni), providing more nourishment to your skin, which may be depleted and lacking lubrication, substance, and fullness. Without adequate nourishment, your collagen layer thins and a kind of wasting takes place. Over time, your skin can shrivel up like a plant without water — due *not* to a lack of estrogen, but to these largely correctable imbalances.

Gunam (Inner Beauty)

Inner beauty is authentic beauty, not the kind that shows on a made-up face, but the kind that shines through from your soul, your consciousness, or inner state of being. Gunam reflects that your mind and heart are in harmony, not at odds and causing emotional confusion, loss of confidence, stress, or worry. When you are not at peace, an illusionary appearance prevails, and your outer beauty has little meaning.

Maintain your self-confidence and a warm, loving personality by paying attention to lifestyle and daily routine, managing stress through meditation, eating your main meal at midday, and going to bed early. Herbal supplements can help, as well. Remember, kindness, friendliness and sincerity can make a person attractive, while being uptight or tense makes people want to walk the other way, regardless of your facial structure, body weight, or other outer signs we associate with attractiveness.

Vayastyag (Lasting Beauty)

Lasting beauty means eternal beauty that is ageless. This is the pillar most relevant to women over forty, because it addresses the issues of antiaging and rejuvenation. Modern science and MAV agree that aging is due in great part to the damage caused by free radical oxidation of your cells and tissues. Free radicals are created when you are exposed to pollutants, chemicals, and poor nutrition, and even stress, all of which hasten the aging process. In contrast, retarding free radicals by reducing stress, eating well, and cleansing your body of toxic wastes slows the aging process. MAV prescribes a specific anti-aging regimen of diet, lifestyle recommendations, herbal skin care products, and herbal supplements, such as *Amrit Kalash* shown in published research to slow biological aging and offer 1,000 times more powerful protection against free radicals than the popular antioxidants vitamins C and E.

MAV also looks at social and psychological factors involved in aging. A peaceful home life and nourishing relationships are important to curb social aging. To prevent psychological aging, a low-stress lifestyle and spiritual practices such as the Transcendental Meditation technique have a profound effect on how you feel on the inside—which determines how radiant and beautiful you look on the outside.

A Balanced Approach

In MAV, all three pillars of beauty are considered equally important when treatments and care regimens are introduced. For example, *roopam*, the outer appearance of beauty, is approached by first restoring balance at the fundamental level of your physiology. Then, your body will naturally create more healthy and structurally sound skin cells continuously as you age, supporting vayastyag, or lasting beauty. Without inner beauty, *gunam*, the other kinds of beauty will seem empty and superficial, a kind of false beauty we see so often in the soulless expressions of many supermodels and some popular movie stars.

In contrast, Western care regimens emphasize outer beauty only, making for a lopsided approach that sacrifices a person's overall well-being for an immediate, short-term result. We see this when harsh chemicals are used in a skin care product to dry up oily skin, but ultimately cause dryness and premature wrinkles. The three pillars allow us to treat not only outer appearance, but all other levels, including the senses, mind, and spirit, laying the foundation for a truly balanced and holistic approach to beauty care.

Ideal Routine for Ideal Skin

To understand how significantly lifestyle impacts your skin, a mini-lesson in Ayurvedic physiology of the skin is in order. The most important principle to understand is that your skin is a mirror of the purity of the blood that feeds it. If you have toxic, preservative-laden, trans-fatty foods in your blood from a heavy restaurant meal the night before, you can expect that these pro-inflammatory substances in your bloodstream will promote inflammation, irritation, hyperpigmentation, or other disfiguring conditions.

Fortunately, our skin has a daily cleansing cycle that helps it purify toxins and protect its youthful, healthy glow. This cycle occurs during the nighttime "pitta" time from 10 P.M. to 2 A.M. If you are sleeping during this time, your skin and body can effectively cleanse themselves of leftover toxins and wastes accumulated in the cells during the day. But if you are up and about after 10 P.M., your energy is being used for other activity and your body's cleansing cycle is weakened. Not only that, but after 10 P.M., your pitta-fired appetite "kicks in" demanding the proverbial "midnight snack." The end result is food coming *in* at a time the body wants to get *rid* of leftover food and toxins, further thwarting your skin's nighttime "beauty cycle."

Another beauty buster occurs when we sleep in to try to make up for staying up late. Lying in bed after 6 A.M. tends to increase kapha, your sluggish, liquidy dosha. The result is a puffy face and bags under the eyes. This situation is compounded if you ate a rich or heavy meal later in the evening, another kapha-increasing habit. These kapha-aggravating habits can also make you gain weight.

Five Magical Tips for Ageless Beauty

To keep your face looking youthful and beautiful, your figure trim, and to improve your overall health, follow these five magical tips to ageless beauty. I call these "magical," because I have found that within only a few days, most women notice a new-found healthy glow and freshness in their faces just from following even one of these simple tips.

• Go to bed and turn your light off by 9:45 P.M. and get up by 6 A.M.

• Take a walk for at least ten minutes outdoors in the fresh air within an hour or two of sunrise.

• Eat fresh, pure, organic foods with lots of sweet, juicy fruits and vegetables during the day.

• Drink plenty of pure spring water during the day (room temperature or warm, not cold).

• Eat a light evening meal without meat, rich sauces, or cheese by 7 P.M. at the latest.

YOUR SKIN AND LASTING BEAUTY

Your skin, the sense organ that covers your entire face and body, is perhaps the foremost marker of your physical beauty. It is also the first place to show signs of aging, such as wrinkles, brown spots, sagging, and drooping. Because your skin is so pivotal in causing an aging appearance, I will concentrate my explanations and recommendations in the remainder of this chapter on the Maharishi Ayurveda understanding and treatment of your skin. The Vedic prescriptions, however, contain a wealth of knowledge to cover other aspects of beauty, such as hair, nails, and sensuality, but they are too lengthy to cover in a single chapter.

Your Skin's Natural Intelligence

According to MAV, your skin, like all of your organs, tissues, and cells, has intelligence. Our modern science supports this claim of the skin's intelligence by pointing out that each square inch of skin contains 1,300 nerve endings, creating a direct link between skin and brain. Think of your skin as an extension of your nervous system, enabling it to be directly influenced by your thoughts and emotions. We know that skin breakouts and rashes go hand in hand with emotional upsets, especially in adolescence, and this may occur again around menopause, when hormones are fluctuating.

MAV understands your mind-body connection in terms of the doshas. *Vyana vata*, a subdivision of vata dosha located throughout the entire body, governs your skin's overall physiology through communication and circulation, and provides the sensitive, *feeling* aspect of your skin. Closely connected to vyana vata is *prana vata*, another subdivision of vata which governs your mind. When your skin senses heat and cold, the information goes via vyana vata to prana vata — from the skin to the brain. "Cold" is information that flows from the skin to the brain. Information flowing from the brain back to the body might be: "I need a blanket!"

Because your skin is suffused with nature's intelligence, it can rejuvenate naturally when this intelligence is supported and enhanced. In other words, aging skin can become young again. MAV prescribes specific diet, lifestyle, care regimens and herbal formulations that contain balanced and enlivening ingredients to awaken the inherent power of your skin to stay youthful.

Your Skin after Menopause

We have seen that loss of estrogen does not necessarily cause your skin to wrinkle and sag, while the effects of aging can. Why then does women's skin show signs of aging more than men's skin? This gender gap is all too painfully apparent when men in their forties and fifties, and sometimes beyond, retain firm, smooth skin. It's even a cliché that men grow more "distinguished" with age, while we women simply lose our beauty.

Despite such culturally reinforced beliefs, there *is* a real biological reason for the differences in aging male and female skin. Female hormones make women's skin softer and thinner, while male hormones, such as testosterone, give men thicker and harder skin which is more resistant to wrinkling. Also, in women, the secretion of oil from the fat layer in the skin is generally less than for a man, so women's skin is drier and thinner, making it more prone to the effects of aging.

All the factors that contribute to women's skin aging faster than men's become even more pronounced when hormones fluctuate at menopause. As estrogen levels decline, your skin's sebaceous glands produce less oil, and the underlying lipid, or fat, layer becomes even thinner. Without its natural emollients, your skin has a tendency to dry out more easily and lose its softness, all signs of this vata-dominated time of life. Wrinkles and lines appear on your face. There is also a thinning of the protective layer on top of the skin, making it more photo-sensitive and less tolerant of dry and windy weather which can easily irritate it. As skin gets more sensitive, it becomes more prone to infection, inflammation, dermatitis, breakout, sunburn, and allergens. Doshically, this kind of stress to the skin aggravates your pitta dosha, further adding to the irritability of your skin.

Other structural changes happen with menopause. The flow of blood to your skin decreases as you age, bringing less nutrition to skin cells and causing skin to heal more slowly. Lack of oils and fatty substances due to hormonal fluctuations and increasing vata deprive your skin of essential nutrients, further depleting it. Undernourished skin looks sallow, nonvital and drained of color and brightness, as if it were starving or wasting away. Collagen synthesis falls off due to hormonal fluctuation, further decreasing your skin's firmness and elasticity.

Katerina's Story

Katerina is fifty-eight-year-old writer from California who has followed the program outlined in this book for several years and has also been to The Raj for Maharishi Rejuvenation Treatment. She was so pleased with the effects of her MAV treatments that when I asked her if she would write a brief account of her experience, she was thrilled. Here is her story in her own enthusiastic words:

"Wow! What did you do? You look ten years younger." That's what I keep hearing since following Maharishi Ayurveda for menopause. I have to admit that facing menopause scared me. I thought my skin would sag, my muscle tone would go and I would start to look like my grandmother — old before her time. Hormone therapy seemed like the magic pill and I took it. When Dr. Lonsdorf suggested that I follow Maharishi Ayurveda for menopause including stopping the hormones, I thought, "Here I go. I'll be healthy, but I'll look like my grandmother."

Following her advice and treatment, I am healthier and believe me, I look nothing like my grandmother! Following the simple diet and lifestyle changes of Maharishi Ayurveda for menopause I look younger and am the absolute envy of my friends. I feel younger and healthier than I have in years. At my recent forty-year high school reunion, people told me I looked the same as I did forty years ago, only now I glow. Someone recently came up to me at a meeting and said, "I hope you feel as good as you look!" I do.

THE MAHARISHI AYURVEDA APPROACH TO SKIN CARE

The MAV approach to skin care and treatment is first of all holistic. It recognizes that your skin is not separate from the rest of your body, any more than your arm or head is. The skin on your face is also not separate from the skin that covers the rest of your body, and responds by giving you feedback when affected by environmental or dietary factors. Therefore, whatever facial skin therapies we use in MAV are assumed to touch the whole skin, the whole body, and the whole person. For this reason, MAV doesn't treat the skin in isolation, but in the context of the whole physiology and the whole person.

The MAV approach also addresses your skin's natural intelligence with specific dietary, behavioral, and skin care regimens aimed at balancing your doshic tendencies. The dietary and behavioral recommendations for balancing each dosha given in Chapter 4, when followed, will support your skin's health and beauty. Additionally, knowledge of your doshic skin type can give you a precise road map for prevention, diagnosis, and treatment of skin problems when they arise.

Your Doshic Skin Type

For simplicity, we can translate your doshic tendencies here as *skin types*: vata skin type, pitta skin type, and kapha skin type. Each doshic skin type will be described in terms of skin qualities, inclination toward certain problems, and the ideal regimen to make your skin type radiant. As you read the descriptions of skin types below, try to identify which is yours, then follow my prescriptions and care regimens for any imbalances you may be experiencing.

Vata Skin

Vata is composed of the elements of air and space. If you have a vata skin type, your skin will be dry, thin, fine-pored, delicate and cool to the touch. If vata skin is imbalanced, it will be prone to excessive dryness and may even be rough and flaky. The greatest beauty challenge for your skin is its disposition to symptoms of early aging. Your skin tends to develop wrinkles earlier than the other beauty types, and, if your digestion is not in balance, your skin will begin to look dull and gray even in early life. In addition, your skin may have a tendency for disorders such as dry eczema.

Pitta Skin

Pitta dosha is composed of the elements of fire and water. If you have a pitta skin type your skin is fair, soft, warm, and of medium thickness. Your hair typically is fine and straight, and is usually red, sandy, or blond in color. Your complexion tends toward the pink or reddish, and there is often a copious amount of freckles or moles.

Among the many beauty challenges of pitta skin types is your tendency to develop rashes, rosacea, acne, liver spots, or pigment disorders. Because of the large proportion of the fire element in your constitution, your skin does not tolerate heat very well. Of all the three skin types, pitta skin has the least tolerance for the sun, is photosensitive, and most likely to accumulate sun damage over the years. Tanning treatments and therapies that involve excessive use of facial or whole body steam can be counterproductive for your skin. Whereas vata skin gets aggravated by mental stress, your skin tends to get aggravated by emotional stress, such as suppressed anger, frustration, or resentment.

Kapha Skin

Kapha dosha is composed of the elements of earth and water. If you have a kapha skin type your skin is thick, oily, soft, and cool to the touch. Your complexion is pale, and the hair thick, wavy, oily, and dark. Kapha skin types tend to develop wrinkles much later in life than vata or pitta types. If your skin becomes imbalanced, it can show up as enlarged pores, excessively oily skin, moist types of eczema, blackheads or pimples, and water retention. Kapha skin is also more prone to fungal infections.

MAV Care Regimens for Your Skin Type

Care regimens for your doshic skin type include cleansing, hydrating, moisturizing, and nourishing your skin to keep it glowing with youthful health. Follow my specific recommendations and formulations for each skin type as given below.

Care Regimen for Vata Skin

Because of the predominance of the space and air element in vata skin, the moisture holding capacity of your skin is limited, and so your beauty care program should emphasize hydration. Your skin needs to be hydrated both from internal and external sources. To hydrate the skin from inside, you should drink at least eight glasses of water a day and eat plenty of sweet, juicy fruits. Externally, your skin will benefit from applying a high-quality moisturizing lotion twice per day. Moisturizers made from formulas prescribed in the ancient Vedic texts, provide a superior source of moisture for vata skin. Because vata skin is thin and delicate, it typically does not respond well to the harsh, chemical ingredients that are in most moisturizers today, so choosing a moisturizer that does not use artificial preservatives or ingredients is important.

Vata Cleansing Recipe. The milk, oat, and marshmallow soap substitute described below helps to nourish and lubricate menopausal vata skin. It also provides a safe and nourishing cleanse to enhance firmness, luster, and glow without having any short-term or long-term drying or irritating effect.

70% rolled oats
10% marshmallow root
10% Indian sarsaparilla
10% lavender flowers

Make up a large batch of these ingredients and store in a dry place. For each cleansing of your face and body, put 2 tablespoons in a cheesecloth bag and dip bag in lukewarm, whole, organic milk. Pat your face and body and rinse for five minutes. Apply a very thin layer of pure aloe vera gel or almond oil to finish. If you have a lot of toxins under your skin, however, it won't tolerate full-strength oil without breaking out. So for the first couple of weeks of this regimen, apply a mixture of 99 percent rosewater and 1 percent ylang ylang essential oil as a toner after cleansing. Always use a natural, nourishing, and lubricating day cream or night cream, preferably one that is herbally balanced according to MAV principles. (See the Resources for product information.)

Care Regimen for Pitta Skin

In caring for your pitta skin, emphasize therapies that have a calming influence on the skin, as well as protecting your skin from the sun and heat. Like vata skin, pitta skin is highly sensitive and tends to become irritated by cleansers or moisturizers that contain synthetic chemicals. Be sure to include ghee and rose petal conserve in your diet, favor cool, sweet foods, and avoid spicy foods. A preshower massage with coconut oil is a wonderful way to both cool pitta and to moisturize your sensitive skin.

Externally, your skin will benefit from applying a high-quality moisturizer with herbs that help to calm the nerves of the skin. Moisturizers made from formulas without irritating additives, as prescribed in the ancient Vedic texts, provide a superior source of moisture for sensitive pitta skin, while at the same time providing deep nourishment for the tactile nerves, your skin's emotional mediators.

Pitta Cleansing Recipe. Pitta skin needs a cooling and nurturing cleanser, based on the following recipe:

> 70% rolled oats
> 10% rose petal
> 10% Indian sarsaparilla
> 10% red sandalwood

Use the same method to make a cleansing rinse as described for vata, only use room temperature whole milk. After cleansing, a mixture of 80 percent coconut oil and 20 percent jojoba oil can be applied on the skin. Again, if your skin has much toxicity, it will not tolerate the oil well, and a rosewater toner should be substituted for the first few weeks of your regimen. (Follow the recipe for rosewater toner given in the Vata Care Regimen above, but substitute jojoba oil for ylang ylang oil.) A natural, nourishing, and lubricating day cream or night cream, preferably one that is herbally balanced according to MAV principles is recommended to lock in the moisture gained through your cleansing routine and to further nourish and protect your skin. (See the Resources for product information.)

Care Regimen for Kapha Skin

The key to beauty care for kapha skin types is proper cleansing, as kapha individuals are more prone to accumulating toxins than the other types. Avoid heavy, greasy, cold or sweet foods and do cook with pungent spices, such as ginger and pepper. Include lots of fresh fruits and vegetables in your diet to support cleansing from within.

Your kapha skin needs frequent, in-depth cleansing and facials, using clay to exfoliate and draw out impurities such as dead skin and ama. MAV recommends first loosening the impurities by lubricating your skin. Externally, your skin will benefit from applying a high-quality moisturizer with herbs that help to detoxify the skin. Especially those made from formulas prescribed in the ancient Ayurvedic texts provide a superior source of moisture for the Kapha skin while at the same time helping to eliminate impurities in the skin. (See the Resources for product information.)

Kapha Cleansing Recipe. To cleanse your kapha skin, use the following:

>70% rolled oats
>10% orange peel
>10% Indian sarsaparilla
>10% oat bran

Use the same method for preparing the milk cleanse as described for vata and pitta, this time with warm milk. After cleansing and rinsing, apply a natural, homemade toner. Mix together 3 parts rosewater to 1 part aloe vera gel (fresh from the plant is best, or from a pure, bottled source that has no added ingredients) and gently apply a few drops to your face. Do not use any oil, only the natural *Youthful Skin Cream* (see below) for day or night, since your kapha skin is already rich in oil.

MAV Skin Care Treatments and Products

Skin care treatments and products formulated according to true MAV principles are unique in that they address and support the intelligence level of your skin. A well-balanced formulation that has nature's healing and nurturing power, whether in the form of an internal supplement or a topical cream, can awaken your skin's own memory of perfect functioning. An anti-aging formula of this kind works in the long term as a transformational agent to actually make your skin younger by enlivening each skin cell to remember its youth.

The Problem with Today's Popular Skin-Care Treatments

Sadly, this is hardly the case with the skin care products currently available on the market. When you purchase today's popular products, you are receiving less benefit than advertised, or at best, some mild to severe side effects along with any benefit. Most popular "natural" face creams, even spa quality formulas and those that call themselves Ayurvedic, contain as little as 1 percent herbal ingredients, and in many cases contain only a fraction of a percent of herbal extracts. In addition, many skin products contain harsh chemical solvents used in processing and are subjected to high, potentially damaging temperatures. This can create long-term damage to the deeper layers of the skin, distorting nature's intelligence as it creates new cells.

Most popular skin care products today are unhealthy for your skin because they are made according to the modern medical notion of *single-cause/single-effect*, the infamous "magic bullet" approach. The erroneous belief is that by simply adding multiple ingredients to a cream or gel base you will get multiple benefits. But this is not the case. No modern delivery system or approach to combining ingredients has resulted in a truly effective, side-effect-free botanical product with multiple benefits. Products containing chemical ingredients, such as *alpha hydroxy acids* (AHA), *beta hydroxy acids* (BHA), and *retinal,* are all designed by juggling the amount of chemical extract needed to achieve the desired "dewrinkling" effects versus the side effects of dryness, irritation (and eventually *more* wrinkling) that the chemical ultimately produces.

The common ingredient AHA works by peeling away the top layer of dead cells to reduce the appearance of fine lines. However, women are beginning to discover the problems with this harsh approach, such as increased sensitivity to the sun, and dry, irritated skin. Continued use of these products can actually lead to premature aging and wrinkles — not exactly the effects you expect when you purchase a skin cream!

How MAV Formulations Are Different — and Better

MAV follows a very different approach to the formulation of anti-aging skin care products. Unlike modern products, an authentic MAV formula balances its multiple ingredients, using natural herbs instead of chemical isolates, to create a safe synergy rather than a dangerous hodgepodge of ingredients. This natural herbal balance within the formula supports a natural state of balance within the skin, promoting real beauty by making the skin healthier.

The purity of the delivery system is also important. When you apply a product to your skin, it is absorbed by your pores and then into your bloodstream via the vessels in the second layer of your skin. Such transdermal delivery is the reason it's important to use only all-natural products that are free of synthetic ingredients. Otherwise, as you apply your skin cream, you will be introducing toxic substances (additives, preservatives, and other chemicals) into your blood which can aggravate your liver, your immune system, your pitta dosha, and ultimately your skin. In other words, toxins in your face cream can directly aggravate your skin from the *outside in,* and then boomerang back to do the same from the *inside out.*

The Youthful Skin Line of MAV Products

To preserve the lasting beauty of your skin, I recommend products that are based on a natural blend of herbs without isolated chemical additives and that follow

MAV principles. I personally use and endorse the *Youthful Skin* line of products, produced by Maharishi Ayurveda Products International, which contain a precise combination of whole herb extracts that work together in synergy. Again, the whole is greater than the sum of its parts. It took many years of research working with scientists from the West and MAV-trained vaidyas from India to create a skin care line gentle enough for modern-day, Western skin types and that contains 9.5 percent herbal extract — almost 10 times more than popular skin care products. The base of the *Youthful Skin* products is completely natural. It uses grape seed extract as a natural preservative, aroma, and antioxidant all rolled into one.

The two primary herbs in the *Youthful Skin Cream* for the face are *gotu kola* (Centella asiatica) and *sensitive plant* (Lajawanti). Gotu kola is a legendary *vayasthapana* herb, which means that it helps slow aging. Recently, a French scientist published a study showing that gotu kola improves collagen synthesis in the skin. Sensitive plant is known for its ability to heal nerves at both the surface and deep levels of the skin and enhance tactile sensitivity. It is so sensitive itself that its leaves actually curl up if you touch them. It has a similar benefit for your skin, making the skin cells more alive, sensuous, and balanced.

Another botanical used in the face cream, *Flame of Forest* (Butea monosperma), has exceptional sun-protecting qualities that can rejuvenate sun-damaged skin. The bright pigmentation of this plant's flower comes from its bioflavonoids, which are known to protect the plant itself and provide superb sun protection to skin, as well as cooling down inflamed, pitta-type skin disturbances.

The Youthful Skin Herbal Tablet helps promote mental calm, contented emotions, and the right balance of skin temperature, moisture, and elasticity. It nourishes what MAV calls the *rohini* layer of your skin. The rohini layer acts as an interface between your blood and your skin. The herbal tablets also help nourish and build healthy tissues and fluids which are essential for healthy skin. The herbs in this formulation are sensitive plant, winter cherry (*ashwagandha*), licorice, gotu kola, and saffron, all prepared in the traditional way to help improve bioavailability and assimilation of nutrients.

Why I Use and Endorse the Youthful Skin Products

The products in the *Youthful Skin* line — face cream, cleanser, toner, and oil — are manufactured in a way that protects nature's intelligence, the deep healing force within every botanical and herb. MAV calls this diligence *sanskar*, or protecting the molecular level of the plant from distortion due to excessive heat or chemical interaction, through each step of the preparation process. This degree of care makes these skin care products superior in purity and potency.

In clinical research in an independent laboratory, *Youthful Skin Cream* was proven to reduce fine lines and wrinkles an average of 33 percent in the first month, increasing to an average of 40 percent after just three months. Hydration ranged from 23 percent to more than 70 percent in the same three months. Clarity and firmness improved on average 24 percent.

Ayurveda knows that the potency of any herbal plant varies with the seasons, cycles of the moon and time of day. Herbs used in the *Youthful Skin* products are harvested at precisely the ideal time, which makes their potency one hundred times more powerful. After harvesting, each plant must be inspected, sorted, cleaned, and stored in a unique way to protect it from deterioration. A high percentage of each crop is rejected because it does not meet MAV's strict herbal standards for purity, maturity, and potency.

Finally, the herbal laboratory where these skin care products are made (and nearly all the herbal products mentioned in this book) received a prestigious award from the government of India for its high, pharmaceutical-grade standard of quality. The company recently received the International Standards Organization certification for their factory in India, making them the first of any company in India to receive such certification.

While product purity, effectiveness, and authenticity are indispensable, what is most important to me as a physician (and as a woman) is the Youthful Skin Cream's *gentleness*. In more than five years of clinical use, none of my patients has reported any negative side effects with this product. Even women with the most sensitive skin tolerate it well. (Tip: if you have very sensitive skin, apply a very small amount after spritzing your face with rosewater.) Yet, even being so gentle, it gives great results.

Not All Ayurvedic Spa Treatments Are Alike

A word of caution about skin care treatments and spas commonly advertised as "Ayurvedic." The ancient Vedic texts are filled with treatments and recipes that the royal families of India have used for centuries. Some of the more famous procedures include rinsing the skin with gallons of milk, applying floral water rinses to the face and body, and using herbal mud treatments on the skin and hair. These procedures are becoming more commonly known, but most people do not understand the precision required to ensure they are 100 percent nourishing without any side effects.

In many spas today, Vedic modalities are utilized without a complete understanding of MAV and skin types. If you have very sensitive skin, you must be careful to ensure that your aestheticians are properly trained in Ayurvedic skin care. Unfortunately, Western trained spa aestheticians are usually not very experienced or familiar with Ayurvedic skin care principles and can easily mismatch products and skin types. Furthermore, treatments used successfully in India since ancient times are not all suited to the West. Many would be harsh for Western skin which is thinner and more sensitive to temperature, pressure, and certain herbs. (See the Resources for information on MAV spas and health clinics.)

MAHARISHI REJUVENATION TREATMENT AND AGELESS BEAUTY

In more than seventeen years of practice in Maharishi Ayurveda, I have found authentic, medically-supervised panchakarma in the form of Maharishi Rejuvenation Treatment to be the single most powerful procedure to quickly turn back the clock for your face and body. Those patients of mine who do MRT at least once a year for five days (or better yet, twice a year) truly do not appear to age. They also report fewer and fewer health problems as time goes by, rather than more and more problems, as is the norm in our culture.

Beyond the enormous health benefits, the effects on personal appearance and beauty can be stunning. A number of women have told me after their MRT treatment that they canceled their plans for a facelift because so many friends and associates were telling them how great they looked! One woman was even asked by her closest friend if she had *had* a facelift!

These remarkable rejuvenation results are due to making "each body part auspicious," the Ayurvedic definition of beauty. The purifying diet, cleansing therapies and soothing warm oil treatments that comprise MRT work from both the inside out and the outside in to cleanse and restore youthful vitality to all the body parts. This complete approach creates both a pure, healthy, glowing physiology and a rested, relaxed mind that radiates bliss — the essential components of ageless beauty.

A FINAL WORD ABOUT OJAS

You may recall that *ojas* is the Sanskrit term that describes that most refined and subtle physical essence of perfect health, your immune-boosting, anti-aging "bliss factor" permeates your tissues when ama is cleared. Ojas is responsible for facilitating all communication between your mind and body and enhancing Nature's intelligence at every level. When your ojas is high, you have a healthy glow to your skin, a bright light in your eyes, and your energy, stamina, and immunity are all at their peak. Furthermore, ojas promotes longevity and is an internally generated antidote to aging.

For lasting beauty beyond menopause, you want to maximize the production and maintenance of ojas within your body and mind. The best way to do this is to transcend stress and suffering through practicing the Transcendental Meditation technique, which I have recommended previously for heart, brain, and emotional health. Practicing Transcendental Meditation helps you to achieve deep inner peace and complete freedom from worry, two hallmarks of true spiritual unfoldment. The Vedic texts tell us that after meditating, the glow of ojas appears on your face, and even advises that you bathe or wash *before*, not after your morning meditation session, because the subtle essence of ojas in your skin promotes strength and immunity throughout the entire day.

Given that your skin is an extension of your mind and nervous system, your emotional well-being is critical to the health and radiance of your skin. For any woman who wants to attain and maintain lasting inner and outer beauty, I recommend cultivating the blissful state of mind that comes from meditating regularly and producing optimal ojas.

One of my most distinguished mentors, an Ayurvedic dermatologist, recalls the words of his father, vaidya to India's last royal family and holder of Vedic beauty secrets handed down through the ages: "All blissful beings are beautiful, and all beautiful beings are blissful. There is no beauty without bliss, and no bliss without beauty."

Age knows no boundaries when it comes to bliss. In fact, as we get older, *and wiser*, our capacity for bliss expands. This is the ultimate beauty secret of the ageless woman. As we grow in wisdom and inner fulfillment, we naturally radiate more love, happiness, and peaceful elegance to those around us. As naturally as a clear pool of water brilliantly reflects the splendid rays of the midday sun, our own faces and selves spontaneously convey a beautiful outer radiance, when our inner light is lit with bliss and fulfillment. As we pass on to the next stage of our life's journey, after forty and beyond, Maharishi Ayurveda would advise us: Take care of yourself, be happy, and let your inner bliss flow out — radiating your natural beauty and peacefulness to those around you and through them, to the entire world.

Epilogue

The World is Your Family

When we investigate the invisible mechanics of nature, we find that everything in the universe is directly connected with everything else. Everything is constantly being influenced by everything else. No wave of the ocean is independent of any other.
— Maharishi Mahesh Yogi

At every end is a new beginning. And with every change comes an opportunity. Menopause is both the end of our reproductive years and the beginning of a new phase of life marked by greater freedom. Before us is an opportunity to take fresh initiative in our lives, whether for better health and lifestyle, a new career or creative expressions, or an inward journey of self-discovery. Indeed, 75 percent of postmenopausal women age fifty to sixty-five made health-related lifestyle change around the time of menopause, according to a Gallup poll for the North American Menopause Society.

Women are awake today to the precious opportunity that lies before them. It is my hope that this book will empower you with the understanding and practical tools necessary to make the most of this window of possibility for your health, happiness, and longevity, *naturally* and *profoundly.*

What Leading Women's Health Visionaries Have to Say

Several distinguished women's health writers today are proclaiming that the menopause transition marks a turning point in our lives when it is natural to seek greater meaning and follow higher goals. Along with the physiological shift, they describe a simultaneous transformation that is occurring on a deeper, more spiritual level. Renowned anthropologist Margaret Mead coined the term "menopausal zest" for the liberated energy available to women after menopause, describing it as "the most creative force in the world."

Physician and writer Dr. Christiane Northrup theorizes that the brain actually begins to function differently at menopause, fostering inward reflection and a craving for inner quiet. This inward retreat ultimately blossoms into "a newfound sense of ourselves and our life's purpose" which includes finding larger meaning in life.

Herbalist and author Susun Weed likewise views the years around menopause as a time to retreat, regroup, and reassess our role in society. You are reborn after menopause, she says, into a fully mature "woman of wholeness" who plays a matriarchal role for the whole of society, not just for her own family unit. Ms. Weed explains that the postmenopausal wise woman in ancient times played an important and respected role in society by upholding spiritual values and was "honored as the teller of truth and the keeper of peace."

The Vedic Woman after Menopause

Satyam eva jayate. *(Truth alone triumphs.)*
— *the* Mundaka Upanishad
Heyam duhkham anagatam. *(Avert the danger that has not yet come.)*
— *the* Yoga Sutras

These inspirational leaders in women's health today echo an ancient wisdom that was once a foundation of Vedic culture and is reemerging today. In the Vedic tradition of ancient India, menopause marked the passage from the "householder" phase of life, when raising a family and earning a living are the primary focus, to a time of greater freedom for women and men alike. After age fifty or so, the opportunity arose to "go to the forest," to reorient one's life toward spiritual development. In those days, that meant leaving the village for caves deep within the Himalayan forests, seeking a guru, and dedicating one's life to meditation.

Fortunately, it is no longer necessary to leave home for the woods in order to develop our spirituality. We can practice scientifically proven, time-tested techniques for self-development in our own homes. This is especially important today, because a reorienting of our lives toward spiritual development is no longer a choice. It is a necessity.

World Peace: The Foundation of Personal Health

Today, we cannot consider our own personal health, or that of our families, without considering the health of the world. On a global level, the most fundamental criterion of health is world peace. Without world peace, no one's health is secure. No single factor affects our health more completely and profoundly than the condition of peace or war in the world. We can never be truly healthy in a war-torn world.

As wise women of the 21st century, we can no longer think only of ourselves, our families, our communities, or even our country. Perhaps the greatest wisdom lies in beginning to think of the world as a whole and asking: What is my part to play? How can I make a difference? After all, we are all one family, on one planet.

Our world changed on September 11, 2001. The terrorist attack on the great towers of world trade in New York City and on the Pentagon greatly moved and saddened the family of nations around the world — and it is bringing about a profound change for all of us. We now realize that we are in urgent need of an entirely new approach to maintaining peace. Security today can't be ensured by any weapon, radar, or satellite. Once an attack is launched, it is already too late. As with our health, *prevention* is the only real solution. We must avert the danger before it arises.

The Global Country of World Peace is a nation without borders founded to provide a global home for peace-loving people everywhere and to offer governments proven, prevention-oriented solutions to critical social problems. Its defense minister, Major General Kulwant Singh, says, "There will never be lasting peace while enmity seethes in the hearts of the people."

With the means of mass destruction lying within the grasp of individuals, no country can afford to have an enemy. We are beginning to understand that the *real* enemies are hatred and enmity. With them, acts of violence will forever continue to occur. Without them, there will be an end to terrorism and wars for all time. We have a choice and an opportunity. We must disallow the birth of an enemy.

THE VEDIC APPROACH TO WORLD PEACE

In the vicinity of transcending, hostile tendencies are eliminated.
— *the* Yoga Sutras

As women entering our most powerful years, we are in a position to lead the way in this largest and most divine change that must occur within our world family. There is a popular saying today: "Think globally, act locally." We can act no more locally than within our own hearts and minds. In the Vedic tradition, it is said, "What you want to do for the world, do first for yourself." If we want to make a peaceful world, we must first make *ourselves* infinitely peaceful.

To bring peace, we must first settle our minds down to the field of infinite silence that already exists within us. The Vedic texts say we must transcend mental activity and experience the silent ocean of pure consciousness that lies at the source of thought, the unified field of natural law. It is this field that connects us all to each other and to all of Nature, that nourishes us all, and that alone can harmonize and unify the tremendous diversity that exists in our world — just as it harmonizes every aspect of the entire universe, effortlessly and spontaneously.

The Vedic text *Yoga Sutras* says, "In the vicinity of transcending, hostile tendencies are eliminated." When we transcend our differences to experience pure consciousness, there can be no hostility. Over the past several decades, this ancient prediction has been tested time after time and found to be true, with results published in more than forty scientific journals. These studies demonstrate that when large groups of people practice Maharishi's Transcendental Meditation and TM-Sidhi program (an advanced program that includes yogic flying) together in hot spots of violence around the globe, hostilities are reduced — including war deaths and injuries. This phenomenon has been titled the Maharishi Effect by social scientists. It demonstrates that just as stress in the individual is relieved through the personal practice of the Transcendental Meditation program, social stress is dissolved when large groups of individuals practice Transcendental Meditation together. One of these well-controlled studies, published in 1988 in the *Journal of Conflict Resolution,* (a leading journal in peace studies) showed an astounding 76 percent reduction in war deaths and injuries during the war in Lebanon when this Vedic peace technology was used. Forty research studies clearly show the Maharishi effect works, and the need is urgent. We just have to implement it fully *now,* on a global scale.

Wise Woman, You Can Lead the World to Peace and Heaven on Earth

United be your purpose, harmonious be your feelings, collected be your mind, in the same way as all the various aspects of the universe exist in togetherness, wholeness.
— *the* Rig Veda, Tenth Mandala

Our bodies are changing, our medicine is changing, and now our world is changing. It is a time for transformation in so many ways. We women of the baby boom generation have led the way in transforming our menopause, transforming our medicine, and now we can lead the way in transforming our world.

We are a special generation of women. Growing up in the sixties, we proclaimed loudly to the world our passion for peace and love. "Make love, not war" and "Flower power, not firepower" were two of our guiding slogans. Yet, lacking a formal technology to actualize our dream of a peaceful world, we turned to our private lives to try to realize our dreams within our own families. But as recent world events are teaching us, we cannot create peace in isolation because we are all connected.

Fortunately, today we have a proven technology that can actually *create* peace, and this technology is now being applied on a global scale. The Global Country of World Peace, under the guidance of Maharishi Mahesh Yogi, is spearheading the assembly of a permanent group of forty thousand Vedic pandits — a calculated number based on the principles of coherence generation in quantum physics — on the banks of the Ganges River in India. This group, which already numbers well over eight thousand, will practice these scientifically verified peacekeeping technologies to ensure perpetual world peace for us all.

Creating health, wholeness, and transcendence within ourselves, we create peace and harmony in the world. What could be more fulfilling, or more important? We can no longer afford not to do it.

Good Health and Peace to You and the World

Vasudhaiv Kutumbakam. *(The world is my family.)*
— *the* Maha Upanishad

It is my heartfelt wish that the knowledge and practical tips you have learned in this book will empower you to transit your menopause smoothly and that, as a result, you enjoy radiant good health for many years to come. And collectively, through the application of Vedic approaches to world health, may we quickly establish lasting world peace and heaven on earth for all generations to come.

Glossary of Ayurvedic Terms

abhyanga a specialized oil application and massage

agni digestive and metabolic fire

ama poorly digested food material that accumulates in the body

ama visha an especially harmful, disease-promoting type of ama that contains highly reactive toxins

Amrit Kalash literally means "container of immortality"

asana a yoga posture

asthi one of the seven bodily constituents, mainly bone and bone metabolism

asthi soshirya porous or brittle bones; osteoporosis

Ayurveda a division of the Vedic literature that deals with health, literally "knowledge of the totality of life"

bala strength or immunity

basti an herbal enema

Bhagavad-Gita a classical text of the Vedic literature

Charaka Samhita a classical text of Ayurveda

dahl a small lentil

dhatu one of seven divisions of the body, it correlates with the modern scientific concept of "tissue"

dhi the mind's ability to learn or acquire knowledge

dhriti the mind's ability to process and store what it has learned

doshas three governing principles in nature that guide the functioning of the mind and body

ghee clarified butter

gunam inner beauty

hridayam that which is especially nourishing and healing for the heart

kanjee a nourishing, easily digested rice-water drink

kapha the dosha governing all strength, substance, and structure of the body

kichari a nourishing, easily digested porridge made of rice and dahl

kshaya reduction of the body, whether through purification and weight-loss measures, inadequate nutrition, or poor assimilation

lassi a drink made of organic plain yogurt blended with water, cardamom powder, organic sugar, and rosewater

Maharishi Amrit Kalash (MAK) proprietary name for a traditional herbal formula of MAV for health and longevity

Maharishi Ayurveda (MAV) the complete system of natural medicine from the Vedic civilization of ancient India

majja one of the seven bodily constituents, mainly the bone marrow and its metabolism

malas bodily wastes; includes urine, feces, sweat, and others

mamsa one of the seven bodily constituents, mainly muscle and its metabolism

meda one of the seven bodily constituents, mainly fat and metabolism of fat, carbohydrates, and hormones

medhya that which is especially nourishing and supportive to the mind and brain

MRT Maharishi Rejuvenation Treatment; traditional cleansing and balancing treatments (*panchakarma*), specifically prescribed for each individual by a medical doctor trained in Maharishi Ayurveda

ojas the subtle, health-promoting substance through which consciousness and Nature's intelligence are connected with the body

panchakarma a series of traditional cleansing and balancing treatments

panir a type of soft, fresh cheese

pitta the dosha governing all digestion, metabolism, and transformation in the body

prana life force

prana vata the chief subdivision of vata, it governs the mind, the heart, respiration, and life itself

pranayama a Vedic breathing exercise

rakta one of the seven bodily constituents, mainly the red blood cells

rasa one of the seven bodily constituents, mainly the plasma (clear part of the blood)

rasa vaha srotas those channels or blood vessels that carry the plasma throughout the body; includes the coronary arteries in the heart

rasayana herbs, foods, or behaviors that support immunity, good health, and long life; that which causes ojas to be produced

rishi literally "seer"; refers to one who sees the reality of life as described in the Veda and Vedic literature

roopam outer beauty

sadhaka pitta a subdivision of pitta dosha that governs how we process our experiences, it coordinates thinking, feeling, and emotions and is responsible for the fulfillment of our desires

shirodhara a treatment of warm oil poured gently on the forehead to balance the mind and nervous system

shukra one of the seven bodily constituents, mainly the ova and their supportive tissue

smriti memory

srotas channels or spaces through which flow occurs

sthapatya Veda the Vedic science of architecture

subdosha a subdivision of a dosha; each dosha has five subdoshas that carry out different functions in the body

subhanga karanam true beauty, in which every aspect of the body is radiantly healthy

Sushruta Samhita a classical text of Ayurveda

tripti a feeling of being deeply nourished and satisfied by your food

vaidya an Ayurvedic physician

vastu vidya the precise rules of construction and design of Vedic architecture

vata the dosha governing all motion and flow in the body

vayastyag lasting, ageless beauty

vyana vata a subdivision of vata dosha that governs all circulation and is associated with moisture balance and sensation in the skin

REFERENCES

Chapter 1

Archer, D. F., et al. "Effects of lower doses of conjugated equine estrogens and medroxyprogesterone acetate on endometrial bleeding." *Fertility and Sterility* 2001; 75: 1080-88.

Beckham, N. "Phyto-oestrogens and compounds that affect oestrogen metabolism." *Australian Journal of Medical Herbalism* 1995; 7 (1).

Bungay, G. T., et al. "Study of symptoms in middle life with special reference to the menopause." *British Medical Journal* 1980; 28 (6234): 181-183.

"Easy on the Antioxidants." *Journal of the American Medical Association* 2000; 283(19), 2514.

Eisenberg, D., et al. "Trends in Alternative Medicine Use in the United States, 1990-1997: Results of a Follow-Up National Survey." *Journal of the American Medical Association* 1998; 280: 1569-1575.

Follingstad, A. "Estriol, the forgotten estrogen." *Journal of the American Medical Association* 1978; 239 (1): 29-30.

Grady, D., et al., "Cardiovascular disease outcomes during 6.8 years of hormone therapy: Heart and estrogen/progestin replacement study follow-up (HERS II)." *JAMA* 2002; 288: 49-66.

Heaney, R. P. "Estrogen-calcium interactions in the post menopause: a quantitative description." *Bone and Mineral* 1990; 11: 67-84.

Hreshchyshyn, M. M., et al. "Effects of natural menopause, hysterectomy, and oophorectomy on lumbar spine and femoral neck bone densities." *Obstetrics and Gynecology* 1988; 72: 631.

"Institute of Medicine advisory on vitamins C and E." *Washington Post*, January 26, 2000.

Kuller, L. H., et al. "Women's Healthy Lifestyle Project: a randomized clinical trial. Results at 54 months." *Circulation* 2001; 103: 32-37.

Kushi, L. H., et al. "Dietary antioxidant vitamins and death from coronary heart disease in postmenopausal women." *New England Journal of Medicine* 1996; 334(18): 1145-1149.

Lee, H. P., et al. "Dietary effects on breast cancer risk in Singapore." *Lancet* 1991; 337: 1197-1200.

Lees, B., et al. "Differences in proximal femur bone density over two centuries." *Lancet* 1993; 341: 673-675.

Leiberman, S. "A review of the effectiveness of *Cimicifuga racemosa* (black cohosh) for the symptoms of menopause." *Journal of Women's Health* 1998; 7 (5): 525-529.

Love, S., and K. Lindsey. *Dr. Susan Love's Hormone Book: Making Informed Choices About Menopause.* New York: Random House, 1998.

Lu, L.-J., et al. "Phytoestrogens and healthy aging: gaps in knowledge; a workshop report." *Menopause* 2001; 8 (3): 157-170.

Menaguchi, et al. "Effect of estriol on bone loss in postmenopausal women: a multicenter prospective open study." *Journal of Obstetrics and Gynaecology Ressearch* 1996; 3: 259-265.

Nawaz, H., and D. L. Katz. "American College of Preventive Medicine Practice Policy Statement: Perimenopausal and postmenopausal hormone replacement therapy." *American Journal of Preventive Medicine* 1999; 17: 250- 254.

New England Research Institute, Inc. *Women and Their Health in Massachusetts: Final Report.* Watertown, Massachusetts: 1991.

"NIH Consensus Development Panel on Osteoporosis Prevention, Diagnosis and Therapy." *Journal of the American Medical Association* 2001; 285 (6): 785-795.

Perez, C. A., et al. "Management of locally advanced carcinoma of the breast. I. Noninflammatory." *Cancer* 1994; 74(1 suppl): 453-465.

Prestwood, K.M., et al. "Ultralow-dose micronized 17 beta-estradiol and bone density and bone metabolism in older women: a randomized controlled trial." *Journal of the American Medical Association* 2003; 290 (8):1042-1048

Rodriguez, C., et al. "Estrogen replacement therapy and ovarian cancer mortality in a large prospective study of U.S. women." *Journal of the American Medical Association* 2001; 285 (11): 1460-1465.

Schairer, C., et al. "Menopausal estrogen and estrogen-progestin replacement therapy and breast cancer risk." *Journal of the American Medical Association* 2000; 283: 485-491.

Stamm, W. E., and R. Raz. "A controlled trial of intravaginal estriol in postmenopausal women with recurrent urinary tract infections." *New England Journal of Medicine* 1993; 329 (11): 753-756.

Steinberg, K. K., et al. "A meta-analysis of the effect of estrogen replacement therapy on the risk of breast cancer." *Journal of the American Medical Association* 1991; 265: 1985-1990.

Stephenson, J. "Estrogen as a carcinogen." *Journal of the American Medical Association* 2001; 285 (3): 284.

Stolze, H. "An alternative to treat menopausal complaints." *Gynecology* 1982; 3: 14-16.

Wang, C., and M. S. Kurzer. "Effects of isoflavones, flavinoids and lignans on proliferation of estrogen-dependent and independent human breast cancer cells." *Proceedings of the American Association for Cancer Research* 1996; 37: 277.

Chapter 2

Cummings, S. R., et al. "Endogenous hormones and the risk of hip and vertebral fractures among older women." *New England Journal of Medicine* 1998; 339 (11): 733-738.

Kuller, L. H., et al. "Women's Healthy Lifestyle Project: a randomized clinical trial. Results at 54 months." *Circulation* 2001; 103: 32-37.

Wise, P. M. "The 'menopause' and the aging brain: causes and repercussions of hypoestrogenicity." *Biogerontology* 2, 2001; 113-115.

Chapter 4

Albright, D., et al. "Circadian rhythms in hot flashes in natural and surgically induced menopause." *Chronobiology International* 1989; 6: 279-284.

Angier, N. "Radical new view of role of menstruation." *New York Times*, September 21, 1993.

Argyle, N., et al. "Maharishi Ayurveda in the Diagnosis and Treatment of Premenstrual Syndrome." (unpublished paper) Department of Physiology, MIU, Fairfield, Iowa, 1990.

Gabbay, F. H., et al. "Triggers of myocardial ischemia during daily life in patients with coronary artery disease: physical and mental activities, anger, and smoking." *Journal of the American College of Cardiology* 1996; 27: 585-592.

Salerno, J. W., and D. E. Smith. "The use of sesame oil and other vegetable oils in the inhibition of human colon cancer growth in vitro." *Anticancer Research* 1991; 11: 209-216.

Smith, D. E., and J. W. Salerno. "Selective inhibition of a human malignant melanoma cell line by sesame oil in vitro." *Prostaglandins, Leukotrienes, and Essential Fatty Acids* 1992; 46: 145-150.

Smolensky, M., and L. Lamberg. *The Body Clock Guide to Better Health*. New York: Henry Holt, 2000.

Chapter 5

Bravata, D.M., et al. "Efficacy and safety of low-carbohydrate diets; a systematic review." *JAMA*, 2003:28 (14); 1837-1850.

Ansell, B. "The metabolic syndrome: an interplay of multiple subtle cardiovascular risk factors." *Journal of Clinical Outcomes Management*. 2002: 9 (1); 41-49.

Consumer Reports, as reported in CNN on the Web, May 7, 2002.

Chapter 6

Zava, D. T., et al. "Estrogen and progestin bioactivity of foods, herbs, and spices." *Proceedings of the Society for Experimental Biology Medicine* 1998; 217: 369-378.

Chapter 7

The Alpha-Tocopherol, Beta Carotene Cancer Prevention Study Group. "The effect of vitamin E and beta carotene on the incidence of lung cancer and other cancers in male smokers." *New England Journal of Medicine* 1994; 330: 1029-1035.

Alexander, C., et al. "A randomized controlled trial of stress reduction on cardiovascular and all-cause mortality in the elderly: results of 8 year and 15 year follow-ups." *Circulation* 1996; 93 (3) (abstract).

Alexander, C. N., et al. "The effects of Transcendental Meditation compared to other methods of relaxation and meditation in reducing risk factors, morbidity and mortality." *Homeostasis* 1994; 35: 243-264.

American Heart Association. *Heart and Stroke Facts: Statistical Update*. Dallas, Texas: 2001.

Anda, R., et al. "Depressed affect, hopelessness, and the risk of ischemic heart disease in a cohort of U.S. adults." *Epidemiology* 1993; 4: 285-294.

Barrett-Connor, E., and V. Miller. "Estrogens, lipids, and heart disease: Care of the older woman." *Clinics in Geriatric Medicine* 1993; 1(9): 57-67.

Bharani, A., et al. "Salutary effect of *Terminalia arjuna* in patients with severe refractory heart failure." *International Journal of Cardiology* 1995; 49: 191-199.

Bujatti, M., and P. Riederer. "Serotonin, noradrenaline, dopamine metabolites in Transcendental Meditation technique." *Journal of Neural Transmission* 1976; 39: 257-267.

Castillo-Richmond, A., et al. "Effects of Stress Reduction on Carotid Atherosclerosis in Hypertensive African Americans." *Stroke* 2000; 31: 568-573.

Davis, L., and G. Kuttan. "Immunomodulatory activity of *Withania somnifera*." *Journal of Ethnopharmacology* 2000; 71(1-2): 193-200.

Dillbeck, M. C., and D. W. Orme-Johnson. "Physiological differences between Transcendental Meditation and rest." *American Psychologist* 1987; 42: 879-881.

Dogra, J., et al. "Lipid peroxide in ischemic heart disease (IHD): inhibition by Maharishi Amrit Kalash (MAK-4 and MAK-5) herbal mixtures." *Journal of the Federation of American Societies for Experimental Biology* 2000; 14 (4):A121 (Abstract).

Dwivedi, S., and M. P. Agarwal. "Antianginal and cardioprotective effects of *Terminalia arjuna*, an indigenous drug, in coronary artery disease." *Journal of the Association of Physicians of India* 1994; 42: 287-289.

Eisenberg, D. M., et al. "Cognitive behavioral techniques for hypertension: are they effective?" *Annals of Internal Medicine* 1993; 118: 964-72.

Gallup Survey Findings: Overview of Perceived and Real Health Threats. Gallup Survey, 1995.

Herrington, D., et al. "Effects of estrogen replacement on the progression of coronary-artery atherosclerosis." *New England Journal of Medicine* 2000; 343: 522-529.

Herron, R. E., and J. B. Fagan. "Lipophil-mediated reduction of toxin body burdens." *Alternative Therapies in Health and Medicine*. 2002; 8(5): 40-51.

Hu, F. B., et al. "Frequent meat consumption and risk of coronary heart disease in women: a prospective cohort study." *Journal of Nutrition* 1998; 129 (6): 1135-1139.

Hulley, S., et al. "Randomized trial of estrogen plus progestin for secondary prevention of coronary heart disease in post-menopausal women. Heart and estrogen/progestin replacement study (HERS) research group." *Journal of the American Medical Association* 1998; 280: 605-613.

Kawachi, I., et al. "Symptoms of anxiety and risk of coronary heart disease: the normative aging study." *Circulation* 1994; 90: 2225-2229.

Kuller, L. H., et al. "Women's Healthy Lifestyle Project: a randomized clinical trial. Results at 54 months." *Circulation* 2001; 103: 32-37.

Lacey, J. V., et al. "Menopausal hormone replacement therapy and risk of ovarian cancer." *Journal of the American Medical Association*. 2002; 288(3): 334-341.

Love, S., and K. Lindsey. *Dr. Susan Love's Hormone Book: Making Informed Choices About Menopause*. New York: Random House, 1998.

MacLean, C. R. K., et al. "Effects of the Transcendental Meditation Program on adaptive mechanisms: changes in hormone levels and responses to stress after four months' practice." *Psychoneuroendocrinology* 1997; 22(4): 277-295.

Manson, J. E., et al. "Estrogen plus progestin and the risk of coronary heart disease." *New England Journal of Medicine*. 2003; 349: 523-534.

Mosca, L., et al. "Hormone replacement therapy and cardiovascular disease: A statement for health care professionals from the American Heart Association." *Circulation* 2001; 104: 499-503.

Nader, T. *Human Physiology: Expression of Veda and Vedic Literature*. Vlodrop, Holland: Maharishi University Press; 1995.

Nagelberg, J., and B. Tunick. "The pressure's on: everything you need to know about hypertension." *The Female Patient* June 1999; (Suppl): 4-8.

Niwa, Y. "Effect of Maharishi 4 and Maharishi 5 on inflammatory mediators—with special reference to their free radical scavenging effect." *Indian Journal of Clinical Practice* 1991; 1(8): 23-27.

Omenn, G. S., et al. "Effects of a combination of beta carotene and vitamin A on lung cancer and cardiovascular disease." *New England Journal of Medicine* 1996; 334: 1150-1155.

Ornish, D., et al. "Can lifestyle changes reverse coronary heart disease?" *Lancet* 1990; 336: 129-133.

Schneider, R. H., et al. "A randomized controlled trial of stress reduction for hypertension in older African Americans." *Hypertension* 1995; 26: 820-827.

Schneider, R., et al. "Randomized, controlled trials of effects of the Transcendental Meditation Program on cancer, cardiovascular and all-cause mortality: a meta-analysis." Paper presented at the Society for Behavioral Medicine Annual Meeting, March 3-6, 1999, San Diego, CA.

Sharma, H., et al. "Inhibition of human low-density lipoprotein oxidation in vitro by Maharishi Ayur-Veda herbal mixtures." *Pharmacology, Biochemistry and Behavior* 1992; 43: 1175-82.

Sharma, H., et al. "Improvement in cardiovascular risk factors through Maharishi Panchakarma (PK) purification procedure." *Journal of the Federation of American Societies for Experimental Biology* 1993; 7(4): A8012 (Abstract).

Sharma, H, et al. "Antineoplastic properties of Maharishi Amrit Kalash, an Ayurvedic food supplement, against DMBA-induced mammary tumors in rats." *Journal of Research and Education in Indian Medicine* 1991; 10 (3): 1-8.

Singh, R. B., et al. "Hypolipidemic and antioxidant effects of commiphora as an adjunct to dietary therapy in patients with hypercholesterolemia." *Cardiovascular Drugs and Therapy* 1994; 8: 659-664.

Srivastava, A., et al. "Maharishi Amrit (MAK) reduces chemotherapy toxicity in breast cancer patients." *Journal of the Federation of American Societies for Experimantal Biology* 2000; 14(4): A720 (Abstract).

Stampfer, M. J., et al. "Primary prevention of coronary heart disease in women through diet and lifestyle." *New England Journal of Medicine* 2000; 343 (1): 16-22.

Wallace, R. K., et al. "A wakeful hypometabolic physiologic state." *American Journal of Physiology* 1971; 221: 795-799.

Walton, K. G., et al. "MAV and reduced stress-related disease: Do reductions in cortisol lower heart disease in postmenopausal women?" Paper presented at Northwestern University's Rice Foundation Symposium on Stress and Human Disease, Lake Bluff, Illinois, October 22-24, 1999.

Wassertheil-Smoller, S., et al. "Effect of estrogen plus progestin on stroke in postmenopausal women: The Women's Health Initiative: a randomized trial." *Journal of the American Medical Association*. 2003: 289(20): 2673-2684.

Writing Group for the Women's Health Initiative Investigators. "Risks and benefits of estrogen plus progestin in healthy postmenopausal women: principal results from the Women's Health Initiative randomized controlled trial." *Journal of the American Medical Association* 2002; 288(3): 321-333.

Chapter 8

Ahlborg, H.G., et al. "Bone loss and bone size after menopause." *New England Journal of Medicine*. 2003; 349:327-34.

Alekel, D. L., et al. "Isoflavone-rich soy protein isolate attenuates bone loss in the lumbar spine of perimenopausal women." *American Journal of Clinical Nutrition* 2000; 72: 844-852.

Altkorn, D., and T. Vokes. "Treatment of postmenopausal osteoporosis." *Journal of the American Medical Association* 2001; 285 (11): 1415-1418.

Clements, D., et al. "Bone loss in normal British women: a five-year follow-up." *British Journal of Radiology* 1993; 66: 1134-1137.

Cummings, S. R. Special Guest lecture at the NIH on results of the Fracture Intervention Trial (FIT), April 2000.

Cummings, S. R., et al. "Effect of alendronate on risk of fracture in women with low bone density but without vertebral fractures; results from the Fracture Intervention Trial." *Journal of the American Medical Association* 1998; 280: 2077-2082.

Dawson-Hughes, B., et al. "Effect of calcium and vitamin D supplementation on bone density in men and women 65 years of age or older." *New England Journal of Medicine* 1997; 337: 670-676.

Ettinger, B., and D. Grady. "The waning effect of postmenopausal estrogen therapy on osteoporosis." *New England Journal of Medicine* 1993; 329 (16): 1192-1193.

Grady, D., and S. Cummings. "Postmenopausal hormone therapy for prevention of fractures: how good is the evidence?" *Journal of the American Medical Association* 2001; 285(22).

Grady, D., et al. "Hormone therapy to prevent disease and prolong life in postmenopausal women." *Annals of Internal Medicine* 1992; 117: 1016-1037.

Heaney, R. P. "Estrogen-calcium interactions in the post menopause: a quantitative description." *Bone and Mineral* 1990; 11: 67-84.

Lees, B., et. al., Differences in proximal femur bone density over two centuries. *The Lancet.* 1993; 341: 673-675.

Leonetti, H. B., et al. "Transdermal progesterone cream for vasomotor symptoms and postmenopausal bone loss." *Obstetrics and Gynecology* 1999; 94: 225-228.

Lu, L. J., et al. "Phytoestrogens and healthy aging: gaps in knowledge; a workshop report." *Menopause: Journal of the North American Menopause Society* 2001; 8 (3): 157-170.

Michelson, D., et al. "Bone mineral density in women with depression." *New England Journal of Medicine* 1996; 335(16): 1176-1182.

Nelson, H., et al. "Osteoporosis and fracture are common in older postmenopausal women using estrogen." *Bone* 1998; 23: S152.

NIH Consensus Development Panel on Osteoporosis Prevention, Diagnosis and Therapy. *Journal of the American Medical Association* 2001; 285 (6): 785-795.

Orwoll, E. "Does estrogen adequately protect postmenopausal women against osteoporosis? An iconoclastic perspective." *Journal of Clinical Endocrinology and Metabolism* 1999; 84: 1872-1874.

Potter, S.M., et al., "Soy protein and isoflavones: their effects on blood lipids and bone density in postmenopausal women." *American Journal of Clinical Nutrition* 1998; 68(6 Suppl.): 1375S-9S.

Prestwood, K.M., et al. "Ultralow-dose micronized 17 beta-estradiol and bone density and bone metabolism in older women: a randomized controlled trial." *Journal of the American Medical Association* 2003; 290(8):1042-1048.

Riis, B. J. "The role of bone loss." *American Journal of Medicine* 1995; 98(Supp. 12A): 2A/29S-2A/32S.

Seeman, E. "Periosteal bone formation — a neglected determinant of bone strength." *New England Journal of Medicine.* 2003; 349: 320-323.

Sellmeyer, D. E., et al. "A high ratio of dietary animal to vegetable protein increases the rate of bone loss and the risk of fracture in postmenopausal women." Study by Osteoporotic Fractures Research Group. *American Journal of Clinical Nutrition* 2001; 73 (1): 5-6.

Spindler, A. "Bone mineral density in a native population of Argentina with low calcium intake." *Journal of Rheumatology* 1995; 22 (11): 2148-2151.

Torgerson, D., and S. Bell-Syer. "Hormone replacement therapy and prevention of nonvertebral fractures; a meta-analysis of randomized trials." *Journal of the American Medical Association* 2001; 285(22): 2891-2897.

Writing Group for the PEPI Trial. "Effects of hormone therapy on bone mineral density: results from the Postmenopausal Estrogen/Progestin Interventions (PEPI) Trial." *Journal of the American Medical Association* 1996; 276: 1389-1396.

Writing Group for the Women's Health Initiative Investigators. "Risks and benefits of estrogen plus progestin in healthy postmenopausal women: Principal results from the Women's Health Initiative randomized controlled trial." *Journal of the American Medical Association* 2002; 288(3): 321-333.

Chapter 9

Alexander, C., et al. "Transcendental Meditation, mindfulness and longevity: an experimental study with the elderly." *Journal of Personality and Social Psychology* 1989; 57 (6): 950-964.

Alexander, C., et al. "Transcendental Meditation, self-actualization and psychological health: a conceptual overview and statistical meta-analysis." *Journal of Social Behavior and Personality* 1991; 6 (5): 189-247.

Bhattacharya, S. K., et al. "Antioxidant activity of *Bacopa monniera* in rat frontal cortex, striatum and hippocampus." *Phytotherapeutic Research* 2000; 14 (3): 174-179.

Castillo-Richmond, A., et al. "Effects of stress reduction on carotid atherosclerosis in hypertensive African Americans." *Stroke* 2000; 31: 568-573.

Eppley, K., et al. "The differential effects of relaxation techniques on trait anxiety: a meta-analysis." *Journal of Clinical Psychology* 1989; 45 (6): 957-974.

Fortes, C., et al. "Diet and overall survival in a cohort of very elderly people." *Epidemiology* July 2000; 11 (4): 440-445.

Freedman, R., et al. "Biochemical and thermoregulatory effects of behavioral treatment for menopausal hot flashes." *Menopause: Journal of the North American Menopause Society* 1995; 2 (4): 211-218.

Geerlings, M., et al. "Reproductive period and risk of dementia in postmenopausal women." *Journal of the American Medical Association* 2001; 285(11): 1475-1481.

Gelderloos, P., et al. "Influence of Maharishi Ayurvedic herbal preparation on age-related visual discrimination." *International Journal of Psychosomatics* 1990; 37 (1-4): 25-29.

Hommer, D. W., et al. "Evidence for a gender-related effect of alcoholism on brain volumes." *American Journal of Psychiatry* 2001; 158: 198-204.

"Lack of sleep impairs reactions like alcohol." Reuters online news service, September 18, 2000.

LeBlanc, E., et al. "Hormone Replacement Therapy and cognition; systematic review and meta-analysis." *Journal of the American Medical Association* 2001; 285 (11): 1489-1499.

Lehrer, P. M., et al. "Stress management techniques: are they all equivalent, or do they have specific effects?" *Biofeedback and Self-Regulation* 1994; 19: 353-401.

MacLean, C. R. K., et al. "Effects of the Transcendental Meditation Program on adaptive mechanisms: changes in hormone levels and responses to stress after four months' practice." *Psychoneuroendocrinology* 1997; 22 (4): 277-295.

Maharishi Mahesh Yogi. *Maharishi Gandharva-Ved: The classical music of the ancient Vedic civilization to create balance in nature and peace in the world.* Fairfield, IA: MIU Press, 1990.

Mayeux, R. "Can estrogen or selective estrogen-receptor modulators preserve cognitive function in elderly women?" *New England Journal of Medicine* 2001; 344 (16): 1242-1244.

Milano, C. "Sleep soundly through menopause." *Medscape*, February 2000.

Mills, P., et al. "The effects of a traditional herbal supplement on anxiety in patients with generalized anxiety disorder." *Journal of Clinical Psychopharmacology*, 2001.

Mitka, M. "Aging patients are advised to stay active to stay alert." *Journal of the American Medical Association* 2001; 285(19): 2437-2438.

Narayan, P., et al. "Effects of pulsating magnetic fields on the physiology of test animals and man." *Current Science* 1984; 53 (18): 959-965.

Orme-Johnson, D., and K. Walton. "All approaches to preventing or reversing effects of stress are not the same." *American Journal of Health Promotion* 1998; 12: 297-299.

Rajeswari, K., et al. "Effect of extremely low frequency magnetic field on serum cholinesterase in humans and animals." *Indian Journal of Experimental Biology* 1985; 23: 194-197.

Rapp, S.R., et al. "Effect of estrogen plus progestin on global cognitive function in postmenopausal women, The Women's Health Initiative Memory Study: a randomized controlled trial." *Journal of the American Medical Association.* 2003; 289(20): 2663-2672.

Schneider, R., et al. "Randomized, controlled trials of effects of the Transcendental Meditation Program on cancer, cardiovascular and all-cause mortality: a meta-analysis." Paper presented at the Society for Behavioral Medicine Annual Meeting, March 3-6, 1999, San Diego, CA.

Schneider, R., et al. "A randomized controlled trial of stress reduction for hypertension in older African Americans." *Hypertension* 1995; 26: 820-827.

Sharma, H., et al. "Effect of herbal mixture Student Rasayana on lipoxygenase activity and lipid peroxidation." *Free Radical Biology and Medicine* 1995; 18: 687-697.

Shumaker, S.A., et al. "Estrogen plus progestin and the incidence of dementia and mild cognitive impairment in postmenopausal women, The Women's Health Initiative memory study: a randomized controlled trial." *Journal of the American Medical Association.* 2003; 289(20): 2651-2662.

Stough, C., et al. "The chronic effects of an extract of *Bacopa monniera* (Brahmi) on cognitive function in healthy human subjects." *Psychopharmacology* (Berlin) 2001; 156 (4): 481-484.

Vohra, B. P., et al. "Effect of Maharishi Amrit Kalash, an ayurvedic herbal mixture, on lipid peroxidation and neuronal lipofuscin accumulation in ageing guinea pig brain." *Indian Journal of Experimental Biology* 2001; 39 (4): 355-359.

Vohra, B. P., et al. "Maharishi Amrit Kalash rejuvenates ageing central nervous system's antioxidant defence system: an in vivo study." *Pharmacological Research* 1999; 40 (6): 497-502.

Wallace, R. K., et al. "Effects of the Transcendental Meditation and TM-Sidhi program on the aging process." *International Journal of Neuroscience* 1982; 16: 53-58.

White, L., et al. "Brain aging and midlife tofu consumption." *Journal of the American College of Nutrition* 2000; 19 (2): 242-55.

Yaffe, K., quoted in Study finds walking, memory loss in aging women link. Reuters online news service: May 9, 2001.

Yaffe, K., et al. "Cognitive function in postmenopausal women treated with raloxifene." *New England Journal of Medicine* 2001; 344: 1207-13.

Yaffe, K., et al. "Estrogen therapy in postmenopausal women: effects on cognitive function and dementia." *Journal of the American Medical Association* 1998; 279: 688-95.

Yaffe, K., et al. "Cognitive decline in women in relation to non-protein-bound oestradiol concentrations." *Lancet* 2000; 356: 708-712.

Zandi, P.P., et al., Hormone Replacement Therapy and incidence of Alzheimer's disease in older women, The Cache County study. *Journal of the American Medical Association* 2002; 288(17): 2123-2129.

Chapter 10

Avis, N. E., et al. "A longitudinal analysis of the association between menopause and depression." Results from the Massachusetts Women's Health Study. *Annals of Epidemiology* 1994; 4: 214-220.

Avis, N. E., et al. "Is there an association between menopausal status and sexual functioning?" *Menopause*, 2000; 7: 297-307.

Bason, R. "Postmenopausal sexual dysfunction: fact or fiction?" *Women's Health in Primary Care* 2001; 4 (7): 479-489.

Blehar, M. C., and D. A. Oren. "Women's increased vulnerability to mood disorders: integrating psychobiology and epidemiology." *Depression* 1995; 3: 3-12.

Desai, H. D., and M. W. Jann. "Major depression in women: a review of the literature." *Journal of the American Pharmaceutical Association* 2000; 40: 525-537.

Endicott, J. "The menstrual cycle and mood disorders." *Journal of Affective Disorders* 1993; 29: 193-200.

Gelfand, M.M. "Sexuality among older women." *J Womens Health Gend Based Medicine.* 2000; 9(suppl 1): S15-S20.

Hopkins, M.P., Androff L, Benninghoff, A.S. "Ginseng face cream and unexplained vaginal bleeding." *Am J Obstet Gynecol.* 1988; 159: 1121-1122.

Kendler, K. S., et al. "Gender differences in the rates of exposure to stressful life events and sensitivity to their depressogenic effects." *American Journal of Psychiatry* 2001; 158: 587-593.

Kessler, R. C., et al. "Lifetime and 12-month prevalence of DSM-III-psychiatric disorders in the United States." Results from the National Comorbidity Survey. *Archives of General Psychiatry* 1994; 51: 8-19.

Meguid, A. S., and T. Wise. "Depressive disorders and the menopause." *Menopause Management* 2001; 10-20.

Nader, T.A., et al. "A double blind randomized controlled trial of Maharishi Vedic Vibration Technology in subjects with arthritis." *Frontiers in Bioscience* 2001; 6: 7-17.

Nicol-Smith, L. "Causality, menopause, and depression: a critical review of the literature." *British Medical Journal* 1996; 313: 1229-1232.

Nidich, S. I., et al. "Maharishi Vedic Vibration Technology on chronic disorders and associated quality of life." *Frontiers in Bioscience* 2001; 6: 1-6.

Pearce, J., et al. "Psychological and sexual symptoms associated with the menopause and the effects of hormone replacement therapy." *British Journal of Psychiatry* 1995; 167: 163-173.

Rosen, R.C., et al. "Prevalence of sexual dysfunction in women: results of a survey study of 329 women in an outpatient gynecological clinic." *J Sex Marital Ther.* 1993; 19: 171-188.

Schmidt, P. J., et al. "The perimenopause and affective disorders." *Seminars in Reproductive Endocrinology* 1997; 15 (1): 91-100.

Stafford, N. "Germany may ban kava kava supplement." Reuters News online, November 19, 2001.

Chapter 11

Castelo-Branco, C., et al. "Skin collagen changes related to age and hormone replacement therapy." *Maturitas* 1992; 15: 113-119.

Gelderloos, P., et al. "Influence of Maharishi Ayur-Vedic herbal preparation on age-related visual discrimination." *International Journal of Psychosomatics* 1990; 37 (1-4): 25-29.

Kolata, G. and Peterson, M. "Hormone replacement study a shock to the medical system." *The New York Times On the Web*, July 10, 2002

Maquart, F. X., et al. "Stimulation of collagen synthesis in fibroblast cultures by a triterpene extracted from *Centella asiatica*." *Connective Tissue Research* 1990; 24 (2): 107-120.

Savas, M., et al. "Type III collagen content in the skin of postmenopausal women receiving oestradiol and testosterone implants." *British Journal of Obstetrics and Gynaecology* 1993; 100(2): 154-156.

Sharma, H., et al. "Inhibition of human low-density lipoprotein oxidation in vitro by Maharishi Ayur-Veda herbal mixtures." *Pharmacology, Biochemistry and Behavior* 1992; 43: 1175-1182.

Wilson, R. *Feminine Forever* (out of print), New York, NY: Evans, 1966.

Epilogue

Maharishi Mahesh Yogi. *The Bhagavad-Gita: Translation and Commentary.* New York, NY: Penguin Books, 1983.

Mead, M. *Male and Female: A Study of the Sexes in a Changing World.* Revised edition. New York, NY: William Morrow, 1975.

Northrup, C. *The Wisdom of Menopause: Creating Physical and Emotional Health During the Change.* New York, NY: Bantam Books, 2001.

Orme-Johnson, D. W., et al. "International peace project in the Middle East: the effect of the Maharishi Technology of the Unified Field." *Journal of Conflict Resolution* 1988; 32 (4): 776-812.

Weed, S. *The Wise Woman Way: Alternative Approaches for Women 30-90.* Woodstock, NY: Ash Tree Publishing, 1992.

Resources

NOTE: The information in this section was current at the time of publication of this book.

Women's Health Education from Maharishi Ayurveda and Nancy Lonsdorf, MD

See Dr. Lonsdorf's website at www.drlonsdorf.com for further Ayurvedic health knowledge and resources for women and to participate in personalized Ayurveda education including self-tests and personalized recommendations for stress and gut health.

Maharishi Ayurveda Health Consultations

For information on Dr. Lonsdorf's practice, including phone or skype sessions:

Email: **healthoffice@drlonsdorf.com**
Web: **www.drlonsdorf.com**
+1 (641) 469-3174

Maharishi Ayurveda Health Center—The Raj

The Raj Health Spa offers complete and authentic Maharishi Rejuvenation Treatment (MRT) under the supervison of an experienced Ayurvedic practitioner trained in Maharishi Ayurveda. Scientifically documented treatment programs are available for a wide variety of chronic health disorders as well as for overall stress reduction, rejuvenation, beauty, and spiritual development.

The Raj
1734 Jasmine Avenue
Maharishi Vedic City, IA 52556
1 (800) 248-9050
641-472-2496 (fax)
E-mail: TheRaj@lisco.com
www.TheRaj.com

How to Obtain Maharishi Ayurveda Products Mentioned in This Book

For information on obtaining Maharishi Ayurveda wildcrafted herbs, spices and other products mentioned in this book: call Maharishi Ayurveda Products International at 1 (800) 255-8332 or go to www.mapi.com.

This "vpk by Maharishi Ayurveda" website also contains detailed recipes for some of the therapeutic Ayurvedic foods mentioned in this book, as well as details and ordering information about Maharishi Ayurveda beauty and skin care products, including the Youthful Skin products.

The Transcendental Meditation Program

To reach the nearest center teaching the Transcendental Meditation Program in the United States or Canada, dial 1 (888) 532-7686 (1-888-Learn TM) or E-mail info@tm.org.

For information and videos regarding the Transcendental Meditation program and related programs, go to www.TM.org.

Maharishi Vedic Vibration Technology

For information on availability in your area, a free video, or to learn more about Maharishi Vedic Vibration Technology, call 1 (800) 431-9680, E-mail: relief@mavf.org, or go to www.VedicVibration.com.

Gandharva Veda Music

Download the Maharishi Veda App for i-Phone or Android for a varied slection of melodies. To acquire Maharishi Gandharva music CD's go to: www.mumpress.com.

Safe Food

For the latest information on genetically modified foods to avoid and genetically natural foods to favor, go to: Non-GMOShoppingguide.com

Recommended Reading

- Bhishagratna, K. L. *Sushruta Samhita*. Varanasi, India: Chowkhamba Press, 1981.

- Lonsdorf, N., Butler, V. and Brown. M. *A Woman's Best Medicine: Health, Happiness, and Long Life through Maharishi Ayur-Veda*. New York, NY: Tarcher/Putnam, 1995.

- Schneider, R., *Total Heart Health: How to Prevent and Treat Heart Disease with Maharishi Consciousness-based Health Care*. Basic Health Publications.

- Sharma, H. and Clark, C. *Ayurvedic Healing*, Kingsley, Jessica, Publishers, 2011.

- Sharma, H., Mishra R., Meade J. *The Answer to Cancer*. New York, NY: Select Books, 2002.

- Sharma, P. V. *Charaka Samhita*. Varanasi, India: Chaukhambha Orientala, 1981.

- Yogi, Maharishi Mahesh, *The Science of Being and Art of Living*. New York, NY: Penguin Putnam, 2001.

For more information on the Global Country of World Peace and its Vedic programs to create permanent world peace, go to:

www.globalcountry.org

INDEX

A

abhyanga (self-massage) 68
Actonel 153
agni
    defined 86
ajwan seed 126
alcohol 183
Alendronate 157
Aloeweed 183
Alora 10
alpha hydroxy acids (AHA) 224
alternative approaches
    safety of 17
ama
    defined 83
    hormones, and 86
    hot water, and 93
    modern medicine, and 89
    mood, and 205
    self-assessment for location of 100
    symptoms of 83
    toxic 140
ama visha 140
American Heart Association 131
amino acids 180
Amrit Kalash. See Maharishi Amrit Kalash.
amyloid-beta-peptide, or abeta 181
androstenedione 30
anger
    dealing with 204
antioxidant supplements
    problems with 139
anxiety 37
    herbs for 197
    tips for balancing 197
    vata imbalance, and 195
arjuna myrabolans 143, 144, 203
ashwagandha 143, 144, 198
asparagus root, Indian 126
asthi
    defined 85
    factors disturbing 120
    lifestyle and dietary tips 120
Atma 184

B

Bacopa 183
bala (strength) 96
bala root 126
basti 186
beauty
    approach to 215
    inner 214
    lasting 214
    new paradigm for 212
    ojas, and 227
    outer 213
    three pillars of 213
    tips for ageless beauty 216
beta hydroxy acids (BHA) 224
bioidentical hormones
    approach compared 10
    described 15
bisphosphonate therapy 153
black cohosh 10
bone remodeling 154
bone turnover rate 152
Brahmi 183, 198
brain
    fat, and 180
    glucose, and 179
    metabolism, tips for improving 182
    protein, and 180
brain fog. See memory.
Butler, Robert 171

C

calcium 157
    common dietary sources 159
    supplementation requirements, and 158
cardamom 126
cholesterol
    bad 140
    dietary tips for 142
    LDL 140
    Maharishi Ayurveda perspective 140
    natural way to lower 142
Climara 10
collagen 212
commiphora mukul 144
constipation
    correcting 123
coriander seeds 126
cravings 92
Crinone 10
critical decade 33

cumin 126
cysteine 180

D

dairy products
    Ayurvedic Medicine, and 180
    ojas, and 180
depression 38
    emotional heart, and 199
    hormonal shifts, and 187
    Maharishi Ayurveda approach to 205–206
    major, signs of 206
    menopause causing 188
    postpartum 8
    sadhaka pitta, and 198
dhatus
    cleansing 117–121
    defined 84
    tissue cascade, and 85
dhi 172
dhriti 172
diadzein 10
diarrhea 124
digestion
    modern lifestyle, and 88
    strengthening, based on type 88
    types of 88
Dong Quai 10
dopamine 180
doshas
    across the lifespan 54
    described 43
    imbalance described 47
    keys for balancing 59–61
    overview 45–47
    seasons, and 54
doshic clock 52
dry skin 37
dysmenorrhea 8

E

emotional heart
    balance quiz 201
empty nest syndrome 189
essential fatty acids (EFAs) 180
Estraderm 10
estradiol 6, 30, 32
estriol 6
estrogen
    backup system 29
    deficiency, myth of 6
    defined 7
    low-dose 14
    receptors 15
    types of 6
estrone 6, 29, 30
Ettinger, Bruce 156
Evista 11
exercise
    weight loss, and 92

F

fatigue 38
Feminine Forever 211
FemPatch 10
fennel 126
Flame of Forest (Butea monosperma) 225
Fosamax 153, 157
foundation program
    described 106
    overview 105–108
    precautions 108
    research on 106
Fracture Intervention Trial (FIT) 153
fracture risk, after fifty 147

G

genestein 10
ghee (clarified butter) 180
glucose 179
gotu kola 183, 225
grains, power. See power grains.
guggulu 143, 144
gunam (inner beauty) 214

H

headaches 37
heart
    emotional balance quiz 201
Heart and Estrogen/Progesterone Replacement Study (HERS) 130
heart disease
    fast-food, and 132
    hormone therapy, and 130
    lifestyle, and 130
    prevalence of 129
    reversal through Transcendental Meditation

reversing via Ornish program 132
Transcendental Meditation, and 133
heart health
    adopting a lifestyle for 146
    dietary tips for 144
    Maharishi Rejuvenation Treatment, and 145
heavy metals 182
herbs
    mood, and 203
    quality control 116
    safety of 19
HERS. See Heart and Estrogen/Progesterone Replacement Study.
hibiscus, Indian 126
hippocampus 184
homeostasis 23
homocysteine 181
hormonal adjustment 31
hormone
    bioidentical, defined 7
    defined 6
    delivery to tissues 30
    female 6
    natural, defined 7
hormone therapy
    Alzheimer's disease, and 170
    approached compared 11
    blood clots, and 12
    breast cancer, and 12
    common side effects, and 13
    dementia, and 12
    depression, and 188
    heart attacks, and 12
    heart disease, and 130
    memory, and 170
    osteoporosis, and 153
    ovarian cancer, and 12
    strokes, and 12
    traditional, risks of 12
    ultra-low dose 153
hot flashes 37
    metabolic waste, and 89
hot water
    ama, and 93
How Balance Are You? (Quiz) 37
HT. See Hormone Therapy.
hypothalamus 30

I

imbalance
    correcting tissue and waste 116
    meal plan for healing all 61
imbalances
    self-assessment quiz 56
Indian pennywort 183
indigestion 38
insomnia 37
International Longevity Center USA 171
isoflavones 21, 157

J

joint pains 38

K

kapha
    detailed description of 47
    dietary tips for 79
    exercise, and 78
    function and qualities 44
    functions after menopause 47
    how to balance 75–79
    skin type 220
    substance, and 47
kava kava (Piper methysticum) 198

L

Lee, John 154
leftovers
    weight loss, and 95
libido
    lack of 38
licorice 10
Love, Susan 14

M

Maharishi Amrit Kalash 138, 183
Maharishi Ayurveda
    approach compared 10
    description 4
    naturalness of 21
    Nature's intelligence, and 27
    NIH funding, and 4
    research on 4
    skin care treatments and products 223
Maharishi Effect 232

Maharishi Mahesh Yogi 133
Maharishi Rejuvenation Treatment
    ageless beauty, and 227
    description 209
    heart disease, and 141
    memory, and 185
    mood disorders, and 207
Maharishi Vedic Vibration Technology
    described 208
    mood disorders, and 207
majja
    defined 85
    factors disturbing 120
    lifestyle and dietary tips 121
MAK. See Maharishi Amrit Kalash.
malas
    defined 96
    purifying 122–125
    self-assessment for impurities 102
mamsa
    defined 85
    factors disturbing 118
    lifestyle and dietary tips 119
manjistha 126
marshmallow root 126, 191
Massachusetts Women's Health Study 188
Matthews, Karen 133
Mead, Margaret 230
meda
    defined 85
    factors disturbing 119
    lifestyle and dietary tips 119
    oily skin, and 214
memory
    diet and exercise, and 171
    Gandharva Veda music, and 186
    herbs for 183
    Maharishi Ayurveda understanding of 172
    nourishing the brain, and 179
    prana vata, and 174
    problems 38
    sleep disturbance, and 177
    vata dosha, and 173
menopause
    bone changes, and 152
    chemotherapy-related 32
    cultural differences 7
    defined 8
    depression, and 188
    health advantage 5
    men, and 7
    natural part of life 5
    natural, defined 8
    premature, defined 8
    rural Indian women, and 28
    sexuality, and 190
    skin, and 217
    surgical 32
    symptom relation to balance 34
metabolic syndrome 91
migraine 37
Mills, Paul 198
mood
    ama, and 205
    herbs for 203
mood swings 37
muscle aches 38
muskroot (N. jatamamsi) 198
MVVT. See Maharishi Vedic Vibration Technology.

N

National Institutes of Health 4
natural treatment
    spectrum of 9
neprilysin 182
neurotransmitters (brain messenger chemicals) 180
North American Menopause Society 229
Northrup, Christiane 230

O

ojas
    beauty, and 227
    behavioral rejuvenatives, and 139
    defined 97
    heart health, and 136
    mood swings, and 203
    rejuvenatives, and 138
    signs of 99
    tips for enhancing 140
Ornish, Dean 132
osteoblasts 152
osteoclasts 152
osteopenia 152
osteoporosis
    age and bone strength 151
    aging's role in 148
    calcium supplementation 157
    defined 149

digestive fire, and 163
elimination, and 166
estrogen levels, and 148
exercise, and 159
hormonal and drug treatments for 152
hormone therapy, and 153
low bone density, and 165
Maharishi Rejuvenation Therapy for preventing 166
modifiable factors 150
myths surrounding 156
nonmodifiable factors 150
peak bone mass, and 149
prevention, and 149
soy products, and 157
vata, and 160, 162
vata-balancing recommendations 162
vitamin D 158
waste and ama-reducing recommendations 164
ovaries
    postmenopause estradiol production, and 29

P

palpitations 38
panchakarma 10
peak bone mass 149
perimenopause
    defined 8
physiological rhythms 31
physiology
    usage defined 47
phytoestrogens 20
    approach compared 10
    defined 7
    diet, and 20
    extracted 10
    isolated, safety of 21
pitta
    detailed description of 46
    dietary tips for 74
    energy production, and 46
    function and qualities 44
    how to balance 68–75
    metabolism, and 46
    mood swings, and 198
    mood swings, balancing 201
    perimenopause, and 46
    sadhaka, heart health, and 137
    skin type 220

    three-day cleanse 76
pitta-vata shift 55
Postmenopausal Estrogen/Progestogen Intervention Trial (PEPI) 155
postmenopause
    defined 8
power grains
    adding to diet 114
    gathering 115
    preparing 115
prana vata 137
    skin, and 217
pranayama 176
Premarin 11, 16
premenopause
    defined 8
premenstrual dysphoric disorder (PMDD) 187
premenstrual syndrome 8
premenstrual syndrome (PMS) 187
principle of opposites 49
principle of similarity 48
Profet, Margie 73
progesterone 6
    bioidentical 154
    defined 7
    natural, safety of 16
progesterone, natural 154
progestin
    defined 7
progestogen
    defined 7
Prometrium 10
Provera 16

R

rakta
    defined 85
    factors disturbing 117
    lifestyle and dietary tips 118
    skin inflammations, and 214
Raloxifen 11
rasa
    defined 85
    factors disturbing 117
    lifestyle and dietary tips 117
    wrinkles, and 214
rasayanas
    ojas-enhancement, and 138
red clover 10
remodeling 152

retinal 224
rohini layer of skin 225
roopam (outer beauty) 213
rosa centifolia (literally "a hundred petals") 202
rose 202

S

sadhaka pitta 137, 198, 199
sadhaka pitta, quiz 201
sarsaparilla, Indian 126
Sellmeyer, Dr. 157
sensitive plant (Lajawanti) 225
SERMs
    approach compared 11
    described 9, 14
    side effects 11
serotonin 180
sexuality
    diminishing sexual desire 192
    menopause, and 190
Shankapushpi (Aloeweed, Convolvulus pluricaulis) 183
Shatavari 191
shirodhara 186
shukra
    defined 85
    factors disturbing 121
    lifestyle and dietary tips 121
skin
    doshic type 219
    kapha care regimen 222
    kapha type 220
    Maharishi Ayurveda approach to ??–223
    pitta care regimen 221
    pitta type 220
    popular skin care products 224
    routine, and 215
    vata care regimen 221
    vata type 219
    wrinkling and hormone therapy 212
    Youthful Skin product line 224
sleep
    memory, and 177
    menopause, and 177
    tips for improving 178
sleep difficulty 37
smriti 172
soy products, osteoporosis 157
spa treatments compared 226
spice mixture, smart
    preparing 113
    using 114
spices
    quality control 116
stool 97
    loose 124
    purifying 123
subhanga karanam (MAV definition of beauty) 213
sweat 97
    purifying 125

T

Tamoxifen 11
terminalia arjuna 144
Testosterone 6
tissues. See dhatus.
tofu
    dementia, and 181
    recommendations for consumption 181
Transcendental Meditation 27
    blood pressure, and 134
    compared to hormone therapy 135
    effectiveness compared to other meditations 185
    heart disease, and 133
    Maharishi Effect, and 232
    mental stress, memory, and 184
    mood disorders, and 207
    prevention, and 135
    research on 184
    reversal of heart disease, and 134
    world peace, and 232
tridosha theory 43
tripti 179

U

University of Kentucky 31
University of Pittsburgh Graduate School of Public Health 33
urinary frequency 38
urinary incontinence 38
urinary tract infections 38
urine 96
    purifying 122

V

vaginal dryness 37

improving through natural approach 191
lack of estrogen, and 191
sanitary products, and 191
sexual function, and 190
valerian root (Valeriana, spp.) 197
vata
anxiety
tips for balancing 197
anxiety, and 195
assessing brain's balance 175
detailed description of 45
dietary tips for 67
digestion during midlife, and 87
flow, and 45
functions and qualities 44
how to balance 61–68
memory, and 173
midlife transition, and 46
movement, and 45
prana, heart health, and 137
prana, memory and 174
prana, tips for balancing 175
qualities of 46
regular routine, and 64
self-massage, and 66
skin type 219
vyana, heart health, and 137
vayastyag (lasting beauty) 214
vitamin B12 181
vitamin C 138
vitamin D 157
osteoporosis, and 158
vitamin E 19, 138
Alzheimer's disease, and 172
vitamins
safety of 19
Vivelle 10
vyana vata 137, 217

W

wastes
bodily 96
Weed, Susun 230
weight
diet tips for losing 94
metabolism, and 90
pitfalls to losing 91
weight gain 37
WHI. See Women's Health Initiative
wild yam 17

Wilson, Robert 211
wise water
formulating 109
ingredients for 110
instructions for drinking 112
preparing 109
specific bodily wastes, and 111
specific midlife symptoms, and 111
worksheet for personalizing 111
Wise, Phyllis 31
withania somnifera 144
Women's Healthy Lifestyle Project 33
Women's Health Initiative 3, 5, 131, 147, 212
world peace 231
Worry Free herbal supplement 198

Y

yeast infections 123

CPSIA information can be obtained
at www.ICGtesting.com
Printed in the USA
FFOW01n1733091117
43382454-41966FF